Y0-BVO-313

Times of Heroism,
Times of Terror

Times of Heroism, Times of Terror

American Presidents and the Cold War

Martin Thornton

PRAEGER

Westport, Connecticut
London

Library of Congress Cataloging-in-Publication Data

Thornton, Martin, 1955–
    Times of heroism, times of terror : American presidents and the Cold War /
Martin Thornton.
        p.   cm.
    Includes bibliographical references and index.
    ISBN: 0-275-98001-4 (alk. paper)
    1. United States—Foreign relations—1945–1989. 2. United States—Politics and
government—1945–1989. 3. Presidents—United States—History—20th century.
4. United States—Military policy. 5. Cold War. I. Title.
        E744.T53   2005
        327.73′009′045—dc22   2005004211

British Library Cataloguing in Publication Data is available.

Library of Congress Catalog Card Number: 2005004211
ISBN: 0 275-98001-4

First published in 2005

Praeger Publishers, 88 Post Road West, Westport, CT 06881
An imprint of Greenwood Publishing Group, Inc.
www.praeger.com

Printed in the United States of America

The paper used in this book complies with the
Permanent Paper Standard issued by the National
Information Standards Organization (Z39.48–1984).

10   9   8   7   6   5   4   3   2   1

Times of heroism are generally times of terror. . . .
But whoso is heroic will always find crisis to try his edge.

—Ralph Waldo Emerson

Contents

Preface

Two civilian aircraft were deliberately crashed into the twin towers of the World Trade Center in New York City, a third aircraft was successfully targeted against the American Department of Defense headquarters (known as the Pentagon), and a fourth aircraft was crashed into a field in Pennsylvania. These events of September 11, 2001, were a significant turning point in the history of the United States and its people, and of such magnitude that they affected international relationships with a host of very different nation states; and they took place after the cold war. Whether or not the actions and consequences of September 11, 2001, prove to be a watershed in American foreign policy, as the ending of the cold war proved to be, is yet to be seen, but the irony is apparent. America had "girded its loins" in fear of a potential attack from the Soviet Union for some four decades, but suffers a direct attack from non-communist civilian terrorists.

The circumstances of September 11, 2001, make Ralph Waldo Emerson's words on crises, used as a frontispiece, seem exceedingly apposite. Although his words have resonance for the history of the cold war, they have added brevity under the tragic circumstances of a direct, undeclared attack on America itself, and the consequences that had to be addressed by President George W. Bush. Not only were these events indicative of the nature of modern political terrorism, but also the pivotal role of the American president for the American political system and world events. President George W. Bush responded to the unexpected attack with a call to arms and mobilization of American and associated forces to fight terrorism and to launch a major war in Afghanistan against the base of al-Qaeda terrorism. This was followed in 2003 by waging war on Iraq, a foreign policy conducted with allies, to remove Saddam Hussein and his regime from power and authority.

Although many events illustrate the unpredictability of international events, the attacks on the United States on September 11, in particular, reflect the dilemmas faced by American presidents because of notable foreign policy events. The carefully prepared policy positions drawn up by the State Department, Department of Defense, National Security Agency, the Central Intelligence Agency, and think tanks are exposed for their limitations when such seminal events occur. Political choices exist within existing political structures, but crises help to redefine the substance of choice and sometimes to change the structures in which they take place. The period of the cold war was beset with a number of crises that tested the mettle of those directly involved and the institutions they worked within.

The cold war between the United States and the Soviet Union now appears more definitive in terms of specific ideological differences that have been brought to a conclusion. The end of the cold war is a seminal event in American foreign policy. The collapse of the Soviet Union gave the United States unrivalled global power status. Capitalism as a system of modernization was left with few rivals, and even communist China has moved to selling goods in the international and United States marketplaces. Whether or not the economic, political, and strategic "realism" that followed the end of the cold war is fundamentally shaken by the events and consequences of September 11, 2001, is already being debated.[1] The cold war worries and scenarios developed by a number of American presidents and their administrations are recent but clearly definable history.

Notes

1. F. Cameron, "Utilitarian Multilateralism: The Implications of 11 September 2001 for US Foreign Policy," *Politics* 22, 2 (2002). A. Lieven, "The Secret Policemen's Ball: The United States, Russia and the International Order After 11 September," *International Affairs* 78, 2 (2002).

Acknowledgments

This book was conceived and partly researched while in the United States as a Visiting Professor at Vanderbilt University in Nashville, Tennessee. The good provisions of the Department of History and the Jean and Alexander Heard Library at Vanderbilt University were gratefully received. Having taught courses where students exhibited strong interest in the role of individual American presidents, I set about writing this book.

In the course of researching and writing this work I visited eight of the ten presidential libraries and museums that relate to the American presidents between 1945 and 1991. Six of the libraries provided interesting material that I have incorporated into this work. All of the presidential libraries have Web sites with fascinating material ranging not only from finding aides, but biographical material, National Security Council memoranda, and some very personal documents.

The material gathered from the depository of Richard M. Nixon's material relating to his time as vice president has also proven to be useful, and the archivist Fred Klose was generous with his time. John H. Taylor, director of the Richard Nixon Library and Birthplace in Yorba Linda, California, was kind enough to send to me in England post-presidential speeches of Richard M. Nixon.

The hospitality and help from the Dwight D. Eisenhower Library in Abiline, Kansas, was channeled through Barbara Constable, a staff archivist who was particularly helpful with a number of avenues of research. My first interest at the library had been the relationship of President Eisenhower with Canadian statesman Lester Bowles Pearson but this broadened to an interest in President Eisenhower as commander in chief. The excellent published collections of documents on Eisenhower have provided memoranda of Eisenhower's communications with political subordinates and foreign dignitaries.

Archivist William H. McNitt was very expeditious in providing files and direction for me at the Gerald R. Ford Library in Ann Arbor, Michigan. I was pleased to receive expert reference assistance and patience over my photocopying.

Brief visits were made by me to the Truman Library and Museum in Independence, Missouri, and the Johnson Library and Museum in Austin, Texas. The Truman Library and Museum was having a very good exhibit on Truman and Israel. The later visit to the Johnson Library and Museum coincided with rather good hospitality provided for the Society for Historians of American Foreign Policy Conference in June 2004. The Perry-Castaneda Library at the University of Texas in Austin had impressive secondary resources.

I made a fruitful visit to the George H. W. Bush Library and Museum at Texas A&M University in College Station, Texas. This is an under-used resource at the moment despite having a sizable number of papers available to researchers. I was grateful that material was delivered to me with great speed and professionalism.

Help at the extremely picturesque John F. Kennedy Library and Museum in Boston, Massachusetts, was much appreciated. Stephen Plath was kind enough to direct me toward the Sorensen and Schlesinger papers and a David Ormsby-Gore interview transcript. The library has also been generous with its time in dealing with enquiries from some of my postgraduate students from the School of History, University of Leeds.

No library, museum, institution, or other individual takes any responsibility for the contents of this book. All blame can be attributed to the author.

The writer acknowledges support and patience of his family, including a considerable debt of gratitude to Eileen, Ethan, and Sean Thornton. My American wife has an inherent interest in the American presidency; my prediction is that my two sons may someday share that interest.

CHAPTER 1

Introduction

Of all manifestations of power, restraint impresses men most.[1]
—*Thucydides*

Under the eighteenth-century Constitution of the United States of America, the checks and balances of the political system inherent to the separation of powers, designed to control and demarcate responsibilities of the legislature, executive, and judiciary, were eloquently defined. The fact that the American Constitution is still a prized working document of the American political and legal system is testament to its inherent quality, and also to its adaptability. As a defined set of rules and obligations, the Constitution was likely to give the appearance of rigidity, and to confine as well as define the role of decision makers. Yet the Constitution is arguably as relevant to the modern political process of the United States as it was at its triumphal inception. The words of the Constitution and Bill of Rights, with limited formal amendments, have largely been preserved as they were expressed by the founding fathers.

The words of the American Constitution remain, but the political fabric of the American political system has been restructured within the constitutional framework. Women and African Americans were not initially accepted as integral components of the political system and had to win acceptance within the system defined by the Constitution. Conflicting social, economic, and racial groups in the United States have been involved in debates and struggles over the relevance of the Constitution and the protection afforded by the Constitution to particular sections of society.

How has the American executive branch of government fared in the development and reinterpretation of the Constitution? Arthur M. Schlesinger Jr., in his famous 1973 book *The Imperial Presidency*, eloquently mapped the increased powers granted to, seized by, and manipulated by the executive branch of government in modern times in the United States.[2] When Lyndon B. Johnson was president in the White House, Schlesinger could claim that the powers of the chief executive over foreign policy issues had become "The Presidency Rampant," particularly because of Johnson's commitment of American military forces to the Vietnam War in 1965.[3] Foreign policy developments and the elevated role of the executive within foreign policy decision-making were major reasons for the increased powers afforded to the American president. Both changes in the international environment and the expectation that an American president would be able to satisfactorily advance American foreign policy led to an extraordinary increase in the political, economic, and military power of American presidents.

Whether or not the founding fathers intended the president to be only a titular commander in chief is moot as a historical point and an issue for debate, but clearly the president has become the commander in chief in a literal sense. Article II of the Constitution posits that"[t]he President shall be Commander in Chief of the Army and Navy of the United States, and of the Militia of the several States, when called into the actual Service of the United States."[4] As if to reinforce the president's responsibility to protect American democracy, the oath of office requires a president to declare his defense of the Constitution. As recorded by Arthur Schlesinger Jr. and Samuel P. Huntington, this designation as commander in chief left the actual functions that the president would perform in this position undefined and provided the opportunity for these functions to be subsequently expanded.[5]

Presidents and Military Service

Has military command been the raison d'être of the presidency and the function of commander in chief? Of the forty-one presidents to hold office by the end of the cold war in 1991, including President George H. W. Bush, twenty-five American presidents experienced some form of military service, although some were not as active as others. Because sixty-one percent of this group participated in military duties, it would appear that military experience prior to obtaining the presidency has been a reasonably useful career characteristic. Moreover, all nine American presidents since Franklin D. Roosevelt up to 1991 have had military service credentials; eight of these presidents served in the American armed services during World War II and one during World War I.

General George Washington, as commander in chief of the Continental Army during the Revolutionary War, was inaugurated as the first American president, thus setting an early association between military prowess and the office of the presidency. World War I produced only one president associated with direct combat, Harry S. Truman, although he was not picked as Franklin D. Roosevelt's vice president in 1944 for his World War I military record. Nevertheless, Truman had commanded an artillery battery in France during the closing American involvement in World War I and left the American army as a brevet major.

In contrast, Dwight David Eisenhower's popularity and nomination for the presidency did stem from an exemplary and well-publicized military record. Like Ulysses S. Grant, Eisenhower was trained at West Point, commanded a victorious army, and claimed no political experience before being nominated for the presidency. It would appear, however, that Grant felt far more uncomfortable as president than Eisenhower ever did. During World War II, U.S. Army Chief of Staff George C. Marshall chose Eisenhower to lead the Allied invasion of North Africa. Following this success he became the supreme Allied commander for the invasion of Europe and reaped the political benefits of the allied victories in Europe. The fact that Eisenhower had not voted in a national election and was a political novice did not prevent both the Democratic and Republican political parties seeking his candidacy for the presidency. Eisenhower, as a Republican candidate with his war record juxtaposed against the Korean War and with campaign buttons declaring "I like Ike" was able to sweep away the Democratic challenge of the more academic Adlai E. Stevenson.

A number of post–World War II presidents experienced U.S. Navy service, including John F. Kennedy, Lyndon B. Johnson, Richard M. Nixon, Gerald R. Ford, Jimmy Carter, and George H. W. Bush. John. F. Kennedy was a lieutenant junior grade (j.g.) and commander of a P.T. boat in the South Pacific. He contracted malaria, suffered an injured intervertebral disc, and won a Purple Heart and a Navy-Marine Corps medal. Although initially a lieutenant commander and then a commander in the U.S. Naval Reserve, Lyndon B. Johnson saw active duty between December 1941 and July 1942. Richard M. Nixon received a Navy commission as lieutenant j.g. in 1942 and finished the war as a lieutenant commander, seeing service overseas from June 1943 to August 1944. Gerald R. Ford entered naval service during World War II as an ensign and emerged as a lieutenant commander, serving on the USS *Monterey*. The longest presidential naval career was held by Jimmy Carter, who entered the U.S. Naval Academy in Annapolis in 1943 (although his appointment was accepted in 1942 and he spent a year as a Naval Reserve Officer Training Corps student in Atlanta at Georgia Tech) and subsequently served as a lieutenant commander, leaving the Navy in 1953.[6] Ronald Reagan's successor as president, George H. W. Bush, had a very active and distinguished Navy flying career, flying fifty-eight combat missions in the Pacific theater of operations during World War II.

Although President Ronald Reagan spent the World War II years in the United States of America, he was also officially on active duty. He was a second lieutenant in the U.S. Army Reserve and then a captain on active duty with the U.S. Air Force from 1942 to 1945.

The association of military men with the White House should not suggest that presidents have acted belligerently or led the nation to war as a consequence of their previous military service. Interestingly, Frederick W. Marks

III has pointed out that there has been an inverse relationship between military men occupying the presidency and the waging of war.[7] High-ranking military personnel have avoided war after becoming president, whereas some presidents from a civilian background or of an "intellectual" disposition have taken the United States to war. Presidents with significant military records who are associated with avoiding major conflicts include George Washington, James Monroe, Andrew Jackson, William Henry Harrison, Zachary Taylor, Franklin Pierce, Ulysses S. Grant, Rutherford B. Hayes, James A. Garfield, Benjamin Harrison, Theodore Roosevelt, and Dwight D. Eisenhower. Marks puts forward the strong argument that "[n]ot a single one of these individuals led the nation to war despite numerous opportunities."[8]

Whether or not active military service was a significant benefit to the presidents who have possessed it is a debatable point. Some presidents who were the product of military academies behaved in a very unmilitary way in office (i.e., Grant, Eisenhower, and Carter). World War II military service has certainly proven to be a useful credential for those aspiring to the presidency, based on the profiles of presidential candidates from 1945 to 1992. Nevertheless, candidates with "superior" military records have also been defeated in some presidential elections. These include George McGovern, Walter "Fritz" Mondale, Bob Dole, and the incumbent presidents Jimmy Carter and George H. W. Bush. Of course, their service was not an exclusive factor for election, nor did it guarantee specific advantages to candidates (with the notable exception of General Dwight D. Eisenhower). However, in a cold war political climate where the Soviet Union was considered a constant cause of international unrest and military tensions were significant being perceived as able to respond rationally and efficiently to strategic and military international problems was a valuable attribute for a president of the United States. Even if the cold war is characterized as a lack of overt military conflict between the United States and the Soviet Union, it was still a period with regional conflicts and the threat of World War III.

American presidents have become extremely powerful through America's rise to global power and because of the capability to intervene in every part of the world. All American presidents since 1945 have been called upon to make strategic foreign policy decisions and to decide on appropriate responses to military conflicts and crises. They were certainly not omnipotent or exclusive decision-makers; nevertheless, their significance is clear in a number of areas. Harry S. Truman was intimately involved in the use of atomic bombs against Japan, responded to the Berlin crisis, and orchestrated the response to the Korean War; Dwight D. Eisenhower was also involved in the Korean War and the growing problem of Southeast Asia; John F. Kennedy had a dramatic showdown with the Soviet Union over the attempted positioning of missiles in Cuba and increased the number of "quiet Americans" in Vietnam; Lyndon B. Johnson's legacy is intertwined with the Vietnam War, and he also took direct action in the Dominican Republic; Richard M. Nixon's policies in Southeast Asia were dramatic and controversial; Gerald R. Ford showed his mettle in the foreign policy arena over the *Mayaguez* affair; Jimmy Carter suffered through events in the Middle East and Soviet aggression in Afghanistan; and Ronald Reagan is remembered for both his tough stance against the Soviet Union and his more awkward policies toward Central America. In the post–cold war period, George H. W. Bush pursued strong military policies and prosecuted the Persian Gulf War against Iraq. In the new millennium his son and successor to President William Jefferson Clinton, George W. Bush, launched himself into a war against international terrorism.

The Cold War

The term "cold war" is a general and imprecise one, although it is widely used, and understood, to describe a situation in which two or more antagonists avoid becoming involved in direct conflict, and often carries associations of an ideological conflict or propaganda war. It is neither a rigorously defined social-scientific concept nor a historical period that can be precisely demarcated. The term has, nevertheless, become associated with the period of hostilities between the Soviet Union and the United States in the post–World War II period of history that comes to an end with the collapse of the Soviet Union. It might be applied more generically to Western and Eastern world political divisions or to the incompatibility of Soviet-style communism and Western-style democracy. This simplification, however, would tend to ignore periods of peaceful cooperation and détente, internal divisions within the rival blocs, and the development of a multipolar rather than a bipolar world.

The exact dating of the beginning, and for that matter the ending, of the cold war are significant and arguable points in their own right. Joseph M. Siracusa has cited a "Cold War Certificate" of the Department of Defense defining the start of the cold war from the end of World War II on September 2, 1945, and its culmination as the lowering of the flag of the Soviet Union on December 26, 1991.[9] The origins of the cold war developments of the 1940s and 1950s can be traced back as early as the Bolshevik Revolution of 1917 and the creation of a communist state in the Soviet Union. Nineteenth-century socialists, and Karl Marx in particular, diagnosed a fundamentally antagonistic character in industrial societies. Marx and his followers would come to see the logical development of history producing an inevitable conflict between two opposing camps, represented by the bourgeoisie and the proletariat.

Once a communist state had been established, whether as an aberration or as an adaptation of Marxism, the creation of further ideological extremes followed. In the interwar years, the competition of fascism with liberal democracy, and communism was important in the development of Italy's domestic and external policies, in Germany's foreign and domestic policies, in producing the Spanish Civil War with its considerable international involvement, and ultimately in producing World War II. Soviet and American isolationism helped to keep the cold war latent in the interwar years. American, British, and French diplomats had attempted to reconcile the contradictions inherent in Soviet foreign policy in the 1930s and 1940s, but even the Allied cooperation during World War II could not overcome the ideological antagonism between capitalism and communism. It was the American journalist Walter Lippmann, whose articles were syndicated around the world, and some published in book form, who popularised the term "cold war" for the postwar years.

The cold war period from 1945 to 1991 is beset with heroic attempts to find peaceful solutions to conflicts: summit diplomacy, détente, peace accords, and strategic nuclear arms limitations. Throughout this period, the president, as the chief executive and commander in chief of a superpower state, has been involved in international problem solving, peace initiatives, traditional diplomacy, and the prosecution of wars. With foreseen and unforeseen outbreaks of international violence, presidents have found themselves in "times of heroism and times of terror."[10] The personalities and actions of presidents have been significant factors in the handling of American foreign policy crises.

To focus on the president's role in conducting the foreign policy of the United States emphasizes and accepts that foreign policy power has been centralized in the hands of the executive. Of course, it cannot be ignored that there are other loci of power in the making of U.S. foreign policy residing with individuals and processes involving the Department of State, Department of Defense, National Security Council (NSC), Congress, other national bureaucracies, the mass media, domestic and multinational corporations, the military and the military-industrial complex, and public opinion. Nevertheless, the present work is a study of the presidency and foreign policy, and operates within more confined, manageable, and personalized parameters. The interaction between the president and other, possibly conflicting loci of power and influence will be covered when they interpose themselves between the president and the ultimate foreign policy decisions.

Edwin S. Corwin captured the relationship between the United States Congress and the president in his remarks in 1941: "Contrary to a common, but quite mistaken impression, no President has a mandate from the Constitution to conduct our foreign relations according to his own sweet will. If his power in that respect is indefinite, so is Congress's Legislative power, and if he holds the 'sword', so does Congress hold the 'purse strings.'"[11]

Before leaving office, President Eisenhower raised the specter of a military-industrial complex as a significant force in American foreign policy. Some sociologists and new-left historians have accepted much offered in this view, and feature film director Oliver Stone even made it a central thesis of his conspiracy theory about the Vietnam War and the assassination of John F. Kennedy, depicted in his film *JFK*.[12]

The eminent academic Graham T. Allison was to look to organizational, bureaucratic, and rational-actor models for explanations of the Cuban missile crisis.[13] Much of Allison's wisdom has been accepted in academic analyses of foreign-policy decision-making. A number of alternative approaches to a rational-actor model as an explanation of the president's role in the making of American foreign policy can be found elsewhere. This study charts the significance of acting presidents to American foreign policy during the complex period of the cold war and captures some of their frustrations, confusions, hopes, intentions, ambitions, and in some cases overweening power in the postwar period. Whether or not each president, over the forty-six years of the cold war, has shown the appropriate levels of restraint in foreign policy decisions has been open to much debate. Each post–World War II president has found a "crisis to try his edge."[14]

Notes

1. This quotation from the Athenian historian Thucydides (c. 470–400 BC) was, according to Bob Woodward, a quotation favored by the chairman of the Joint Chiefs of Staff, Colin Powell, a copy of which was kept in his glass-topped desk in the Pentagon. B. Woodward, *The Commanders* (New York: Simon & Schuster, 1991), 153.

2. A. M. Schlesinger Jr., *The Imperial Presidency*, revised edition (Boston: Houghton Mifflin, 1989).

3. Ibid., 177–207.

4. In the appendix of G. B. Tindall, D. E. Shi, *America: A Narrative History*, 3rd edition (New York: W.W. Norton & Company, 1984), A18.

5. Schlesinger, *The Imperial Presidency*, 62.

6. This aspect of his career is explained in J. Carter, *Why Not the Best?* (Eastbourne: Kingsway Publications, 1977).

7. F. W. Marks III, "Power and Peace in American Diplomatic History," *The Society of Historians of American Foreign Relations (S.H.A.F.R.) Newsletter*, March, 1996.

8. Ibid., 15.

9. J. M. Siracusa, "The 'New' Cold War History and the Origins of the Cold War," *Australian Journal of Politics and History* 47, 1 (2001), 1 49. In footnote 2, Siracusa points out: "The flag of the former USSR was lowered for the last time on Christmas day, 25 December 1991, but Congress was apparently loath to assign the anniversary of the death of communism to the same day as the birth of Christ."

10. R. W. Emerson, *Essays, First Series* (Boston: Houghton, Mifflin and Company, 1883), 246–247.

11. E. S. Corwin, "Some Aspects of the Presidency," *Annals*, 218, November 1941, 122–131, cited in W. LaFeber, *The American Age: U.S. Foreign Policy at Home and Abroad, 1750 to the Present*, 2nd edition (New York: W. W. Norton & Company, 1994) 410, endnote 73.

12. *JFK*, directed by Oliver Stone (Warner Bros., 1991).

13. G. T. Allison, *Essence of Decision* (Boston: Little, Brown and Company, 1971).

14. Emerson, *Essays, First Series*, 246–247.

CHAPTER 2

Total War and the Quest for Peace, 1945

Franklin's illness gave him strength and courage he had not had before. He had to think out the fundamentals of living, and learn the greatest of all lessons–infinite patience and never-ending persistence.[1]

—Eleanor Roosevelt

These words by Eleanor Roosevelt, the president's wife, are etched into a wall behind a bronze statute of Franklin Delano Roosevelt in his wheelchair as part of the Franklin Delano Roosevelt Memorial in Washington, D.C. Unveiled in January 2001, the statue exposes Franklin Roosevelt to the public as he was hardly ever seen during his lifetime. Almost no photographs or film footage show him struggling with his physical disability, a disability caused by a form of polio that he contracted in 1921. Yet this is the image we now retain of Roosevelt, a man of great courage, patience, and persistence whose domestic reputation was enhanced by the leadership he exhibited during World War II. He went beyond being a man of fireside chats and sound economic policies to become an international statesman. His reputation as a decision-maker on the international stage is not without its critics, but his personal courage and his dominance of American foreign policy is widely accepted by historians and political commentators. World War II produced a range of crises that tested Roosevelt's resolve, determination, and patience.

By 1945, the longevity of Roosevelt's tenure as president, which had begun in 1933, had made him a formidable and experienced political leader. Roosevelt, the British prime minister, Winston Churchill, and the secretary general of the Communist Party of the Soviet Union, Joseph Stalin, represented the "Big Three" within the Grand Alliance during World War II, and they would be key players in determining the peace. Although the Grand Alliance would be made up of as many as fifty nations, the decision-making process was dominated by the United States, Great Britain, and the Soviet Union.

Many students of modern history see the wartime Grand Alliance as an aberration or hiccup in an otherwise latent cold war that existed since 1917. In the Soviet Union, the effort to win World War II pushed aside considerations of class consciousness, and, as in the United States, the Soviet Union found itself promoting nationalism and patriotism during the war. The German invasion of the Soviet Union in June 1941 in Operation Barbarossa created a temporary respite in ideological rivalry between capitalism and communism as the Soviet Union allied itself with the West. The attack on Pearl Harbor by the Japanese and the subsequent German declaration of war against the United States in December 1941 not only brought the United States into the war, but also brought about a Soviet-British-American understanding. Not only was there much to be lost in World War II, there was much to be gained. The Grand Alliance of the Soviet Union, the United States, and Britain and the associated Allies changed the balance of the war against the Axis of Germany, Japan, and Italy.

Roosevelt and World War II

President Roosevelt delivered a war message to the Congress of the United States on December 8, 1941. This message was in direct response to the attack by Japanese naval and air forces on Pearl Harbor in Hawaii on December 7. Besides declaring December 7 "a date which will live in infamy," Roosevelt went on: "As Commander-in-Chief of the Army and Navy I have directed that all measures be taken for our defense. But always will our whole nation remember the character of the onslaught against us. No matter how long it may take us to overcome this premeditated invasion, the American people in their righteous might will win through to absolute victory."[2]

In declaring war against the United States, Germany and Italy miscalculated the strength and determination of the United States. The Axis became the declared enemy of the United States, and the considerable military and economic power of the United States that had hitherto been used sparingly in the war effort was eventually unleashed. As a further consequence of Pearl Harbor, both the House of Commons and House of Lords of the British parliament voted on December 8 for Great Britain to be at war with Japan.

World War II lasted over three and a half years for the United States and required a myriad of decisions that affected its conduct and determined the shape of the peace to follow. President Roosevelt was to follow the details and battles of the war and was an "activist commander," as he was described by Eric Larrabee.[3] Further, the president worked hard to inject idealism into the propaganda of the American war effort and to convey the same idealism into diplomacy and the strategy for a postwar peace. What helped Roosevelt enormously in his wartime decision-making was the amity and nonpartisanship of the Democratic and Republican political leadership in the United States. Of course this could not be guaranteed to continue into the postwar peace process.

Winston Churchill and Franklin Roosevelt

Roosevelt had served since March 1913, as assistant secretary of the Navy under President Woodrow Wilson for seven years and five months, a period which thus included World War I. Winston Churchill had served as first lord of the admiralty in the British government for periods of both World Wars. This naval interest was to reappear in some of the 1,700 pieces of correspondence that passed between Churchill and Roosevelt during World War II.[4] Churchill chose his own code name as "Naval Person," which he subsequently changed to "Former Naval Person." Their correspondence reflects a mutual respect that existed between Roosevelt and the older Churchill and that went beyond their affection for the navy.[5]

Churchill considered himself half-American and had a respect for the Anglo-American political culture that he felt Britain and the United States represented. Although the "special relationship" tag has become somewhat clichéd and Britain has come to been seen as rather dependent on the United States, the solid personal relationship established between Franklin Roosevelt and Winston Churchill during the crises of World War II is still widely accepted as accurate. Nevertheless, it would appear that Roosevelt attached less importance to the idea of a transatlantic Anglo-American association than Churchill did, and historian John Charmley has suggested some negative long-term consequences of the Roosevelt-Churchill relationship for the British Empire.[6]

During World War II Churchill and Roosevelt met nine times.[7] The first meeting of Churchill as prime minister and Roosevelt as president took place at Placentia Bay, Newfoundland, on August 14, 1941. The importance of the relationship was made clear ten days after this meeting to Churchill. Churchill commented on the comradeship established with Roosevelt and on the Anglo-American association that he believed to be inevitable. "When I looked upon that densely-packed congregation of fighting men of the same language, of the same faith, of the same fundamental laws and the same ideals . . . it swept across me that here was the only hope, but also the sure hope, of saving the world from measureless degradation."[8]

Although the United States had not entered the war at the time the Atlantic Charter was produced, the future postwar shape of the world was discussed, rather than just the question of the Allies winning the war. There was a clear emphasis on peacetime aims, including the principles that came to be associated with the Atlantic Charter: national self-determination and territorial integrity. These principles later provided a guide for the State Department in its briefings concerning Eastern Europe for the Yalta and Potsdam conferences in 1945. There was at the Atlantic Charter meetings clear concern over the shape of the postwar world, premature though this may have appeared in 1941. Churchill mentioned the provision of a second front in Europe at the Atlantic meeting; he felt a second front was liable to be a bloody experience reminiscent of the World War I campaigns. In January 1942, after Pearl Harbor, Churchill's reservations were repeated and further expressed to Roosevelt at which time he largely accepted them.

Churchill and Roosevelt discussed military matters more formally at the Casablanca conference, held from January 14–24, 1943. This conference planned the British and American occupation of Sicily and Italy. It also produced the Allied call for unconditional surrender from Japan, Italy, and Germany. Roosevelt wished to show the Soviet Union that no deals would be made with the enemy. Unconditional surrender, however, did not leave much room for diplomatic concessions. This problem was to particularly affect Allied policies toward Japan and was a factor in the use of the atomic bomb and atomic diplomacy as the Pacific War drew to a close.

Roosevelt and Churchill met twice, with premier of the Soviet Union, Joseph Stalin, at the wartime summit meetings at Teheran from November 28 to December 1, 1943 and at Yalta in the Crimea during February of 1945. The first meeting of Roosevelt and Stalin was at the Teheran conference. Stalin appeared preoccupied with considerations of a second front, although he had much less need of a second front by December 1943. The Soviet Union had largely saved Stalingrad and Moscow, and Red Army forces were on the offensive. Roosevelt may have underestimated Stalin's reading of diplomacy. Promises of a second front, or rather the unwillingness of the United States and Britain to launch one, meant Stalin could expect conciliation on other issues, particularly that of Poland. Stalin wanted to regain territory in Poland that the Soviet Union had temporarily occupied as a result of the infamous Nazi-Soviet Pact of 1939. He also wanted a future Polish government to be friendly towards the Soviet Union and satisfy Soviet security fears. Yet the Polish government-in-exile, based in London, wanted a reasonable and fair settlement of Polish interests in line with principles of national self-determination. These issues largely had to wait for the Yalta conference for them to be aired in formal discussions. Stalin and Churchill at Teheran were happy to discuss Poland informally after Roosevelt had retired to bed. Roosevelt did not wish to make domestically unpopular decisions over Poland, because Polish-Americans might take offense at a pro-Soviet policy, which could be a problem for Roosevelt in seeking a fourth presidential term of office in 1944. He also did not wish to offend constituents in significant congressional districts in the United States because he also wanted support in Congress for a postwar international organization.

Over the problem of a French government that had collaborated with the Germans, Roosevelt was less reticent. He felt Indochina should not be returned to France as part of its colonial empire at the conclusion of the War, although this policy was not undertaken because it proved necessary to have the diplomatic support of France at the end of the war. The Teheran conference did not show signs of cold war hostility, but was a fairly cordial event where Roosevelt and Churchill believed the Soviet Union to be indispensable to victory and the postwar peace.

Yalta and the High Costs of Peace

The Yalta conference was an eight-day conference held from February 4 to 12, 1945. Franklin Roosevelt, Joseph Stalin, and Winston Churchill, along with their foreign ministers, interpreters, and advisers, met at the Livadiya Palace in Yalta in the Crimea. It is a testament to the determination of Roosevelt to meet and do business with Stalin that he should have travelled so far to meet with him, particularly since his own suggestions of Scotland, Athens, Cyprus, and Malta were rejected by Stalin. W. Averell Harriman records a cable that Harry Hopkins, special assistant to the president, sent to Roosevelt about the choice of venue: "Churchill . . . says that if we had spent ten years on research we could not have found a worse place in the world than MAGNETO [the code name for Yalta] but that he feels that he can survive it by bringing an adequate supply of whiskey."[9]

Roosevelt was aware of Congressional worries about the conduct of executive foreign policy, and he put together a very nonpartisan delegation for the Yalta visit. Roosevelt's secretary of state Edward R. Stettinius Jr. was known for agreeing with the president. Other luminaries with Roosevelt included Harry Hopkins; chief of staff, Fleet Admiral William Leahy; Averell Harriman, ambassador to the Soviet Union; James F. Byrnes, director of the Office of War Mobilisation; and George C. Marshall, chief of staff of the United States Army. Charles Bohlen served not only as assistant to the secretary of state, but also as a translator because of his knowledge of Russian.

Stettinius wrote his book *Roosevelt and the Russians* in 1950 as a defense of Roosevelt's record at Yalta. *Life* magazine had, as early as September of 1948, pilloried the Yalta conference as being a case of appeasement of the Soviet Union. The previous American ambassador to the Soviet Union, William C. Bullitt, was damning of Roosevelt at Yalta in the same issue of *Life*. Stettinius attempted to counter Bullitt's harsh claims, including the following criticism: "He [Roosevelt] was ill. Little was left of the physical and mental vigour that had been his when he entered the White House in 1933. Frequently he had difficulty in formulating his thoughts, and greater difficulty in expressing them consecutively. But he still held to his determination to appease Stalin."[10]

Roosevelt at Yalta did not wish to give the impression of a united front made up of the United States and Britain, a condition that might upset the Soviet Union. Roosevelt sought a commitment from Stalin that the Soviet

Union would enter the war in Asia and also join a postwar international organization. The atomic bomb was still under development at this time, the war against Japan appeared to be a potentially long and difficult one. The costs of defeating Japan, both in terms of human and financial losses, were expected to be high, and General George Marshall saw the wisdom of involving the Soviet Union against the Japanese. Further, a postwar international peacekeeping organization without the Soviet Union could lead to problems parallel to those experienced with the League of Nations after World War I. With this in mind, Roosevelt did not wish to offend Stalin.

The dominant issue discussed at Yalta was that of Poland, which was on the agenda at seven of the eight plenary sessions. Roosevelt's major problem was trying to "square the circle" of upholding principles he had put forward in the earlier Atlantic Charter while providing assurances of security for the Soviet Union. Could Poland be a sovereign and independent state, yet also reside within the sphere of influence of the Soviet Union?

Roosevelt clearly had a belief in his leadership abilities and pursued what Daniel Yergin has described as a "Grand Design."[11] The exact form of the democratic political institutions that should be established in Eastern Europe were not clear. In many ways the detail was not important to Roosevelt if the important foreign-policy principles that concerned the United States were perceived as being upheld. Harriman felt that Roosevelt did not always understand the complexities of the issues being discussed, or care too much about the language used in draft agreements and final protocols.[12] Harriman may also have believed that his own diplomatic role was marginalized at the conference, as did James F. Byrnes, director of the Office of War Mobilization, early on in the conference.[13]

In contrast to Harriman, Admiral Leahy has claimed that Roosevelt understood that the Yalta agreements were elastic, particularly the Declaration on Liberated Europe and the Declaration on Poland. In his view, Roosevelt knew that Stalin perceived democracy differently than Roosevelt and Churchill did. It was apparent to Roosevelt and Churchill that Stalin could exploit the development of a Provisional Government of National Unity for Poland. On Saturday, February 10, 1945, Leahy noted the following about the Declaration on Liberated Poland:

> I saw the now-familiar phrases, such as "strong, free, independent and democratic Poland," Russia "guaranteeing" the liberated country "unfettered election," "universal suffrage," "secret ballot," and so on. I felt strongly that it was so susceptible to different interpretations as to promise little toward the establishment of a government in which all the major Polish political parties would be represented. I handed the paper back to Roosevelt and said: "Mr. President, this is so elastic that the Russians can stretch it all the way from Yalta to Washington without ever technically breaking it." The President replied: "I know, Bill. I know it. But it's the best I can do for Poland at this time."[14]

The Yalta agreements were cleverly sold to the American public and were met with acclaim. Winston Churchill believed it was the best that could be negotiated. Stalin was provided with a temporary moral legitimization for what he had effectively already achieved. If Yalta marks the beginning of the cold war, this was far from evident at the time. It was later, in the more clearly established stage of the cold war, that the Yalta agreements were denounced. In fact they provided a useful standard against which Stalin could be judged as duplicitous in not living up to the agreements. Both Averell Harriman and Charles Bohlen would denounce Stalin for violating the agreements.

Critics of Roosevelt have argued that he had the opportunity to be tough with Stalin, but he did not pursue the opportunity. Concrete settlements were avoided in the spirit of compromise and appeasement. Was Roosevelt an ill, if not dying, sixty-three-year-old man at Yalta? He clearly had failing health, but it is not clear that this impaired his mental capabilities and his ability to deal with Stalin.[15] Ambassador Harriman has speculated, "I suppose that if FDR had been in better health, he might have held out longer and got his way on a number of detailed points. But I can't believe that it would have made a great difference on, say, the Polish question. At the time of Yalta, the Red Army was in full control of the country and no amount of careful drafting could have changed that."[16] It must also not be forgotten that the Soviet Union was an ally of the United States, and its participation was clearly required if an inclusive postwar international organization was to function. The background to the Yalta agreements is the total war situation that the Soviet Union, Britain, and the United States have been locked into since 1941.

The editors of *Roosevelt and Churchill: Their Secret Wartime Correspondence* draw the conclusion that "Roosevelt and Churchill did not anticipate and made no contingency plans for the possibility of renewed friction with the Soviet Union in 1944–1945 or for the coming of the cold war."[17] However, a letter from Roosevelt to Churchill on March 29, 1945 illustrates Roosevelt's post-Yalta concern over the Soviet Union:

> I have likewise been watching with anxiety and concern the development of Soviet attitude since the Crimea conference. I am acutely aware of the dangers inherent in the present course of events not only for the immediate issues involved and our decisions at the Crimea but also for the San Francisco conference and future world cooperation. Our peoples and indeed those of the whole world are watching with anxious hope the extent to which the decisions we reached at the Crimea are being honestly carried forward.[18]

Roosevelt's China Policy

Although Roosevelt had approved making the winning of the war in Europe a priority, he did not forget or neglect the war in Asia. Despite the fact that Roosevelt had not been to Asia, he felt an affinity with and good will toward China. China was expected to be a significant political power in Asia after World War II, and Roosevelt believed that it could achieve the status of a great power. Roosevelt adopted a legislative program concerning China that suited his approach to crisis and problem management. In 1943 the president obtained the approval of the American Senate and a treaty was ratified that relinquished American claims in China and the exemption of Americans from Chinese law.[19] It had been an embarrassment to the Chinese that foreigners were exempt from laws in China. A second piece of legislation withdrew the harsh discrimination against Chinese who wished to settle in the United States. It was a sane, democratic, and rational approach to crisis.

As the Chinese requested a new military front from the Allies in 1943, Roosevelt had to consider alternative military and strategic plans for China. Despite the military priority accorded to Western Europe, Roosevelt did not drain supplies away from the Far East. James MacGregor Burns summarized, "Roosevelt could not allow himself the simplicity of one set tactic. He was following his usual multichanneled approach to a number of goals. He wanted to keep China in the war. . . . He wanted to prepare China for a major postwar role, so that it would become a member of the highest council of world organization."[20]

Roosevelt's Approach to Crisis

President Roosevelt commented, dramatically, "It's a terrible thing to look over your shoulder when you are trying to lead–and to find no one there." [21] Yet an American president is not short of advice or advisers in times of crisis. As commander in chief, Roosevelt did not lack for formal or informal advisers, and there were plenty of competent and qualified officials to proffer advice, if Roosevelt sought it. He was, of course, correct in believing that executive decisions and ultimate decisions on the conduct of World War II for the United States lay with him.

In many ways President Roosevelt's approach to decision-making was determined by whom he was dealing with and the circumstances of World War II. In the Soviet Union, Roosevelt was dealing with a dictator with a legendary concern with secrecy and with unrivalled authority. Stalin's control of purges, secret police, and a gulag environment made rather bizarre personal diplomacy necessary if this unholy alliance between the Soviet Union and the United States was not to unravel rather swiftly. If Roosevelt was to achieve his postwar aims, he had to confront, negotiate with, and reassure Stalin. Diane Clemens has reminded us that the diplomacy of Yalta was very suspect: "Negotiations with the Soviet Union are themselves unacceptable and constitute a type of compromise, reminiscent of Munich and 'appeasement.'"[22] It is also widely acknowledged, including by Clemens, that a substantial difference between the German appeasement at Munich and the Yalta agreements is that Stalin, Roosevelt, and Churchill were trying to turn victory into an enduring peace.[23]

Roosevelt rose to the challenge of making important decisions through summit diplomacy and through regular correspondence and communication with Allied leaders, including Stalin. His style and notable confidence enabled him to carry out American foreign policy under his own personal direction and to ignore advice when he so desired. However, Roosevelt's decisions at Yalta were executive agreements. They may have been morally binding on Roosevelt, but did not have the status of official treaties until approved by a two-thirds majority in the Senate. Congress would also control the purse strings for any agreement that required funding, and this could not be considered a foregone conclusion for any president of the United States.

World War II was a series of crises of such magnitude that it would be difficult to conceive of United States foreign-policy decision-making procedures staying entirely as they were. A new rationalization was brought to foreign policy as a consequence of the war. New structures and organizations had to be developed to deal with wartime emergencies, such as the War Food Administration, Office of Lend-Lease Administration, the Office of War Mobilization, and the Office of War Information. The reorganization, modernization, and efficiency was delivered not so much through the efforts of Roosevelt's secretary of state, Cordell Hull, but those of his undersecretary of state (and successor to Hull), Edward Stettinius.

There was a pressing demand for reorganization. The task was carried out during 1944 by Undersecretary of State Edward R. Stettinius, a skilled administrator from the world of business–General Motors and U.S. Steel. Stettinius refashioned and rationalized the geographical and functional divisions of the department, putting similar tasks in the same offices and drawing more efficient lines of reporting to relieve top officials of routine decisions and give them more time for policy analysis and long-range planning.[24]

Roosevelt put in place new structures and had a range of very competent administrators in Stettinius, Dean Acheson, William L. Clayton, Admiral W. Leahy, Joseph C. Grew, and James F. Byrnes. Yet, as demonstrated by circumstances and events surrounding the Yalta decisions, Roosevelt was capable of making sweeping foreign-policy decisions with or without State Department assistance. Eleanor Roosevelt summed this up on one occasion suggesting "the President never 'thinks'! He decides."[25]

President Roosevelt disdained arguments with his subordinates, and his preferred role was that of a mediator and a manager who had confidence in his own counsel and leadership. Succeeding presidents would also often disdain arguments with their staff, but they would have different ways of avoiding disputes and imposing their own strategic thinking. Although Roosevelt influenced a significant body of policies, he of course did not live to put his final imprint on how World War II should be concluded and he was not there to oversee the postwar peace.

Truman's Inheritance and Dilemmas

The death of Franklin Roosevelt from a brain hemorrhage on April 12, 1945, thrust forward a vice president allegedly inexperienced in foreign affairs. Harry S. Truman, vice president only since January 1945, became president of the immense military and economic powerhouse of the United States. Was Truman qualified for the job? All new presidents are by definition inexperienced in the position, and it is extremely difficult to gain all the necessary expertise to be a chief executive, head of state, and commander in chief. Unlike Roosevelt, Truman did have battle experience. He had been a captain of artillery in France during World War I, and he came out of military service a brevet major.[26]

The image of Truman having been ill-prepared for foreign-policy decision-making comes at least partly from the fact that Roosevelt had not taken him into his confidence in revealing to him the secret of the atomic bomb program, the Manhattan Project. Of course, very few people in the Roosevelt administration knew of its existence, and as successor to the four-times-elected Franklin Roosevelt, Truman would immediately appear inexperienced for the office of president. Truman also portrayed himself as a novice in world affairs, which was a useful diplomatic ploy, as well as a strategy for limiting expectations of him. Harry Truman cultivated an earthy approach that worked against the image of personal grandeur and statesmanship associated with Roosevelt.

Truman was happy to see himself portrayed as an unsuccessful haberdasher from Missouri, yet he had been a judge in his county and a senator in Congress since his election to the position in 1934. During World War II, Truman launched a Special Committee Investigating the National Defense Program and was a well-respected member of the Democratic Party. Although he was launched into the presidency at a traumatic time in the history of the United States and would be faced with unparalleled decisions, Truman was not ignorant of foreign affairs.

The new president was not short on advice and advisers. The normal State Department briefing papers were provided for Truman to acquaint him with the major issues in world affairs. "Hawks" and "Doves" within the Administration attempted to influence the direction of American policy towards the Soviet Union. The American Ambassador to the Soviet Union, W. Averell Harriman, made his anti-Soviet views known to Truman in the White House in April of 1945. "Doves" like the secretary of war, Henry Stimson, and the secretary of commerce, Henry Wallace, would also try to influence Truman's views. Congress was equally determined to influence the new president, and the prominent senator Arthur H. Vandenberg recorded in his diary on April 13, 1945, the day after Roosevelt's death, "Truman came back to the Senate this noon for lunch with a few of us. It shattered all tradition. But it was both wise and smart. It means that the days of executive contempt for Congress are ended; that we are returning to a government in which Congress will take its rightful place."[27]

A State Department briefing paper summarizing the international problems facing Truman was prepared for him for the afternoon of April 13. The new president had requested this from Secretary Stettinius. It advised him that "[s]ince the Yalta Conference the Soviet Government has taken a firm and uncompromising position on nearly every major question that has arisen in our relations. . . . In the liberated areas under Soviet control, the Soviet Government is proceeding largely on a unilateral basis."[28] The State Department summary went on to warn the president that the situation in Poland was "highly unsatisfactory."[29] Later in the month of April, Truman was warned by Ambassador Harriman that the Soviet Union perceived the United States as rather weak, and he used the emotional description of the Soviet threat being that of a "barbarian invasion of Europe."[30]

Good news for the Allies at the end of April included the announcement of the death of Adolf Hitler, and by May 2 over one million troops had surrendered in Italy and Soviet forces had control of Berlin. On May 7 the German High Command surrendered unconditionally. This allowed Truman and Churchill the opportunity to declare Victory in Europe Day on May 8, the celebrations of which were slightly muted by minor military skirmishes in Europe and the more significant fact that the war in the Far East was still a considerable problem.

Toward the end of May 1945, in an effort to break the impasse with the Soviet Union over the issues of Poland, the United Nations, and Soviet entry into the war against Japan, Truman was encouraged by Harriman and Charles Bohlen to send Harry Hopkins as an envoy to Moscow, despite his being ill. President Truman told his experienced envoy that he could "use diplomatic language or he could use a baseball bat if he thought that was the proper approach to Mr. Stalin."[31] The latter did not prove necessary when Hopkins, Harriman, and Bohlen met Stalin six separate times in the Kremlin, meetings that began on May 26 and were brought to a close in a final meeting on June 6. These meetings did not include British representatives, and Hopkins felt mildly hampered by not knowing Churchill's exact and current position on issues like Poland. Hopkins cabled Truman and the State Department with a report after each meeting. A cable about the third meeting has fuelled the debate concerning whether or not Truman, armed with knowledge of Stalin's views about Japan, ordered that atomic bombs, when they became available, be used against Japan, ostensibly to keep the Soviet Union out of Japan. Hopkins's cabled report included this ordered list of comments:

1. Japan is doomed and the Japanese know it.

2. Peace feelers are being put out by certain elements in Japan and we should therefore consider together our joint attitude and act in concert about the surrender of Japan. Stalin expressed the fear that the Japanese will try to split the allies. The following are his statements about surrender:

A. The Soviet Union prefers to go through with unconditional surrender. . . .

B. However, he feels that if we stick to unconditional surrender the
Japs will not give up and we will have to destroy them as we did
Germany.

C. The Japanese may offer to surrender and seek softer terms. While
consideration of this has certain dangers as compared with (A) it
nevertheless cannot be ruled out. Should the Allies depart from
the announced policy of unconditional surrender and be prepared to accept a modified surrender, Stalin visualizes imposing
our will through our occupying forces and thereby gaining substantially the same results as under (A). In other words, it seemed
to us that he proposes under this heading to agree to milder peace
terms but once we get into Japan to give them the works.

3. The Marshal expects that Russia will share in the actual occupation
of Japan and wants an agreement with the British and us as to occupation zones.

4. He also wants an understanding between the Allies as to areas of
operation in China and Manchuria.[32]

The question of Poland was still a test case of Soviet-American cooperation. Hopkins did not insist that democracy be established in Poland with all
the same trappings as the United States. However, Truman did expect the
Soviet Union to make symbolic changes that would show good faith on its
part. "He [Hopkins] said the question of Poland per se was not so important
as the fact that it had become a symbol of our [the United States'] ability to
work out problems with the Soviet Union. He said that we had no special
interests in Poland and no special desire to see any particular type of government."[33] Progress was made over Poland in that the Lublin government was
given four more members from democratic groups, including Stanislaw
Mikolajczyk, prime minister of the Polish government-in-exile in London.

Walter Isaacson and Evan Thomas suggest in their book *The Wise Men*
that this mission by Hopkins to the Soviet Union "represented perhaps the
last full-fledged effort to salvage the shaky alliance."[34] In this regard Harriman and Hopkins had some optimism in believing that Stalin was a realist
and would not try to dominate Poland completely. A workable Soviet-
American alliance appeared to still be in play after this mission. Herbert
Feis suggests that "[s]ince the mutual candor of these talks was accepted by
each as a service to the search for friendship, it did not lead to rancor."[35]
This strategy from a senior assistant to the president and the Soviet leader
was very effective as preparation for the Potsdam conference.

What became significant cold war problems were evident to a degree at
the Yalta conference, but the Potsdam conference serves as a more definitive
point of termination of the World War II cooperation between the United

States and the Soviet Union and the onset of cold war problems. Appropriately, the code name for the Potsdam conference was "Terminal," and although it was not the exact ending of World War II, it appears to mark the cessation of a considerable amount of wartime cooperation between the United States and the Soviet Union.

The Potsdam conference, held at the Cecilienhof Palace in Potsdam in Germany from July 17 to August 2, 1945, coincides with the United States' successful test of an atomic bomb at Alamogordo, New Mexico, creating a new atomic age and arguably the advent of atomic diplomacy. Truman was the first president to have an atomic bomb at his disposal, and he is also the only president so far to have used it. It was at the start of the conference, on July 16, that Truman was secretly informed that the United States had detonated an atomic bomb. The coded message was received by Henry Stimson and read in part, "Operated on this morning. Diagnosis not yet complete but results seem satisfactory and already exceed expectations."[36] Stimson informed Truman and the next day also informed Churchill. Details of the nature and ferocity of the explosion at the Alamogordo site were also conveyed to the president. Although Churchill was worried about the disclosure of information, Truman recounts in his memoirs how he rather simply and informally told Stalin on July 24 that he had "a new weapon of special destructive force."[37] This conversation did not include the word atomic or the phrase atomic bomb and Truman did not reveal the exact report of the atomic test to Stalin.

President Truman had gone to the Potsdam conference rather nervous of confronting the elder statesmen, Churchill and Stalin. However, the situation did not remain static; after defeat in the British general election, Churchill was replaced at the conference from July 26 by prime minister Clement Attlee, and foreign secretary Ernest Bevin replaced Anthony Eden. Interestingly, Stalin initially appeared to be a character with whom Truman could do business. Truman's stature at Potsdam was aided by the fact that he chaired the conference sessions, and his military position as commander in chief of American forces was advanced by the news that came from New Mexico about the testing of an atomic bomb.

Many historians have debated the extent to which President Truman pursued atomic diplomacy at Potsdam. It is not always clear what atomic diplomacy refers to. For historian Gar Alperovitz, it concerns how Truman delayed the Potsdam conference, sought diplomatic leverage at Potsdam from the possession of atomic weapons, and used the bombs against the Japanese for other than purely military reasons. Alperovitz argues the New Mexico test had a psychological impact on both Truman and Byrnes, stating that "[t]he emotional impact of the new development added a special psychological dimension to their confidence—and to expectations of a future in which the atomic bomb would play a major role in world affairs."[38] Further, the two atomic bombs dropped on Hiroshima and Nagasaki, it has been argued, were used to gain strategic political and military initiatives against the Soviet Union. No direct statements by Truman at Potsdam confirm the existence then of such a strategy.

The agenda of the Potsdam conference included the questions relating to the future of the Balkan countries, the four-power administration of Germany, and the control of Austria and Poland's eastern borders. For the first formal meeting, the delegation from the United States comprised President Harry Truman; Secretary of State James Byrnes; Admiral William Leahy; the ambassador to the Soviet Union and United States representative on the Polish question, W. Averell Harriman; the United States representative on the Allied Commission on Reparations, Edwin W. Pauley; the chairman of the president's War Relief Control Board, Joseph E. Davies; assistant secretaries James C. Dunn and William L. Clayton, Benjamin Cohen, H. Freeman Matthews, and interpreter, Charles E. Bohlen.[39]

The chairman of the plenary sessions at Potsdam was Truman, and he set about establishing his agenda. Broadly, he wanted the establishment of a Council of Foreign Ministers that would include France and China, the settlement of questions concerning Germany, the reaffirmation of the Yalta protocols, and a clear policy on Italy. Stalin's agenda bore some similarity, but the emphasis was on reparations, the demilitarization of Germany, and diplomatic recognition for East European states under Soviet control. The British agenda emphasized Poland, Germany, Austria, and the Balkans.[40] Truman had been well briefed on board the *Augusta* prior to the conference, but he had no actual experience of this level of diplomacy and he found the work rather frustrating.

The Labour Party victory in the British general election of 1945 elevated Clement Attlee to prime minister and led to Ernest Bevin being flown to Potsdam. The British maintained continuity through the help of Churchill, Eden, and other civil servants, but the style and tone of the conference changed. The United States delegation managed to make more progress, at least in the speed of decision-making, and Churchill's notable interventions no longer held them back.

Truman and his advisers at Potsdam, particularly Byrnes, Clayton, and Pauley, largely felt satisfied with the agreements on Germany in terms of demilitarization, denazification, and reparations. The United States managed to avoid a dollar sum being assigned to reparations, and they felt that they had secured sufficient supplies of food and fuel from the Soviet zone of Germany to make their zone economically viable. However, the United States differed with the Soviet Union on broad strategy towards Germany, and it did not wish to see Germany kept as weak as the Soviets preferred. The view that had been presented by the secretary of the treasury, Henry Morgenthau Jr., to have Germany deindustrialised was not a view prominent for very long, nor was it supported by the State Department. Instead the United States opted for a policy that it hoped would produce a significant measure of German economic recovery. This, it was believed, would help lead to a democratized and hence a peaceful Germany. Secretary

Byrnes, alongside Pauley and Clayton, believed they had obtained a good deal on reparations, although the actual details, parts of which favored the Soviet Union, appear less than straightforward:

> In addition to the reparations to be taken by the U.S.S.R. from its own zone of occupation, the U.S.S.R. shall receive additionally from the Western Zones:
>
> A. 15 percent of such usable and complete industrial capital equipment, in the first place from the metallurgical, chemical and machine manufacturing industries, as is unnecessary for the German peace economy and should be removed from the Western Zones of Germany, in exchange for an equivalent value of food, coal, potash, zinc, timber, clay products, petroleum products, and such other commodities as may be agreed upon.
>
> B. 10 percent of such industrial capital equipment as is unnecessary for the German peace economy and should be removed from the Western Zones, to be transferred to the Soviet Government on reparations account without payment or exchange of any kind in return.[41]

Reciprocity was clearly written into point (a), but this would prove problematic in implementation. The agreement also allowed the Soviet Union to settle Polish reparation claims out of its own share, a decision that clearly puts Poland and the Soviet Union into a working relationship. Despite these features, the delegation of the United States appeared to be initially satisfied with the result.

Ultimately, however, James Byrnes rather appropriately called chapter four of his book *Speaking Frankly* (published in 1947), "Potsdam–The Success That Failed," and wrote, "We considered the conference a success. We firmly believed that the agreements reached would provide a basis for the early restoration of stability to Europe. The agreements did make the conference a success but the violation of those agreements has turned success into failure."[42] Truman can be criticized for allowing too many decisions to be passed on to a future Council of Foreign Ministers. In particular, the diplomatic recognition of the "satellite" states in Eastern Europe would be left for future examination, and peace treaties with these countries remained to be established. No binding arrangements for Poland's frontiers were agreed upon, although the borders that were eventually introduced would later reflect much that had been discussed previously. The vague agreements from Yalta stood, but the United States did not formally invite the Soviet Union to enter the war against Japan. Truman may no longer have wanted the Soviet Union to be involved in the war against Japan, for he of course now had a bigger ally, the atomic bomb.

The decisions to drop two atomic bombs on Japan at Hiroshima and Nagasaki are clearly two of the most dramatic and monumental events in history. Truman had been unhappy with the rejection by the Japanese of the unconditional surrender required by the Allies in the Potsdam Declaration. Truman was to recount, "They told me to go to hell, words to that effect."[43] The Americans do not explicitly warn the Japanese about the first bomb to be dropped. It is unclear if this was because the United States did not wish to potentially waste one of the two bombs in a demonstration in Tokyo Harbor or some other, more benign site, but whatever the reason, the first bomb was dropped, on Harry S. Truman's orders, on the industrial city of Hiroshima, and he always said that he did not lose a night's sleep over the decision.

Truman was always characteristically brief in claiming the dropping of the atomic bombs was for military reasons. "Four cities were finally recommended as targets: Hiroshima, Kokura, Nagasaki, and Niigata."[44] These he described as appropriate military targets, and he investigated the details for a final choice of the first target with Secretary Stimson, General Marshall, and General Henry H. Arnold of the U.S. Army Air Forces.[45] Truman unreservedly recounted, "The final decision of where and when to use the atomic bomb was up to me. Let there be no mistake about it. I regarded the bomb as a military weapon and never had any doubt that it should be used."[46] While still returning home from Potsdam aboard the *Augusta* on August 6, Truman received the report that Hiroshima had been hit with the atomic bomb. While the world digested this news, three days later, on August 9, a second atomic bomb was dropped on Japan at Nagasaki. It was a military weapon developed and used during war to end a military conflict. Of course, this may not have been its exclusive use and not only did it shorten the war against Japan, but it also rendered redundant the Soviet Union's declaration of war against Japan. The United States had made it apparent to the Soviet Union that they had awesome military power and the willingness to use it.

The amount of controversy that the alternative views on the reasons behind the use of the atomic bombs can cause was evident in January 1995. A major exhibition at the National Air and Space Museum of the Smithsonian Institution in Washington, D.C. was cancelled and only a very small exhibition commemorating the *Enola Gay's* bombing of Japan fifty years previously went ahead. The revisionist text of the cancelled exhibition expressed skepticism about the necessity of using atomic bombs against Japan. It was designed to be controversial and evoke how scholarship on the matter posed awkward questions and answers. On the issue of the significance of Japanese peace feelers and the rather counterfactual areas of how the war might have ended, the original script read: "It is . . . clear that there were alternatives to both an invasion and dropping atomic bombs without warning–for example guaranteeing the Emperor's position, staging a demonstration of the bomb's power, or waiting for blockade, firebombing and a Soviet declaration of war to take their toll on Japan." [47]

Truman would justify the necessity of the bombs in the context of saving American lives. Gar Alperovitz cites the "chief historian of the U.S. Regulatory Commission," J. Samuel Walker in defence of his revisionist views and claims they were influential in his writing *The Decision to Use the Atomic Bomb and the Architecture of the American Myth*.[48] Walker wrote in an article in 1990: "The consensus among scholars is that the bomb was not needed to avoid an invasion of Japan and to end the war within a relatively short time. It is clear that alternatives to the bomb existed and that Truman and his advisers knew it."[49] The extent to which the Japanese were seeking a peace before the atomic bombs and how much unconditional surrender could have been redefined by the Allies is much debated in literature dealing with the use of the atomic bombs. Barton Bernstein has also been critical of the Truman premise for dropping the bomb and the number of American lives that might have been saved.

Perhaps in the aftermath of Hiroshima and Nagasaki, Truman developed a need to exaggerate the number of U.S. lives that the bombs might have saved by possibly helping render the invasions unnecessary. It is probably true, as he contended repeatedly, that he never lost any sleep over his decision. Believing ultimately in the myth of 500,000 lives saved may have been a way of concealing ambivalence, even from himself. The myth also helped deter Americans from asking troubling questions about the use of the atomic bombs.[50]

Yet as Samuel Walker has pointed out in the context of collective memory outside critical scholarly research: "Most Americans, it seems safe to say, would accept without serious reservation the assertion of President George H. W. Bush in 1991 that dropping the bombs 'spared millions of American lives.'"[51]

Notes

1. Franklin Delano Roosevelt memorial in Washington, D.C.
2. "Roosevelt's War Message, 1941," in T. G. Paterson and D. Merrill, *Major Problems in American Foreign Relations,* Vol. II, *Since 1914* (Lexington, Massachusetts: D. C. Heath and Company, 1975), 146–147.
3. E. Larrabee, *Commander in Chief: Franklin Delano Roosevelt, His Lieutenants, and Their War* (New York: Simon and Schuster, 1987).
4. Ibid., 33. See also, in particular, F. L. Lowenheim, H. D. Langley, and M. Jonas, eds., *Roosevelt and Churchill: Their Secret Wartime Correspondence* (London: Barrie & Jenkins, 1975). They point out (p. 4) that between September 1939 and April 1945 of all the letters, messages and telegrams that passed between Roosevelt and Churchill "over 700 [were] from Roosevelt and over 1,000 from Churchill."
5. Churchill was eight years older than Roosevelt.
6. J. Charmley, *Churchill's Grand Alliance: The Anglo-American Special Relationship, 1940–1957* (London: Hodder and Stoughton, 1995).
7. August 1941, at Newfoundland; December 1941, at Washington, D.C.; January 1943, at Casablanca; May 1943, at Washington D.C.; August 1943, at Québec;

November 1943, at Cairo; November 1943, at Teheran; September 1944, at Québec; and February 1945, at Yalta. Counting the stopover at Cairo after the Yalta conference, the total number is ten.

8. British Broadcasting Company broadcast, August 24, 1941, in *Churchill* (London: BBC Education, 1992), 154–155.

9. W. A. Harriman and E. Abel, *Special Envoy to Churchill and Stalin 1941–1946* (London: Hutchinson, 1975), 390.

10. E. R. Stettinius, *Roosevelt and the Russians* (London: Jonathan Cape, 1950), 15.

11. See chapter 1, part II, "The Yalta Axioms: Roosevelt's Grand Design," D.Yergin, *Shattered Peace: The Origins of the Cold War and the National Security State* (Boston: Houghton Mifflin, 1977), 42-68.

12. Harriman and Abel, *Special Envoy to Churchill and Stalin,* 399.

13. Ibid., 395.

14. W. D. Leahy, *I Was There* (New York: McGraw Hill, 1950), 370.

15. Robert Ferrell argues that President Roosevelt's failing health in his final years in office had a crucial effect on his performance as president. R. H. Ferrell, *The Dying President: Franklin D. Roosevelt, 1944–1945* (Columbia, Missouri: University of Missouri Press, 1998).

16. Harriman and Abel, *Special Envoy to Churchill and Stalin,* 390.

17. Loewenheim, et. al., *Roosevelt and Churchill,* 72.

18. Ibid., 689–690.

19. J. MacGregor Burns, *Roosevelt: The Soldier of Freedom, 1940–1945* (London: Weidenfeld and Nicholson, 1971), 375

20. MacGregor Burns, *Roosevelt: The Soldier of Freedom,* 378.

21. J. G. Clifford, "Bureaucratic Politics and Policy Outcomes," in T. G. Paterson and D. Merrill, *Major Problems in American Foreign Relations,* Vol. II, *Since 1914* (Lexington, Massachusetts: D. C. Heath and Company, 1995), 21.

22. D. S. Clemens, "Yalta: Conference of Victory and Peace," in P. Brundu Olla, editor, *Yalta: Un Mito Che Resiste* (Roma: Edizioni Dell'Ateneo, 1988), 7.

23. Ibid., 13.

24. J. E. Dougherty and R. L. Pfaltzgraff Jr., *American Foreign Policy: FDR to Reagan* (New York: Harper and Row, 1986), 43.

25. Larrabee, *Commander in Chief,* 644 (citing a conversation between John Gunther and Eleanor Roosevelt).

26. A brevet rank meant that the person carried the higher title, while remaining at a lower rank in terms of authority and pay.

27. A. H. Vandenberg Jr., editor, *The Private Papers of Senator Vandenberg* (Boston: Houghton Mifflin, 1952), 167.

28. H. S. Truman, *Memoirs,* Vol. 1, *Year of Decisions, 1945* (Suffolk: Hodder and Stoughton, 1955), 15.

29. Ibid., 15.

30. Ibid., 73.

31. W. Isaacson and E. Thomas, *The Wise Men: Six Friends and the World They Made* (London: Faber and Faber, 1986), 283.

32. R. E. Sherwood, *Roosevelt and Hopkins: An Intimate History* (New York: Harper & Brothers, 1948), 903–904. An account of the conversation has also been recounted by Charles Bohlen: See "Memorandum by the Assistant to the Secretary of State," May 27, 1945, *Foreign Relations of the United States, The Conference of Berlin, 1945,* Vol. 1

(Washington, D.C.: Government Printing Office, 1960), 44. (Hereafter cited as *FRUS, The Conference of Berlin.*)

33. *FRUS, The Conference of Berlin*, p. 38.

34. Isaacson and Thomas, *The Wise Men*, 283.

35. H. Feis, *Between War and Peace: The Potsdam Conference* (New Jersey: Princeton University Press, 1960), 101.

36. Ibid., 72. See also G. Alperovitz, *Atomic Diplomacy: Hiroshima and Potsdam* (London: Pluto Press, revised edition, 1994), 195.

37. Truman, *Memoirs,* Vol. 1, 346.

38. G. Alperovitz, *The Decision to Use the Atomic Bomb and the Architecture of an American Myth* (London: Fontana Press,1996, first published 1995) 224.

39. Truman, *Memoirs,* Vol. 1, 269.

40. See "Preparation of the Agenda," *FRUS, The Conference of Berlin,* 156–245.

41. M. E. Pelly and H. J. Yasamee, eds., *Documents on British Policy Overseas, Series 1,* Vol. 1, *The Conference at Potsdam* (London: Her Majesty's Stationery Office, 1984), 1268–1269.

42. J. F. Byrnes, Speaking Frankly (New York: Harper & Brothers, 1947), 87.

43. R. H. Ferrell, *Harry S. Truman: A Life* (Norwalk, Connecticut: The Easton Press, 1994), 215.

44. Truman, *Memoirs,* Vol. 1, 350.

45. Ibid., 350.

46. Ibid., 350.

47. Richard H. Kohn, "History and the Culture Wars; The Case of the Smithsonian Institution's Enola Gay Exhibition," *Journal of American History* 82, 3 (December 1995), 1045.

48. Alperovitz, *The Decision to Use the Atomic Bomb,* 7.

49. Ibid., 6-7. Also see, J. S. Walker, "The Decision to Use the Bomb: A Historiographical Update," *Diplomatic History* 14, 1 (Winter 1990).

50. B. Bernstein, cited in Walker, ibid., 422–23, endnote 25.

51. J. S. Walker, "History, Collective Memory, and the Decision to Use the Bomb," *Diplomatic History* 19, 2 (Spring 1995), 320.

CHAPTER 3

Harry S. Truman and Containment, 1946–1952

I'm tired of babying the Soviets.[1]
—*President Truman*

Whether or not President Truman had strong anti-Soviet feelings in 1945 and 1946 is the subject of a considerable amount of academic debate. Truman as a cold war warrior is the image that Truman portrayed in his two volumes of memoirs. If we accept Truman's account, then he was a man who did not suffer fools, was capable of making tough decisions quickly, and would put subordinates in their place when he felt that they usurped their powers. A good example of this last point is the relationship between President Truman and his secretary of state, James F. Byrnes. Historian Gar Alperovitz has led us to believe that Truman was dependent on James Byrnes, particularly with regard to the atomic diplomacy practiced by Byrnes. Yet Truman's own account of the relationship is that of a president who lost patience with Byrnes when he did not keep him fully informed about the diplomacy being pursued toward the Soviet Union, especially during the meetings of the Council of Foreign Ministers.

Truman claims that he was unhappy with Byrnes as early as December 1945, and on board the presidential yacht, the *Williamsburg*, Truman made Byrnes aware of this. It was a criticism that was reinforced when Truman berated Byrnes in the White House in early January 1946. It may tell us much about Truman that he put his thoughts in a letter to Byrnes but never sent it, deciding instead to read it aloud to Byrnes. It appears an incongruous situation, and the events were disputed by James Byrnes. If we accept Truman's account, we have a communication that provides a memorable cold war development as Truman lost patience with the Soviet Union, and we also have the private dressing down of the secretary of state, from which he could not easily recover Yet the image left by the account of Truman's strong personnel management and anti-Soviet stance is largely one provided from Truman. The unsent letter dated January 5, 1946 was a defense of the presidential prerogative to make decisions in foreign policy, and it read in part:

> I received no communication from you directly while you were in Moscow. The only message I had from you came as a reply to one which I had Under Secretary Acheson send to you about my interview with the Senate Committee on Atomic Energy.
>
> The protocol was not submitted to me, nor was the communiqué. I was completely in the dark on the whole conference until I requested you to come to the *Williamsburg* and inform me. The communiqué was released before I even saw it. . . .
>
> At Potsdam we were faced with an accomplished fact and were, by circumstances, almost forced to agree to Russian occupation of Eastern Poland and the occupation of that part of Germany east of the Oder River by Poland. It was a high handed outrage.
>
> At the time we were anxious for Russian entry into the Japanese War. Of course we found later that we didn't need Russia there and the Russians have been a headache to us ever since.
>
> There isn't a doubt in my mind that Russia intends an invasion of Turkey and the seizure of the Black Sea Straits to the Mediterranean. Unless Russia is faced with an iron fist and strong language another war is in the making. Only one language do they understand—"How many divisions have you?"
>
> I do not think we should play compromise any longer. We should refuse to recognize Rumania and Bulgaria until they comply with our requirements; we should let our position on Iran be known in no uncertain terms and we should continue to insist on the internationalization of the Kiel Canal, the Rhine-Danube waterway and the Black Sea Straits and we should maintain complete control of Japan and the Pacific. We should rehabilitate China and create a strong central government there. We should do the same for Korea.
>
> Then we should insist on the return of our ships from Russia and force a settlement of the Lend-Lease debt of Russia.
>
> I'm tired of babying the Soviets.[2]

With Truman's expressed outrage at a number of Soviet policies, it might surprise us that this feeling was not expressed to the American public at the earliest opportunity. The press was given Truman's vote of confidence in Secretary Byrnes shortly after the incident, and Byrnes was later to deny the event ever took place. When illness required Byrnes to resign he was replaced by General George C. Marshall, a man much admired by Truman.

Containment was to provide an intellectual development in American foreign policy and was not a development stemming from a heightened international crisis caused by one significant event. At the time of George F. Kennan's "8,000-word Long Telegram" from the American Embassy in Moscow on February 22, 1946, the issues of Soviet forces in Iran, spies in Canada working for the Soviet Union, and Soviet attitudes to Eastern Europe and the capitalist world were in the public domain. George F. Kennan, as a rather unhappy chargé d'affaires in Moscow, responded rather dramatically to a request for information about Soviet attitudes toward international monetary organizations. Whether or not Kennan intended to have a dramatic impact on the thinking of the Truman administration is unclear. Nevertheless, the rather academic expose of Soviet "paranoia" and ideological vulnerability, coupled with his rather positive suggestions concerning American policy, was greeted with considerable enthusiasm from the State Department and Admiral Forrestal, secretary of the navy. Although Kennan's "Long Telegram" prose did not use the word *containment,* the idea is inherent in his suggestion that the Soviet Union understood the rational use of force and would back down if confronted with superior force in situations that warranted it.

The climate of international affairs had been soured by a Marxist-Leninist speech by Stalin on February 9, 1946. World War II was portrayed as a product of capitalist forces, and thus Stalin's speech in Moscow was more reminiscent of Lenin's views about World War I than Stalin's hitherto attitudes toward the Grand Alliance during World War II. Stalin's views appeared to presage a considerable shift in Soviet rhetoric and propaganda against the West. Kennan's "Long Telegram" came hot on the heels of Stalin's public return to more orthodox Marxist-Leninist roots.

On Iran, the Soviet Union was accused by the United States of not arranging to remove troops from its area of occupation, and the issue was taken to the United Nations for public deliberation. The Soviet Union was further accused of fermenting political unrest in northern Iran by delaying withdrawal of all of its troops from Azerbaijan and encouraging a puppet regime there. Given that after cajoling, the Soviet Union eventually withdrew from Iran, the questions of whether or not the Soviets acted in good faith and had trustworthy intentions toward Iran were worrying the United States in 1946.

Also the Gouzenko spy scandal in Canada, which had been kept under wraps since September 1945, became public in February 1946. A Soviet spy ring in Canada was revealed through the defection of a Soviet cypher clerk, Igor Gouzenko, working in Ottawa. President Truman and Clement Attlee, the British prime minister, had been informed directly of the events by William Lyon Mackenzie King, the Canadian prime minister. None of the direct events surrounding the spy scandal appear to have conspicuously shifted Truman's public foreign policy positions in 1946.

However, the collective importance of such events should not be under-estimated, particularly given a perceived need in the United States for a clear expression of foreign policy ideas. It can be argued that in 1945 Tru-man was more anti-Soviet than Roosevelt had previously been, and the Soviet Union had given Truman further justification for an anti-communist stance in 1946. This was the interpretation that he received from most of his advisers and Winston Churchill.

A few days after the publication of the Canadian Royal Commission report on the Gouzenko spy scandal, and while Kennan's "Long Telegram" was being digested in Washington, Winston Churchill made his own contri-bution to cold war folklore at Westminster College in Fulton, Missouri, in March 1946. Churchill famously took the opportunity to castigate the Soviet Union and provide his own suggestions on how to combat these policies in the international arena. He controversially popularized an important image of the cold war in referring to an "iron curtain" descending across central Europe, an image that illustrated a politically and economically divided Europe. Part of Churchill's speech was "Kennanesque" when he referred to Soviet realism, noting, "There is nothing they [Soviet Union] admire so much as strength and there is nothing for which they have less respect than for military weakness."[3]

Churchill, in March 1946, was not promoting the "iron curtain" analogy as the most important thing he had to say. The title of his lecture was "The Sinews of Peace," and the central focus of his argument was toward an unusual "fraternal association of English-speaking people."[4] In fact, he advo-cated a greater cooperation between the United States and the British Empire and Commonwealth, a subject not entirely warmly received in America nor entirely sanctioned by Truman.

President Truman's involvement with this famous speech began six months before its public delivery by Churchill. When Truman introduced Churchill at Fulton, he explained that he had forwarded an invitation from Westminster College to Churchill "and made a long-hand note at the bottom of it telling him that if he would spend his vacation in the United States, at whatever point he chose to pick, and then deliver this lecture, I would make it a point to come to Missouri and personally welcome him and introduce him for that lecture."[5]

Churchill chose a period from January 14 to March 21, 1946, to visit the United States. After a stay in Miami, Churchill went to Washington, D.C. in February and had discussions in the White House about his intended speech. Truman's meeting with Winston Churchill in the White House on February 10 has been the point of much historical speculation.[6] It is appar-ent that the president knew the general substance of what Churchill was going to say at Fulton, but it is far less clear as to whether he had a direct influence on the content of the speech. Both Admiral William D. Leahy, Truman's military chief of staff and chairman of the Joint Chiefs of Staff, and American secretary of state, James Byrnes, saw full drafts of the speech and reported its contents to Truman. According to Harbutt, Truman was shown a summary of the speech by James Byrnes "but decided not to read it."[7] Of course, despite the suggestion that Truman had a general knowledge of its contents, this does not mean that Truman officially approved of its thesis, and Truman in many ways worked consistently hard to avoid the accusation that he had a personal hand in writing the speech. Despite the fact that Truman read a draft of the speech on the train to Missouri and appeared to sanction Churchill's views by being on the same platform as Churchill, President Truman could still subsequently distance himself from Churchill's views when American press reports were critical of it. It was only after the Fulton speech and after Churchill had completed his engagements in the United States that the White House press secretary, Charles G. Ross, proclaimed, "Mr Truman had no advance knowledge and didn't know what Mr. Churchill was going to say. There is no truth whatsoever in the report that Churchill and Truman spent several hours in the White House going over parts of the drafted speech. The speech was not discussed."[8]

Ideological, Economic, and Military Containment

In 1947, what had hitherto been a private development within the State Department and the White House became a public declaration of containment. The economic worries facing Western Europe and, consequently, the United States had not been alleviated. The political and military situation in Eastern Europe and the Near East had become a growing problem for Truman. In February 1947 the State Department received a memorandum from the British government declaring an inability to maintain military and economic support to Greece. The hawkish advisers to the president had been maintaining that Western Europe and the Middle East were vulnerable to Soviet penetration. The British memorandum may not have determined the policy of the Truman administration, but it clearly affected the timing of a dramatic policy initiative. In a speech to a joint session of Congress in March, Truman put forward a claim for American commitment toward defending democracy and supplying Greece and Turkey with $400 million worth of military and economic aid. The Truman Doctrine was both a domestic and an international propaganda coup. The congressional speech famously promised to help those who were "resisting subjugation by armed minorities or outside pressure," and it happily divided the world into the free and those living under tyranny.[9] It was a simplified bipolarization of the world that would set the stage for American military and economic involvement on a grand scale, notably in peacetime.

Richard Morris and Jeffery Morris, a historian and attorney, respectively, captured Truman's degree of involvement in the doctrine that would carry his name.

The drafting of the President's message to Congress was first entrusted to the State Department, but Truman was dissatisfied with the version that he was offered. The writers "made the whole thing sound like an investment prospectus," he commented. He returned the draft to Dean Acheson, requesting more emphasis on a declaration of general policy. . . . The key sentence in the new draft read, "I believe that it should be the policy of the United States. . . ." Truman pencilled out "should" and wrote in "must." Elsewhere he struck out hedging phrases.[10]

Was the Truman Doctrine a reaction to a crisis or crises? The British had a financial crisis, including a shortage of currency to buy imports, a lack of capital equipment, an energy crisis, and expensive overseas military and administrative commitments. Great Britain had to relinquish itself of commitments to Palestine and Greece and could not afford to support Turkey. Each of these states had a different set of problems, and Palestine became a major issue for the United Nations and an issue over which Britain and America had to agree to differ.

The Greek regime had a financial and military crisis accentuated by their civil war. Greece was vulnerable from communism in a domestic context because of the success of the Greek Communist Party. Great Britain and the United States believed Greece to be vulnerable from the potential intervention of Yugoslavia, Albania, and Bulgaria in Greek problems. The juxtaposition of communists on the borders with Greece led to a Western conclusion that the opportunity for the destabilization of Greece was possible and that the Soviet Union could exploit this situation. It had been an irony of British policy that it was difficult to criticize the Red Army in Eastern Europe while the British maintained a military presence in Greece. The Greek military needed to be supported and a viable Greek Army maintained if Greece was to be able to defend itself, a defense that had internal and external ramifications. With support to the Greek government, the Greek communists might be defeated and the borders protected. However, was there much point protecting Greece from communism if its neighbor Turkey was vulnerable to Soviet penetration in some form?

Averell Harriman, American ambassador to the Soviet Union, as early as October 1945 described Turkey as representing the "principal westerly gap in the Soviet system of defense in depth along its borders."[11] It was a description that emphasized the foreign policy determinants of geography and politics being brought together. In simple terms, the Soviet Union needed the Black Sea Straits to exit from the Black Sea into the more satisfyingly warm seas of the Aegean and the Mediterranean. This was an access that opened up the African continent, the Middle East, the Suez Canal, and ports beyond to easier Soviet reach by sea. This is to see Turkey as being strategically important to the Soviet Union, or an American perception that this was the case, which from the point of view of the Americans would amount to the same thing unless they could be convinced otherwise. The Black Sea Straits were an international waterway covered by the Montreux Convention, but this was clearly out of date given that Japan was also a signatory.

As the eminent historian Stephen Ambrose pointed out, in the beginning of 1947 the military and foreign policies of the United States appeared to have been moving in opposite directions, particularly because of demobilization.[12] Despite the ownership of atomic bombs and technology, the United States was unsure how to combat the perceived Soviet challenge. One answer was to promote prosperity through economic and military aid. Supporting Greece and Turkey with military and economic aid allowed the development of a broader policy of containment. A further consequence of this ideological commitment was a Western European economic package, the European Recovery Program, or the Marshall Plan as it was more popularly known.

Berlin Crisis: Not the Munich Crisis

A major test of Truman's policy of containing communism came with Stalin's surprising blockade of Berlin. The Truman administration did not expect the Soviet Union to enter into a prestige showdown, since they assumed a rational balance of power attitude from their opponents. Yet, in June 1948 Stalin did not appear to have read the containment script that the Americans had prepared earlier. In March a "baby blockade" by the Soviets had restricted military traffic to Berlin, but on June 24 the road, rail, and canal links between the Western zones of occupation in Germany were cut with Berlin. Admittedly, Berlin was an unresolved problem bequeathed by World War II, and a city inside the Soviet zone of Germany, but the blockade of Berlin occurred at a time when the resolve to combat communism was high in the United States. Since the spring of 1948, via the Pentagon negotiations between America, Britain, and Canada (ABC Talks), Truman had begun to accept military obligations that would become the basis of the North Atlantic Treaty and the North Atlantic Treaty Organization (NATO), formed in April 1949.

The decision to stand firm on Berlin and not allow Soviet penetration even into this outpost of Western interests was a spirited decision that reflected an Anglo-American understanding and response that produced a considerable resolve not to capitulate to Soviet demands. Truman had moved a long way from his conciliation toward Stalin, arguably evident at the Potsdam conference three years before. The United States categorically declared that they had an established right of access to Berlin and would "not be induced by threats, pressure or other actions."[13] Truman made the stakes considerable and presented the situation as a crisis for Germany and Western Europe. Particularly after the Marshall Plan, Truman was determined to see United States economic policies prove successful, and he wanted to make it apparent that he would not back away from military risks. The Berlin crisis of 1948 was not going to be an American and British capitulation that could be likened to the Munich crisis of 1938.

An ingenious and measured response to the blockade was evident in the airlift that was accepted by Truman. Pushing tanks through to Berlin to break the blockade was considered too great a risk and potentially a prelude to World War III. Although alternatives could escalate to a similar level, a humanitarian airlift for the people of West Berlin allowed more scope for diplomatic and strategic maneuvering. The airlift of tons of food, coal, medicines, and raw material was designed to help the beleaguered Berliners until the diplomatic stalemate could be broken. A risk of aircraft straying from flight paths or having to be diverted outside the corridors used by America and Britain had the potential to end in disaster. Good planning and considerable resolve produced eleven months of supplies being delivered to Berlin, and this commitment led to the capitulation of the Soviet Union on the blockade.

With the clear perception in the United States that the airlift had been successful, the Truman administration believed they had evidence that containment worked. Ironically, the blockade of Berlin, inaugurated to weaken the unity of Western powers in central Europe, gave impetus to the containment strategy. The vulnerability of Western Europe to Soviet political and military penetration made previously skeptical congressmen and senators address the necessity for more interventionist approaches on behalf of the United States. Although a Western security organization was negotiated in the spring and summer of 1948, the crisis over Berlin made the ratification of the North Atlantic Treaty easier. With the signing of the North Atlantic Treaty, Truman had by April 1949 the three major containment policies: the Truman Doctrine, Marshall Plan, and NATO.

The measured response of Truman over Berlin was not only recognized internationally, but saw Truman elected president in his own right, independent of the direct legacy of Roosevelt. Of course, it can also be emphasized that Truman almost lost the election, and the Jewish vote delivered over the recognition of Israel and international communist scares were fortunate and timely additions for Truman.

During the Berlin crisis, George C. Marshall's illness saw him replaced as secretary of state by Dean Gooderman Acheson. Acheson was extremely experienced in foreign affairs, having been both assistant secretary and under secretary of state. By the time Acheson became secretary of state the policy toward Berlin was in full swing. Acheson's military contribution was to expand the airlift and tighten what was effectively a counter blockade. Although he sidelined the role of the United Nations, he did open diplomatic channels to the Soviet Union that helped the Soviet Union back down. Deputy chief of the United States delegation to the United Nations, Philip Jessup was chosen by Acheson to make approaches to Soviet representative to the United Nations Jacob A. Malik. The Jessup-Malik negotiations were important in convincing the Soviets that a future West German government was not something that would be negotiated over, and the blockade ended on May 12, 1948.

Acheson's tenure as secretary of state was to parallel Truman's last four years in office, and the president often spoke of him in even more glowing terms than General Marshall.

There was never a day during the four years of Dean Acheson's secretaryship that anyone could have said that he and I differed on policy. He was meticulous in keeping me posted on every development within the wide area of his responsibility. He had a deep understanding of the President's position in our constitutional scheme and realized to the fullest that, while I leaned on him for constant advice, the policy had to be mine—it was.[14]

Korean War

It was while at home in Independence, Missouri, that President Truman received a telephone call from Secretary Acheson on June 24, 1950. He stated: "I have very serious news. The North Koreans have invaded South Korea."[15] From this, President Truman adopted his commander-in-chief mentality and issued orders, while otherwise going about his other duties. His daughter, Margaret, recounts how they flew back to Washington, D.C. from Kansas City aboard the *Independence*. The president was troubled with thoughts about the inactivity of democracies to Japanese, Italian, and German actions toward Manchuria, Abyssinia, and Austria, respectively, during the interwar years.[16] He believed the result had been World War II and by implication the aggressors should have been stopped much earlier. Korea was also a further test for the principles of the Truman Doctrine and the underlying policy of supporting non-communist nations resisting aggression.

The Sunday evening of his arrival back at Blair House (a residence across the road from the White House) saw the assembly of advisers, all of whom would get a chance to state his views that night and would be used on future occasions. The party incorporated secretary of state, Dean Acheson; secretary of defense, Louis Johnson; under secretary of state, James Webb; secretary of the army, Frank Pace; secretary of the navy, Francis Matthews; secretary of the air force, Thomas Finletter; assistant secretaries of state, Dean Rusk and John D. Hickerson; General Omar Bradley; General Lawton Collins; General Hoyt Vandenberg; and Admiral Forrest Sherman.[17] Unanimity of approach was evident at the meeting, as advisers put faith in a collective security approach of the United States and the United Nations. A resolution of the Security Council of the United Nations (in the absence of the Soviet Union) had already condemned North Korea's aggression. Dean Acheson had been prompt in calling for a Security Council meeting, much to the gratitude of Truman. President Truman did three things on advice: General MacArthur was to supply South Korea with military munitions, Americans and dependents were to be evacuated from South Korea, and the Seventh Fleet was ordered to move into the

Formosa Straits. On the last point, Truman was both protecting Formosa from being attacked and also discouraging the Nationalist Chinese on Formosa from exploiting the situation and attacking the Chinese mainland. It was seen from Beijing as a more provocative act, although they controlled their intervention in the conflict until the war was taken across the thirty-eighth parallel into North Korea.

With the swift return to the White House, Truman's unintended Monday morning in the White House left the president's appointments "diary" short of any appointments. It consequentially read: "War in Korea."[18] This seems rather symbolic of the drive and subsequent actions of the Truman administration. In conversation with presidential aide George Elsey, Truman appeared concerned about the Soviets exploiting difficult situations elsewhere, particularly that of Iran. He went on to refer to Korea as being like Greece. "If we are tough enough now, if we stand up to them like we did in Greece three years ago, they won't take any next steps. But if we just stand by, they'll move into Iran and they'll take over the whole Middle East. There's no telling what they'll do, if we don't put up a fight now."[19]

Although initially the conflict was restricted to America using air and naval support for the South Korean army, Truman realized that there was some inevitability to him ordering American infantry into action. After a visit to Korea, General Douglas MacArthur painted a grim picture of the prospects for South Korea with only air and naval cover. This was conveyed to the president on Friday June 30. "He [Truman] listened to the grim news and made the most difficult decision of the week without a moment's hesitation. He had known it was coming and had been bracing himself for it."[20] This begs the question whether all weeks had decisions just as difficult or was this an especially traumatic one? Since Truman had a week in which he ordered the atom bomb dropped, he was not immune to difficult decisions or considering the consequences of them.

Truman ordered two American divisions under MacArthur's control to be deployed from Japan to South Korea. The United Nations was happy to pass command of the war to the United States and did so on July 7, 1950. It was a considerable fillip for Truman to have the war endorsed by the United Nations and to have the umbrella of collective security.

Wars rarely run smoothly on a domestic or a foreign front. The military situation in Korea became difficult; Douglas MacArthur became more imperious, the Chinese entered the war with volunteers, and congressional Republicans became increasingly critical of Truman. No formal declaration of war was obtained from Congress, and this can be seen, despite the United Nations involvement, as a domestic constitutional mistake by Truman. A second decision that Dean Acheson advised the president to pursue was taking the war over the thirty-eighth parallel, partly encouraged by Douglas MacArthur's military successes in South Korea. Both Charles Bohlen and George Kennan warned against the move, but Dean Acheson's recommendation and other State Department advice prevailed.[21]

One of the early political casualties of the Korean War was the secretary of defense, Louis Johnson. Secretary Johnson was locked into personal feuding with Dean Acheson, and when Johnson failed to subdue General MacArthur, Truman asked for Johnson's resignation.[22] Although Truman would find firing old friends extremely difficult, he clearly put national interest before personal feelings.

Truman's firing of MacArthur does not resemble the same problem as with Johnson. Truman and MacArthur had no personal friendship, and although Truman admired the World War II record of General MacArthur, they otherwise did not show great mutual admiration for each other. MacArthur's mistakes included not anticipating the contribution of the Chinese People's Republic to the war, wanting to unleash the Nationalist Chinese on the war, threatening to take the war into China, and his contempt for the way the United States and the United Nations were fighting the war. MacArthur continued to give his own press statements, despite being warned against this. His correspondence with Congressman Joseph W. Martin (Republican Party minority leader of the House of Representatives) that was critical of the way the cold war was being fought—and, unfortunately for MacArthur, that was read to the House of Representatives—was a final straw. By April 10, 1951 Truman decided enough was enough and relieved the general of his command. This policy reflected his view of the military that "No good soldier is a speechmaker or a showman."[23] In the publicity that followed, the White House received two hundred and fifty thousand telegrams supporting MacArthur.[24] Yet, Truman hardly drew breath before he was moving on to new issues and problems, many of them domestic. The Korean War continued, often in a state of stalemate, and it was not concluded until the presidency of Dwight D. Eisenhower.

Conclusion

It is appropriate to remember that President Truman was not beset with the same constant pressures from the media that is evident in the daily life of more recent presidents. Visits to the Truman White House by colleagues and friends were not always a circus of media pundits and cameramen. Whether that means we know less or more about Truman is debatable. His writing of a scalding letter to his secretary of state but not sending it shows a degree of self-control, if not weakness.

Truman's desire to take historical responsibility for difficult decisions has been illuminated by himself and some subordinates. His range of difficult decisions included dropping atomic bombs, recognizing the state of Israel, showing grim determination not to capitulate over the Berlin Crisis, ordering American forces into a United Nations action over Korea, sacking General Douglas MacArthur, and replacing Secretary of State Byrnes and Secretary of Commerce Wallace. Congressional disapproval festered over his decision to act on the crisis in Korea without seeking congressional approval first. Yet he weathered this criticism and others through to January 1953. A contemporary cartoon at the time of the Truman-MacArthur controversy aptly summed up the historical place of Truman. The ironic cartoon depicted a senator saying, "Who does Truman think he is? President of the United States?"[25]

The plaque on Truman's desk that read "The buck stops here" was a borrowed idea from the governor of a state penitentiary and could be considered a mere foible. The idea inherent to the statement is more interesting in that it reflects a more serious manipulation of the public presentation of Truman's own image. Other presidents may have taken for granted that authority over many decisions lay with them and did not need to remind themselves or subordinates of this fact. A small plaque does not prove this point, but Truman was at least consistent in showing candor in his explanations of decisions and his feelings toward critics and political opponents. Although Truman had a forthright approach to decision making and captured the image of being an average guy, this image was only part of the persona that was Harry S. Truman.

Legacies of Truman include both the NSC and the CIA. Created by the National Security Act of 1947, both were subsequently significant national bodies to help the president formulate policy. Stanley Falk has examined Truman's attitudes toward and use of the NSC. "Truman did not regularly attend Council meetings. After presiding at the first session of the Council on September 26, 1947, he sat in on only eleven of the fifty-six other meetings held before the start of the Korean War."[26] The NSC would become crucial and controversial for some presidents, but Truman made sure it did not diminish his presidential authority.

A further legacy of Truman includes a policy of containment toward communism that manifested itself in economic, ideological, military, and strategic programs. Severe critics can attribute American involvement in the Vietnam War to the policy of containment, but scholars can also attribute the "winning" of the cold war to the same overall policy.

Notes

1. H. S. Truman, *Year of Decisions, 1945. The Memoirs of Harry S. Truman*, Vol. 1 (Bungay, Suffolk: Hodder and Stoughton, 1955), 493. It appears in a slightly different form in R. H. Ferrell, ed, *Off the Record: The Private Papers of Harry S. Truman* (Norwalk, Connecticut: Easton Press, 1980), 80. Here it reads "I'm tired babying the Soviets."

2. Truman, *Year of Decisions*, 491–493.

3. F. J. Harbutt, *The Iron Curtain: Churchill, America, and the Origins of the Cold War* (Oxford: Oxford University Press, 1986), 184.

4. "Westminster College Bulletin," series 46, 1 (1946). In *President Harry S. Truman's Office Files, 1945–1953, Part 2: Correspondence File*, microfilm (Bethesda, 1989). M. Gilbert recounts how "Churchill had earlier intended to call the speech 'World Peace'."

Letter of February 14, 1946 to Dr F. L. McCluer, Westminster College papers, a footnote in *Never Despair* (London: Heinemann, 1988), 203.

5. "Westminster College Bulletin," series 46, 1.

6. Harbutt, *The Iron Curtain,* 161.

7. Ibid., 180.

8. Press report included in *President Harry S. Truman's Office Files.*

9. The text of the Truman Doctrine is carried in many textbooks. See T. G. Paterson and D. Merrill, *Major Problems in American Foreign Relations,* Vol. II, *Since 1914* (Lexington, Massachusetts: D. C. Heath and Company, 1995), 259–261.

10. R. B. Morris and J. B. Morris, *Great Presidential Decisions: State Papers that Changed the Course of History from Washington to Reagan* (Norwalk, Connecticut: Easton Press, 1992, first edition 1960), 392–393.

11. Harriman to Byrnes, October 23, 1945. This despatch was drafted by George Kennan and John Davies in the American embassy in Moscow. *Foreign Relations of the United States (FRUS), 1945,* Vol. V, *Europe* (Washington, D.C: Government Printing Office, 1967), 901.

12. S. E. Ambrose, *Rise to Globalism,* 3rd edition (Harmondsworth, Middlesex: Penguin Books, 1983), 122.

13. *FRUS, 1948,* Vol. II, *Germany and Austria* (Washington, D.C.: United States Printing Office, 1973), 952.

14. H. S. Truman, *Memoirs,* Vol. 2, *Years of Trial and Hope, 1946–1953* (Suffolk: Hodder and Stoughton, 1956), 455–456.

15. M. Truman, *Harry S. Truman* (Norwalk, Connecticut: Easton Press, 1972), 455.

16. Ibid., 457.

17. Ibid., 458.

18. Ibid., 461.

19. Ibid., 461.

20. Ibid., 469.

21. Ibid., 326.

22. "Johnson was a big, blustering bully of a man with presidential ambitions who undercut Acheson over China policy by leaking information to the Nationalists," in Ferrell, *Harry S. Truman: A Life,* 322.

23. Ibid., 330.

24. Ibid., 335.

25. Ibid., 335.

26. S. L. Falk, "The Role of the National Security Council under Truman, Eisenhower, and Kennedy," in D. Caraley, *The President's War Powers: From the Federalists to Reagan* (New York: Academy of Political Science, 1984), 134.

CHAPTER 4

Dwight D. Eisenhower and the Military Challenge, 1953–1960

> Realizing that common sense and common decency alike dictate the futility of appeasement, we shall never try to placate an aggressor by the false and wicked bargain of trading honor for security. Americans, indeed, all free men, remember that in the final choice a soldier's pack is not so heavy a burden as a prisoner's chains.[1]
> —*Dwight D. Eisenhower, inaugural address, January 20, 1953*

It is very difficult to think of President Eisenhower—at a time of great cold war hostility—as pursuing anything other than a vibrant anti-communist foreign policy. In terms of the considerations of America's allies and Eisenhower's own perceptions of the cold war, he sought a degree of conformity in the international system. This was not unlike the bipartisan political and economic conformity and consensus he encouraged within the United States. However, the conformity he sought within the international system was a consensus in support of American interests and views of a peaceful world system, and support for American opposition to communism around the globe. This attitude required President Eisenhower to make tough decisions toward allies and opponents during a number of crises. These decisions were made so that American economic, ideological, and strategic interests could be preserved and developed. It will become clear that there were some ambiguities in President Eisenhower's foreign policies, and that he made controversial decisions affecting France and Britain.

To have one distinguished career is an accomplishment that may be reserved for the few, but Dwight D. Eisenhower had an astonishing military career before serving as a two-term president of the United States. World War II provided the opportunity for his rise to considerable fame, from the successful direction of the invasions of North Africa, Sicily, and Italy to his position as supreme commander for the Allied Expeditionary Force in Europe to the complex and masterful D-Day landings on the French coast in June 1944. After World War II he took over from General George Marshall as chief of staff of the United States Army, leaving the office in February 1948 to later in the year become president of Columbia University, followed by Truman convincing him to be supreme commander of NATO. He was an organizational man, not a career politician, or for that matter someone who had even voted in national elections. Yet, Eisenhower became the Republican Party presidential candidate in 1952 and was successfully elected.

The traditional view of President Eisenhower (affectionately known by the public as Ike) was that he was not an active president in domestic or foreign policies, that he saw himself as a statesman above politics, and that he much preferred the card game of bridge or to be playing golf (both inside and outside the White House).[2] Stephen Ambrose summarized this view of Eisenhower: "[H]e was an old man, head of an old party, surrounded by old advisors . . . a kindly grandfather."[3] Eisenhower's heart attack in 1955, during his first term as president, furthered the view that Eisenhower had to delegate a number of burdens of his office and was rather lackadaisical. In foreign policy, John Foster Dulles, as secretary of state for six years, was allowed to pursue a militantly anti-Soviet and anti-communist foreign policy driven by containment, brinkmanship, and "roll-back" ideas. However, with the advent of revisionist interpretations of Eisenhower, the opinion developed that he was merely a less-than-enthusiastic public salesman of his own ideas. The view that now prevails in academic scholarship is that he was an active and well-informed decision maker in his own administration, even involved in the development of his own speeches.[4] It is also apparent that Dulles sought approval from Eisenhower before undertaking major policy moves and was not a maverick policy maker. A further post-revisionist variation on Eisenhower's foreign policy outlook is that Eisenhower understood the depths and difficulties of cold war problems, and despite having a cold war warrior as secretary of state, fought against the radical escalation of the cold war and was happy to accommodate various peace processes. In essence, Eisenhower supervised a domestic consensus and conformity while also looking for stability and conformity for essential anti-communist interests of the United States abroad.

Presidents would scarcely be able, either temperamentally or intellectually, to deal with foreign policy issues alone, and Eisenhower is no exception to this. As was stated in a public report in 1937, "The President needs help."[5] Of course, relying on, or appearing to rely on, your secretary of state or your vice president could have advantages.[6] One of the attractions for Ike of relying on his secretary of state was that much of the criticism of Eisenhower's policies could be directed away from the president, with Dulles serving a useful function as a "political lightening rod."[7] Secretary Dulles was attacked by critics for both his aggressiveness in foreign policy and for his personal self-righteousness. Oliver Franks, British ambassador to the United States, has captured the nature of John Foster Dulles. "Three or four centuries ago, when Reformation and Counter Reformation divided Europe into armed camps, in an age of wars of religion, it was not so rare to encounter men of the type of Dulles. . . . Like them, he saw the world as an arena in which the forces of good and evil were continuously at war." [8]

Asian Burdens

On becoming president Eisenhower inherited the problem of the Korean War–a problem that had assisted his election campaign for the presidency in 1952, since he could exploit the publicly perceived failings of the previous administration and the Democratic Party to resolve the war. The conclusion of the Korean War had for some time appeared to be a stalemate in Korea and a return to the position prior to the North Korean attack in June 1950. It was possible for Eisenhower to push a settlement forward by indicating to the People's Republic of China that nuclear weapons had not been ruled out as an option for the United States. He also obtained support from the United Nations in suggesting that future hostilities might not be confined to Korea. Eisenhower pledged support to the president of the Republic of Korea, Syngman Rhee, promising Rhee that he would continue to promote the unification of Korea and provide continued economic aid to the Republic in the south. If Rhee agreed to participate in the Geneva Conference on Korea and was committed to the armistice, then the United States would enter into a mutual defense treaty with the Republic of Korea.[9] The situation in Korea for America and the United Nations had to some extent been helped by the death of the Soviet premier, Joseph Stalin, on March 5, 1953, and the subsequent uncertainty about leadership in the Soviet Union. A cease-fire was signed for the Korean War on July 27, 1953, and America went on to sign a defense treaty with South Korea in October.

On nuclear policy, particularly toward Korea, Eisenhower never ruled out the possibility of deploying American nuclear weapons. In his memoir, *Mandate for Change*, Ike makes his position for 1953 clear. "[I]t would be impossible for the United States to maintain its military commitments . . . did we not possess atomic weapons and the will to use them when necessary. But an American decision to use them at that time would have created strong disruptive feelings between ourselves and our allies. However, if an all-out offensive should be highly successful, I felt that the rifts so caused could, in time, be repaired."[10]

Winston Churchill, the British prime minister, was informed about Eisenhower's military attitude toward North Korea at the Big Three (USA, France, and Britain) conference in Bermuda from December 4 to 8, 1953. Eisenhower told Churchill about the course of action that America would take if the communists broke the armistice in Korea. "I informed him of our intention to strike every military target in the region, but to avoid useless attacks upon civilian centers. I also informed him that we intended to use every weapon in the bag, including our atomic types. To all this he agreed, stating that they were already on official record as approving our idea of refusing to confine the war to the area south of the Yalu."[11]

With a perceived success in containing communist aggression against the Republic of Korea, and having the Panmunjom armistice agreement slightly enlarge the territory administered by the Republic of Korea, Dulles could embark on an even more positive containment policy. Eisenhower's "New Look" foreign policy was to emphasize air power and nuclear weaponry. The secretary of state extended this policy and embarked on a policy of positive containment: brinkmanship, using the threat of nuclear weapons to force opponents to back down from previously held positions. It was the implications of this—Dulles's support for "massive retaliation" with nuclear weapons—that worried America's allies, particularly Britain. Also criticized by allies were the Eisenhower administration's policies on China. The insistence of the United States that Jiang Jieshi (Chiang Kai-shek) was still the representative leader of mainland China was also criticized externally. Nevertheless, this policy of nonrecognition of the People's Republic of China was to be followed by all succeeding presidents until the détente between Chinese communists and America initiated by President Nixon eventually resulted in the formal recognition of the People's Republic of China by the United States in 1979 under President Carter. Eisenhower and Dulles continued Truman's policy that it would be difficult to champion an anti-communist crusade against the People's Republic of China while recognizing them. The establishment of a Bolshevik government in Russia in 1917 had caused similar problems until Franklin D. Roosevelt recognized the Soviet Union and appointed William Christian Bullitt ambassador to the Soviet Union in 1933.[12]

The danger of a Sino-American conflict derived not so much from the issue of Taiwan and American support for Jiang Jieshi, but from the other islands off the coast of mainland China: Jinmen and Mazu (Quemoy and Matsu) and the Tachen islands. Here America seemed confronted with the danger of war over what appeared to be the most trivial of issues, which was arguably a by-product of pursuing the domino theory. The background to American foreign policy thinking was set by the famous domino analogy put forward by Eisenhower in a press conference given on April 7, 1954. In answer to a question about the strategic importance of Indochina, and referring to what was to be a "falling domino principle," Eisenhower stated:

> You have a row of dominoes set up, you knock over the first one, and what will happen to the last one is the certainty that it will go over very quickly. So you could have a beginning of a disintegration that would have the most profound influences. . . . Then with respect to more people passing under this domination, Asia, after all, has already lost some 450 million of its peoples to the Communist dictatorship, and we simply can't afford greater losses.

But when we come to the possible sequence of events, the loss of Indochina, of Burma, of Thailand, of the Peninsular, and Indonesia following, now you begin to talk about areas that not only multiply the disadvantages that you would suffer through loss of materials, sources of materials, but now you are talking really about millions and millions and millions of people.

Finally, the geographical position achieved thereby does many things. It turns the so-called island defensive chain of Japan, Formosa, of the Philippines and to the southward; it moves to threaten Australia and New Zealand.[13]

Dulles would not retreat over the Chinese islands issues and left the policy of the United States in an awkwardly ambiguous situation. The islands issue reached a crisis in 1955, but the People's Republic of China called off their bombardment of the islands. Eisenhower obtained a resolution from Congress in January 1955 for Congress to support him as commander in chief in the defense of Taiwan, and he subsequently deployed United States air and naval forces in the area surrounding Taiwan. Writing to Jiang Jieshi on May 17, 1956, Eisenhower was to confirm his support for the Nationalist Chinese of Taiwan, seeing them as having a key role in contesting the position of Chinese communists in Asia. In this letter containing warm personal remarks, Ike wrote:

I am convinced that the opportunity may arise for your Government to provide leadership to people on the China mainland seeking to free themselves from the yoke of Communism. In the meantime, I feel sure that the close and fruitful cooperation of the past few years between our two Governments will continue. You can rely upon my intention to do what I appropriately can to safeguard the international position of your Government and to ensure that it remains economically and militarily strong.[14]

Despite this apparently strong attitude in support of Jiang Jieshi, it is now clear from State Department documents that the Eisenhower administration was opposed to the use of force in the Taiwan Strait in the 1950s. Leonard Gordon has clearly defended this view in an article on "United States Opposition to Use of Force in the Taiwan Strait, 1954–1962."[15] By 1956 the United States did not expect the Nationalist Chinese to obtain mainland China, and accordingly built up a response concerned with the defense of Taiwan. This would appear to contradict the substance of Eisenhower's May letter to Jiang Jieshi. The common ground is that the United States remained sympathetic to the cause of the Nationalists, but would not give them as much military support as they requested; the United States thought in terms of Taiwan's self-defense. Gordon's overall conclusions correspond to a revisionist view that Eisenhower was committed to not using force. "Both Eisenhower and Dulles had exhibited moderation, vision, and unwavering commitment to settling the Taiwan question without the use of force."[16] This contradicts the traditional view that they both exhibited almost inflexible hostility to communism.

Still within Asia, the United States under Eisenhower became further embroiled in a conflict against communism in Southeast Asia. French Indochina, or more particularly, Vietnam, was an unusual geographical and political area for Eisenhower and Dulles to get involved with, but it was the third area (Korea, Chinese islands, and Indochina) in which Dulles would publicly claim that brinkmanship worked. "We walked to the brink and we looked it in the face."[17] Dulles felt that the threat of nuclear weapons had forced the Vietminh to the negotiating table in Geneva in 1954. Despite the doctrines espoused by Eisenhower and Dulles, it does now appear clear that Eisenhower showed considerable restraint in his policies toward the Vietminh and control over his support for the French in Vietnam. In support of a revisionist view of Eisenhower's decision-making abilities, it can clearly be seen that he showed heroic restraint toward the French in denying them aerial support at the battle of Dien Bien Phu in 1954.

Despite verbal commitments to the anti-communist doctrines of containment and "roll-back," Eisenhower did not commit American forces to help the French garrison at Dien Bien Phu, in the northern part of Vietnam, that was being besieged by Vietminh forces. Admiral Arthur W. Radford of the United States and General Paul Ely of France put together an audacious plan for the Americans to help the French at Dien Bien Phu with substantial aerial bombing. It was a bold plan because it called for American aircraft, including B-29 bombers, to bomb the Vietminh within what would normally have been considered usual French safety perimeters. The French believed themselves to have an ally in this cause, not only because Admiral Radford helped to devise what was ostensibly a rescue plan, but also because Eisenhower and Dulles had pressed upon the French the importance of fighting the war assertively, while also encouraging the French to give assurances of independence to states in the region. Yet President Eisenhower chose not to intervene to help the French. In what can be seen as a salutary lesson that was not adequately digested by his two successors as presidents, Eisenhower does not accept a high-level plan just because it exists and it is pressed upon him, nor would he make a commitment without taking the advice of a number of members of Congress.

Why exactly did President Eisenhower show a clear presence of mind not to intervene at Dien Bien Phu? Having extracted America from the Korean War in 1953, it was untimely for the United States to be pushed into a conflict so soon in Indochina. Having avoided a major military showdown with the People's Republic of China over Korea, the worries of an Indochinese adventure encouraging Chinese communist involvement had to be considered. The Vietnam problem was not of Eisenhower's or America's making, so he felt detached from the issue of responsibility. If American military forces were to be as dramatically deployed as was being requested, then Eisenhower wanted further international support. A multilateral effort might help to remove the taint of colonialism, even if much of that support was from old colonial powers. On April 3 a group of congressional leaders (including Lyndon Baines Johnson) warned the president that he should not act without also having British support.[18] Winston Churchill, the prime minister of Britain, and his foreign secretary, Anthony Eden, were reluctant to furnish such support. To develop the view of one historian about the British and American situation in 1954 that would also appear to be applicable to Dien Bien Phu: The British were unwilling to sign and authorize a shotgun license for Dulles.[19]

In military and strategic terms, Eisenhower and the Joint Chiefs of Staff were unhappy with the plan put forward by Admiral Radford because they believed air support by itself would not determine the results of the conflict. An intervention by America could only produce a few military achievements. Eisenhower did not wish to change the scenario that indigenous military forces should undertake primary responsibility for the fighting. Eisenhower was content to continue to supply money and military supplies and keep open the option of future air and naval support. Furthermore, Dulles was pleased to believe that the Vietminh were forced to accept an unfavorable cease-fire because of American nuclear weapons. Thus, although Eisenhower and Dulles showed considerable restraint over the use of tactical conventional weapons in support of the French at Dien Bien Phu, they never gave up on the policy of deterrence and threatening the use of nuclear weapons to obtain certain interests.

Despite not helping the French at Dien Bien Phu, the United States continued to seek multilateral responses to the problems of Southeast Asia. Although Dulles showed lackluster support for the Geneva Conference on Indochina in 1954 and the United States did not sign the resulting Geneva Accords, the Eisenhower administration did at least give its vocal endorsement to the Geneva Accords that provided a temporary respite in the hostilities in Vietnam. In an attempt to provide a Western-supported mutual defense treaty for the region, Eisenhower helped to set up the South East Asian Treaty Organization (SEATO), which was approved by the American Senate in February 1955. This always appeared an unusual endeavor since SEATO included two previous colonial powers of diminishing political significance in Southeast Asia, Great Britain and France; incorporated Pakistan, but not its larger neighbor India; adopted the Philippines as a member; and took on board the geographically peripheral states of New Zealand and Australia.[20] With the deployment of American military and political power in South Korea, Okinawa, and Japan, the United States had declared itself to have strong interests in Asia. America also retained strategically useful military bases in Guam and the Philippines. With increasing American economic support given to South Vietnam, Laos, and Thailand, and the development of SEATO, America had become a major international player in Asia.

European Dilemmas

Eisenhower's administration was clearly opposed to control of Eastern Europe by communists, yet, it had to accept this *de facto* situation. It was difficult for brinkmanship to manifest itself as a workable policy in Europe, particularly if it meant a direct challenge to the Soviet Union. The United States could not effectively respond to either the East German or East Berlin uprisings of 1953 or the Hungarian uprising of 1956.

For all of the Republican Party criticism of the previous Truman administration's foreign policy, there was considerable continuity toward Europe between both the Truman and Eisenhower presidencies.[21] Eisenhower and Dulles, like Democratic Party predecessors, were prepared to strengthen the economies of Western Europe and recognize the continued division of Germany. America also encouraged the growth of Western European organizations such as the European Coal and Steel Community. John Foster Dulles strongly supported a planned European Defense Community to which the West Germans would send military units, but would not develop their own army. Dulles was very irritated when this scheme was rejected by the French Assembly, and he made vague threats about the future of NATO. The United States continued to support NATO, and with the development of the initiatives of Anthony Eden, the new prime minister in Britain, a small West German army with limited weapons was integrated into NATO in May 1955.[22] Eisenhower's approval of Western European unity had various motives: removing economic burdens from the United States; the military-strategic advantages of avoiding a European war; and slightly less tangible, but still relevant, the flattery America accepted by seeing some of her political and economic ideas accepted in Western Europe. Dulles in particular continued to support the European Economic Community and to oppose British moves to create an alternative European Free Trade Association.

The death of Joseph Stalin in 1953 clearly created an opportunity for less-rigid policies for both the Soviet Union and the United States. In May 1955 a conference in Vienna led to the removal of Soviet troops from Austria, and in July 1955 the American and Soviet heads of government met in Geneva, the first such summit meeting since the Potsdam conference of July and August 1945. An atmosphere of goodwill was achieved, the "Geneva spirit," although very little else is associated with the conference. Ike's suggestion of an "open skies" policy, whereby mutual aerial inspection of military facilities would take place in the Soviet Union and the United States, was largely a propaganda ploy by Eisenhower. He expected the Soviet Union to reject the proposal. A nuclear arms race was to continue and the earlier testing of hydrogen bombs by the Americans and the Soviets, respectively, made the risks from brinkmanship that much greater and the policy less viable in Europe. By 1961 the Soviet Union and the United States "together possessed more than twenty thousand nuclear and atomic weapons."[23]

Eisenhower's second term in office (January 1957 through January 1961) saw much greater sensitivity toward demands for a policy of coexistence with the Soviet Union. It is possible that the view held by Dulles that the Soviet Union was fundamentally immoral and therefore impossible to negotiate with was in decline. In March 1958 a summit conference was accepted in principle; however, the Soviet Union's verbal attacks on the West's position in Berlin destroyed this situation. Although nothing subsequently followed, in November 1958 the Soviet Union pronounced that the West had six months to get out of Berlin.[24] Although this did little for harmonious international relations between the superpowers, Ike showed the restraint of a seasoned president in not being baited by these pronouncements from the Soviets.

In April 1959 Dulles resigned because of ill health, and he died a month later. His successor as secretary of state, Christian Herter, emanated a much less aggressive atmosphere in pursuing American foreign policy interests. Secretary Herter produced a very conciliatory tone at the Foreign Ministers' Conference in May 1959. Nikita Khrushchev with his foreign minister, Gromyko, made their famous visit to the United States in September 1959, and they were entertained by the president at Camp David. At the end of 1959, in conjunction with Charles de Gaulle, president of France, and Harold Macmillan, prime minister of Britain, Eisenhower proposed a four-power summit conference, including the Soviet Union, for Paris in the forthcoming year. These positive moves toward understanding were set back when, on May 1, 1960, the U-2 spy plane of Francis Gary Powers was brought down in the Soviet Union. This event led to the early breakdown of the Paris summit conference in May 1960. The timing of the U-2 flights over the Soviet Union appears to have been a serious error of judgment. Harsh critics of Eisenhower can argue that he did not handle the situation very well, particularly since he would not apologize for the incident and would not disavow presidential responsibility. In fact, Eisenhower appeared on American television and radio in a broadcast from the Oval Office on May 25, 1960, and took complete responsibility, stating that as "[p]resident, charged by the Constitution with the conduct of America's foreign relations, and as Commander-in-Chief, charged with the direction of the operation and activities of our Armed Forces and their supporting services, I take full responsibility for approving all the various programs undertaken by our government to secure and evaluate military intelligence."[25] Eisenhower considered American espionage an unpleasant necessity, and his particular responsibility.[26] There would be no more summit diplomacy during the Eisenhower presidency. If the opportunity for détente between America and the Soviet Union existed in the late 1950s, it was clearly lost by the end of Ike's tenure as president, and would have to wait until the accords of President Nixon in the early 1970s.

The Middle East and West European Interference

A number of major problems for the United States and Eisenhower developed in the Middle East, including problems with European allies. There were various motives for American involvement in the Middle East: oil supplies, fear of Soviet involvement, a strong American commitment to Israel as a nation-state, and the fear of Arab-Israeli conflicts. American containment policies had extended themselves from the Near East countries of Greece and Turkey promoted under Truman to an extended geographical coverage in the region. In May 1950 the Tripartite Declaration of the United States, France, and Britain was announced to help preserve the status quo in the Middle East. This essentially set out principles on the sale of arms to Middle East states and the obligations of the three governments to intervene should borders or armistice lines be violated. To counter the threat of Soviet penetration in the area, Britain proposed the Middle East Defense Organization, but Egypt rejected this. However, in 1954 an Anglo-Egyptian treaty on the Suez Canal was signed whereby Britain would withdraw from its Suez base. To compensate for the dwindling British presence, the Americans sought a new system of defensive alliances. Iraq, in receipt of American aid, signed the Baghdad Pact, which was joined by Britain and Pakistan. When Iran also joined, a northern tier system of defense appeared to exist. Despite all of this strategic posturing, the United States was let down by a rather old fashioned lack of diplomatic communication, partly of its own making, but largely from Britain, France, and Israel.

The circumstances that led to the Suez crisis of 1956 are associated with the problems emanating from the financing of the Aswan High Dam project. The International Bank for Reconstruction and Development (World Bank), with American and British financial support, offered to finance the project for Egypt in December 1955. However, Egypt's political flirtations with the Soviet Union, the continuation of an Egyptian arms deal with Czechoslovakia, and Egypt's recognition of the People's Republic of China led John Foster Dulles to feel aggrieved with President Gammal Abdul Nasser of Egypt, and Dulles withdrew the American offer of support in July 1956. Stephen Ambrose also cites the worries of the Americans about the ability of the Egyptians to effectively operate the Aswan Dam; and the economic policy of helping Egypt become more fertile in order to produce cotton was not irrelevant to members of Congress from the cotton-producing states of the Deep South, and could also appear to be illogical.[27] As the State Department recorded for July 19, 1956: "Secretary Dulles had told Eisenhower that internal economic conditions in Egypt had changed markedly since the initial offer and that the problem of the division of the Nile waters was far from a solution. An additional problem, he said, was the increasing difficulty of close cooperation with the Nasser regime—a necessity for the successful completion of the project. Eisenhower agreed that the United States should withdraw the offer."[28] There is much irony in this decision since a lot that followed, including American criticism of France, Britain, and Israel, would appear to result from this. Nasser's response to the withdrawal of funds for this important Egyptian development project was to nationalize the Suez Canal.

Eisenhower and Dulles appeared to be embarrassed at the prospect of supporting their European allies in what looked to be a blatant colonial and imperialistic stand to maintain their economic interests in the Middle East region and, more particularly, maintain trade and revenue generated from or via the Suez Canal. France took a forceful stance, particularly because of Nasser's support for Algerian independence. America had no particular desire to support these issues, and although Egypt received increasing Soviet support, the United States accurately categorized Nasser as an Arab nationalist. More strident issues of communism and anti-communism elsewhere in the world led future American administrations into different conclusions about indigenous nationalist movements, but here at least Eisenhower and Dulles showed the presence of mind not to be driven by ideological simplifications. Nevertheless, the American stance was further surprising given strong American political commitments to Israel and America's own worries about Nasser that had led them to withdraw funding for the Aswan High Dam project.

When Israel attacked Egypt on October 29, 1956, Britain and France intervened in what had been a prearranged plan between the three parties. Under the pretext of separating Israel and Egypt, the British and French occupied the Suez Canal area.

Why did the United States not support the British and French over Suez? A number of reasons clearly explain this situation, including the fact that the British and French had underestimated world criticism. Eisenhower and Dulles had made it clear to Britain, from an early stage in events, that the use of force against Egypt was a problem for the United States. In a letter to Eden drafted by Dulles but heavily annotated and signed by Eisenhower, they set out an American position that should have served as a warning to Eden. Eisenhower wrote in this letter to Eden on September 2, 1956:

I really do not see how a successful result could be achieved by forcible means. The use of force would, it seems to me, vastly increase the area of jeopardy. I do not see how the economy of Western Europe can long survive the burden of prolonged military operations, as well as the denial of Near East oil. Also the peoples of the Near East and of North Africa and, to some extent, of all of Asia and all of Africa would be consolidated against the West to a degree which, I fear, could not be overcome in a generation and, perhaps, not even in a century particularly having in mind the capacity of the Russians to make mischief. . . . We have two problems, the first of which is the assurance of permanent and efficient operation of the Suez Canal with justice to all concerned. The second is to see that Nasser shall not grow as a menace to the peace and vital interests of the West. In my view, these two problems need not and possibly cannot be solved simultaneously and by the same methods, although we are exploring further means to this end. The first is the most important for the moment and must be solved in such a way as not to make the second more difficult. Above all, there must be no grounds for our several peoples to believe that anyone is using the Canal difficulty as an excuse to proceed forcibly against Nasser.[29]

Looking for support from the United States after the crucial intervention and when military and diplomatic policies began to unravel was not the way for Britain to get the approval and support of Eisenhower. Not to have consulted Eisenhower and Dulles in advance of the very specific military action France, Britain, and Israel undertook was a grave miscalculation. Eisenhower was to complain that he had to read of events in newspapers, which is stretching the truth since he had his own intelligence reports on what Britain and France were undertaking.[30]

However, the point is not lost that Eisenhower was aggrieved because of the lack of early consultation and information supplied from Britain and France. Britain was to regret this, since in the ensuing economic crisis the United States refused to support sterling on the financial markets. Anglo-American relations became particularly tense. Whether or not a greater attempt at conciliation between John Foster Dulles and Anthony Eden would have saved the situation is speculation, but this prospect always seemed unlikely given poor relations resulting from differences over Vietnam. Eden and Dulles held differing views on Vietnam that went back to the Indochina Conference in Geneva in 1954. Dulles would also not concede that Nasser, backed by the Soviet Union, was as great a threat to the world balance of power as Ho Chi Minh, backed by the Chinese and Soviet Union. Brinkmanship appeared to be buried at the Suez crisis. However, the Suez crisis did not prove to be a problem for the re-election of Eisenhower in November of 1956 or as great a threat to America's guarantee of European security as the French speculated. Eisenhower was to verbally counter Soviet aggressive pronouncements against Britain, but much of the assumed Middle Eastern pre-Suez Anglo-American diplomatic understanding appeared to be destroyed.

After the Suez crisis Eisenhower and Dulles looked to construct an alternative approach to the Middle East. In what was to become known as the Eisenhower Doctrine, Ike sought authority from Congress to defend any Middle Eastern state attacked by communists. This was approved along with proposals for economic aid.

In 1958 the pro-Western president of Lebanon was attacked by Syrian forces, but Eisenhower was reluctant to intervene with American military forces until the Iraqi revolution of July. With British troops placed in Jordan to help the king of Jordan, United States forces entered Lebanon. The Iraqi revolution was a great blow to the United States, and in 1959 the Baghdad Pact was reorganized as CENTO (Central Treaty Organization). As in Southeast Asia an escalating American involvement was leading them into increasingly difficult situations.

Eisenhower's Leadership

Eisenhower's foreign policy leadership included a cautious approach to disarmament; a negotiated settlement for the Korean War; support for an ill-fated European Defense Community; military and economic support for Taiwan, South Korea, and South Vietnam; and also disillusionment with seasoned allies the British and French over the Suez crisis. During his eight years in office, President Eisenhower did not involve the United States in a declared war or any lengthy international conflict. Although he committed American marines to Lebanon in 1958, this was a short-lived intervention. John Foster Dulles held a particularly high profile as secretary of state under Eisenhower. However, despite the clear cold war rhetoric of the hawkish Dulles, Ike was happy to accommodate others to produce peaceful settlement of disputes. If Ike was to act forcefully in adopting a military option for foreign policy, then he wished to have a coalition of powers on his side.

In terms of Ike's style and methods of leadership, he would hold exhaustive discussions before making important decisions, including the decisions not to intervene in support of the French at Dien Bien Phu. Also Ike did not push the Nationalist Chinese toward war with the People's Republic of China in their quest for reoccupation of the mainland. During the Suez crisis, it is clear that Dulles and Eisenhower managed a small group of trusted decision makers. As Michael Fry has calculated, there "were twenty-nine recorded decision sessions on the Suez crisis between July 27th and November 6th. The decisions made concerned both substance and legitimation."[31] These were in addition to formal Cabinet meetings and a limited number of NSC meetings. As commander in chief, Eisenhower felt he needed "patience, steadiness, firmness and time."[32]

In many ways, Eisenhower's own military experience led him to expect effective staff support and for this support to be formal, clear, illuminating, and consistent. He, as most senior military personnel would expect, required internal dissension to be minimal and any public dissent to be avoided. Ike created a group spirit through having regular cabinet meetings, even if he had largely made up his own mind about the issues on the agenda prior to these meetings. National security was a high priority for Eisenhower, but his pre-presidential wartime experiences had led him to value cooperation and understanding. From his military career, Eisenhower clearly understood large-scale organizations and how to manage them. As a revisionist view would suggest Eisenhower did not seek narrow sources for advice or limit the sources of information for crucial decisions.

The view that Eisenhower kept tight managerial control of foreign policy has to be qualified with consideration of the growth in power of the CIA during the 1950s. Ike's legacy for the United States was to be not only the apologetic development of a military industrial complex for America and a bipolar view of the world, but also a very active CIA.[33] Eisenhower could be blamed for letting the CIA develop too much independent thinking and allowing them to undertake a vigorous and clandestine anti-communist foreign policy for the United States.

The fall of the Cuban regime under Fulgencio Batista to Fidel Castro's forces in January 1959 seemed to exemplify the difficulties of Eisenhower's foreign policy approach. The broad sweeping doctrines of his first term in office appeared inappropriate by the end of his time in office. As Castro moved toward the Soviet Union politically and Khrushchev embraced Cuba in July 1960, Eisenhower, before leaving office, was to fix the American quota for importing Cuban sugar at zero and sever diplomatic relations with Cuba. The CIA had its own ideas on how to replace Castro, but the simplified view that a pro-American liberal regime could be imposed on Cuba as elsewhere was to materialise and fail badly.

Notes

1. *Public Papers of the Presidents of the United States: Dwight D. Eisenhower, 1953* (Washington, D.C.: National Archives and Records Service, 1960), 5. See also http://www.presidency.ucsb.edu/.

2. John and Jacqueline Kennedy, while occupants of the White House, reputedly had a fondness for showing guests chips in the parquetry flooring caused by Eisenhower's golf practice. Eisenhower was criticized at the time of the Sputnik crisis in August 1957, when the Soviet Union used a ballistic missile to launch a satellite into outer space. He only returned to Washington, D.C. for a press conference after rain prevented him from playing golf at the Gettysburg Golf Country Club.

3. S. E. Ambrose, *Rise to Globalism,* 3rd edition (Harmondsworth, Middlesex: Penguin, 1983), 238.

4. This view of Eisenhower as a skillful chief executive was particularly presented by F. I. Greenstein, *The Hidden-Hand Presidency* (Baltimore, Maryland: Johns Hopkins University Press, 1994), originally published in 1982. He also presented this view in an earlier article, "Eisenhower as an Activist President: A Look at New Evidence," *Political Science Quarterly* 94 (Winter 1979–1980). See also R. H. Immerman, "Eisenhower and Dulles: Who Made the Decisions?" *Political Psychology* 1 (Autumn 1979); V. P. De Santis, "Eisenhower Revisionism," *Review of Politics* 38 (April 1976).

5. From the 1937 report of the President's Committee on Administrative Management, cited in F. H. Heller, "The Eisenhower White House," *Presidential Studies Quarterly* XXIII, 3 (Summer 1993), 509.

6. Vice President Richard M. Nixon was given a rough reception in Peru in 1958 on what was intended as a goodwill visit to Peru and six other Latin American countries.

7. W. LaFeber, *The American Age: United States Foreign Policy at Home and Abroad,* 2nd edition (New York: W. W. Norton & Company, 1994), 538.

8. T. Hoopes, *The Devil and John Foster Dulles* (London: Andre Deutsch, 1973), 491.

9. *Public Papers of the Presidents of the United States: Dwight D. Eisenhower, 1953,* 379.

10. D. D. Eisenhower, *Mandate for Change, 1953–1956* (New York: Doubleday & Co., 1963), 180.

11. *The Papers of Dwight David Eisenhower,* Vol. XV, edited by L. Galambos and D. Van Ee (Baltimore, Maryland: Johns Hopkins University Press, 1996), 728.

12. The American ambassador to Russia, David R. Francis, departed from the Soviet Union on November 7, 1918–the new government still unrecognized. The American ambassador to the Soviet Union, William C. Bullitt, was appointed on November 21, 1933. See D. Mayers, *The Ambassadors and America's Soviet Policy* (Oxford: Oxford University Press, 1995).

13. W. A. Williams, T. McCormick, L. Gardner, and W. LaFeber, *America in Vietnam* (London: W. W. Norton & Company, 1975), 156–157. See also *Public Papers of the Presidents of the United States: Dwight D. Eisenhower, 1954* (Washington, D.C.: U.S. Government Printing Office, 1958), 381–390.

14. *The Papers of Dwight D. Eisenhower,* Vol. XVII, 2170.

15. L. H. Gordon, "United States Opposition to Use of Force in the Taiwan Strait, 1954–1962," *Journal of American History* 72, 3 (December 1985).

16. Ibid., 660.

17. Ambrose, *Rise to Globalism,* 194.

18. Ibid., 199. Also see the comprehensive article by G. C. Herring, R. H. Immerman, "Eisenhower, Dulles, and Dienbienphu: 'The Day We Didn't Go to War' Revisited," *Journal of American History* 71, 2 (September 1984), 353.

19. Anthony Short made his specific reference to the Geneva Conference on Indochina in 1954. "Dulles had, in effect, needed someone to sign his shotgun permit; and Eden had refused." A. Short, *The Origins of the Vietnam War* (London: Longman, 1989), 148.

20. See P. M. Kattenburg, *The Vietnam Trauma in American Foreign Policy, 1945–1975* (New Brunswick, New Jersey: Transaction Books, 1980), 47–50.

21. The Republican Party platform of 1952 had been to criticize the Democrats for being soft on communism. This included the view that the Democrats had abandoned Poland, Czechoslovakia, Estonia, Latvia, and Lithuania. *The Papers of Dwight David Eisenhower,* Vol. XIV, 64, footnote 3.

22. Winston S. Churchill retired as British prime minister in April 1955.

23. T. G. Paterson, D. Merrill, *Major Problems in American Foreign Relations,* Vol. II, *Since 1914* (Lexington, Massachusetts: D.C. Heath and Company, 1995), 417.

24. Ambrose, *Rise to Globalism,* 232.

25. *Public Papers of the Presidents of the United States: Dwight D. Eisenhower, 1960–61* (Washington, D.C.: United States Government, 1961), 437.

26. In the president's news conference on May 11, 1960, Eisenhower, in defence of the U-2 intelligence gathering, stated, "It is a distasteful but vital necessity." Ibid., 404.

27. Ambrose, *Rise to Globalism,* 220.

28. *The Papers of Dwight D. Eisenhower,* Vol. XVII, 2240, footnote 6.

29. Ibid., 2264.

30. The Anglo-French military preparations off Malta were photographed by U-2 flights. R. H. Ferrell, ed., *The Eisenhower Diaries* (New York: W. W. Norton & Company, 1981), 331.

31. M. G. Fry, "Eisenhower and the Suez Crisis of 1956," in S. A. Warshaw, ed., *Re-examining the Eisenhower Presidency* (London: Greenwood Press, 1993), 156.

32. *The Papers of Dwight David Eisenhower,* Vol. XIV, xxiii.

33. On the development of Eisenhower's views on the United States being a military industrial complex, see C. J. Griffin, "New Light on Eisenhower's Farewell Address," *Presidential Studies Quarterly* XXII, 3 (Summer 1992).

CHAPTER 5

John F. Kennedy: The Problems of Foreign Policy Leadership, 1961–1963

> O, what a noble mind is here o'erthrown!
> The courtier's, soldier's, scholar's, eye, tongue, sword,
> The expectancy and rose of the fair state,
> The glass of fashion, and the mould of form,
> The observ'd of all observers.[1]
> —*Act III, Scene I, The Tragedy of Hamlet,*
> *Prince of Denmark*

Inauguration

"Let every nation know, whether it wishes us well or ill, that we shall pay any price, bear any burdens, meet any hardship, support any friend, oppose any foe to assure the survival and the success of liberty."[2] The cold war rhetoric of John F. Kennedy's inauguration in January 1961 is now almost too famous to present as an opening summation of the Kennedy presidency. Both the eloquence of the language and the delivery set a very high standard. In the wake of President Kennedy's problems in Berlin, Cuba, and Southeast Asia, it also appears rather jingoistic and meant to justify intervention abroad. The speech also had what Lance Morrow in *Time* magazine much later described as "reversible-raincoat prose."[3] This is evident in such passages as "Let us never negotiate out of fear. But let us fear to negotiate."[4]

Experience

John F. Kennedy was the first president born in the twentieth century. His early administrative experience was in the navy commanding a PT boat, PT-109 in the Pacific. His years in Congress from 1947 to 1960 were to further serve him well. However, as he stated himself, "There is no experience you can get, that can possibly prepare you adequately for the presidency."[5]

Yet, some might consider him more qualified to deal with foreign policy than domestic policy, and more qualified in discussing foreign policy issues than most presidents have been. His tenure on the Senate Foreign Relations Committee, diplomatic encounters when his father was ambassador to the United Kingdom, and his extensive world traveling built a strong interest in world affairs. The undergraduate thesis he wrote for Harvard University on appeasement in the 1930s was subsequently published as *Why England Slept.* He was also to have strong foreign policy debates with his Republican Party rival for the presidency in 1960, the vice president Richard M. Nixon, a man who also prided himself on foreign policy expertise. In many ways they outbid each other to see who could be more anti-communist.

Although you can hire the most intelligent people that your country can provide, unless the "jigsaw puzzle" fits together, so that intelligent and appropriate decisions are made, then the talent is wasted. In many ways the Kennedy administration fits this picture. Kennedy's staff—including the intellectuals, some anti-communist who were put in high office; McGeorge Bundy, assistant to the president for national security affairs; Walt W. Rostow, director of the policy planning staff at the Department of State; Robert S. McNamara, secretary of defense; and Dean Rusk, secretary of state— found themselves divorced from reality, yet arrogant with their newfound power. This was made worse by the privatization and centralization of presidential foreign policy power from Congress that continued under Kennedy.

His style of command was different to Eisenhower's more formal chain of decision making. Kennedy would elicit information from anyone he felt appropriate, but had a preference for oral reports or brief memoranda delivered to him. He also favored the advice of his very close associates, his brother, Robert (Bobby) F. Kennedy, the attorney general; Arthur M. Schlesinger Jr., special assistant to the president; and Theodore C. Sorensen, the special counsel to the president.

Bay of Pigs Failure

Within three months of his inauguration as president, Kennedy suffered a major setback in foreign policy. President Eisenhower, before leaving office, had authorized plans for the training of a group of Cuban exiles to return to Cuba and launch a counter-revolution against Fidel Castro. These forces made their preparations in Guatemala and believed they were to be given considerable help from the United States when they landed in Cuba. On taking office as president, John Kennedy learned of these plans and had to decide whether or not to give them the go ahead. Even if they were not given the go ahead some explanations would have to be given about the training of the exiles and why they were not supported. After consultation with advisers, including the Joint Chiefs of Staff, he decided to approve the plan. The attempted landing in Cuba at the Bay of Pigs in April 1961 was a complete disaster. The brigade of 1,400 exiles was no match for Castro's forces, and the expected uprising against Castro never materialized.

As a result of the Bay of Pigs failure, Kennedy's prestige suffered both at home and abroad. The domestic criticism was tempered when Kennedy took full responsibility for the disaster, his truthfulness finding resonance with the public in the United States. He ruminated on the events with Arthur Schlesinger Jr. "There's an old saying that victory has a hundred fathers and defeat is an orphan."[6] His recklessness had been exposed, but the perils of taking advice from military and intelligence experts appeared to have been learned. As Schlesinger concluded, "The Bay of Pigs provided Kennedy the warning and confirmed his temperamental instinct to reach deep inside State, Defense and the CIA in order to catch hold of policies before these policies made his choices for him."[7] In an off-the-record press briefing in December 1961 he reflected on the Bay of Pigs. "I think the assessments, and so on, were based on miscalculations. The situation within Cuba, the military situation—I think a good many miscalculations were made in regard to Cuba. I just don't think we're going to make another mistake—I don't think we are ever going to make one like that again."[8] At the very least his judgment was to mature, but the improvisation of his decision making exposed a personal vulnerability for making grand gestures.

Although not apparent to all parties within the Soviet Union, Cuba, and the United States, at the time—and despite the public remorse of John F. Kennedy over the Bay of Pigs—covert operations toward Cuba by the United States were to continue. "Operation Mongoose" was a covert operation to help facilitate the overthrow of Castro, including assassination attempts against Fidel Castro. President Kennedy gave approval for the new clandestine activities in November 1961, and the minutes of the first Operation Mongoose meeting on December 1, 1961, read, "The Attorney General told the Group about a series of meetings which had been held recently with higher authority. Out of these had come a decision that higher priority should be given to Cuba. General Lansdale [Brigadier General Edward Lansdale—counterinsurgency expert] had been designated as "Chief of Operations," with authority to call on all appropriate Government agencies for assistance, including the assignment of senior representatives from State, Defense and CIA."[9] However bizarre some of the activities associated with Operation Mongoose may have been, it is in retrospect not surprising that the Cuban government believed that Cuba might be subject to an invasion from the United States.

Vienna

John Kennedy tried to make the summit meeting with Nikita S. Khrushchev in Vienna on June 3 to 4, 1961, as informal as possible. Issues concerning Berlin, Laos, and disarmament were discussed, but Khrushchev was more truculent than Kennedy expected and little progress was made. The summit had been arranged rather too soon after the Bay of Pigs, and Khrushchev believed he could bully Kennedy, particularly over the thorny problems of Germany and Berlin. Lord Harlech (David Ormsby-Gore) commented on meeting John Kennedy in London, shortly after Vienna:

> Khrushchev obviously tried to brow-beat him and frighten him. He had displayed the naked power of the Soviet Union and this had all been extremely unpleasant and quite unlike what he had hoped their first meeting would be—that they would try to find areas of agreement, instead of which on Berlin and on the test ban treaty it was a very negative result—the only slight crumb of comfort was the Laos Agreement which did not seem to be sticking too well.[10]

The Berlin Wall and Cold War Symbolism

Berlin in 1961 was memorable for the erection of the Berlin Wall, a physical symbol of cold war differences. In turn, John F. Kennedy's remark "Ich Bin ein Berliner" in 1963 made his commitment to a free Berlin symbolic of the commitment of the United States to defend freedom against tyranny.[11]

Late on August 12, 1961, the East Germans began new road and border constructions in East Berlin. "A few days later, the East Germans began to construct what came to be known as the Berlin Wall, a 'permanent' installation of concrete, barbed wire, and watchtowers, bordered by minefields. The Berlin Wall, which reached one hundred miles in length, surrounded West Berlin, sealing it off from East Berlin and neighbouring parts of East Germany. About fifteen thousand East German troops guarded the wall."[12]

The creation of the Berlin Wall acerbated cold war issues. The West German government under Chancellor Konrad Adenauer (chancellor from 1949 to 1963) feared Western abandonment, and the French under President de Gaulle had a fear of American recklessness. Kennedy was seen as a newcomer to European problems and politics. More logically, the erection of the Berlin Wall was an indication of Soviet weakness rather than weakness of the United States. Kennedy always appeared unlikely to abandon Berlin since it had been a major feature of containment since World War II.

Kennedy did not abandon Berlin and made a very memorable speech in defense of a free Berlin on June 26, 1963, at the Rudolph Wilde Platz, Berlin. "Two thousand years ago the proudest boast was *civis Romanus sum.* Today, in the world of freedom the proudest boast is *Ich bin ein Berliner.* . . . Freedom is indivisible, and when one man is enslaved, all are not free. When all are free, then we can look forward to that day when this city will be joined as one and this country and this great Continent of Europe in a peaceful and hopeful globe."[13] It was another Kennedy speech full of impressive rhetoric, but of course the Soviet Union was capable of recognizing rhetoric. At the very least Kennedy was gambling that he could defend West Berlin, if necessary.

Cuban Missile Crisis

When the White House received U-2 aerial photographs showing the Soviet Union was installing nuclear missiles on Cuba, Kennedy accepted that he had to act to prevent this. Analysis of the photographs indicated that the Soviet Union was installing medium-range ballistic missiles (MRBMs) and intermediate-range ballistic missiles (IRBMs) in Cuba. Both types of weapon are surface-to-surface missiles, with the IRBMs having a target range of up to three thousand nautical miles. The photographs provided him with irrefutable evidence to combat Soviet denials. Against the advice of the military, which wanted to bomb the sites, President Kennedy ordered a naval blockade of Cuba. This, if the Soviet Union observed the quarantine, would stop the Soviets from delivering missiles to Cuba. The blockade allowed the Soviet Union to make a considered response rather than provoking them into a retaliatory strike, which the destruction of the missile sites on Cuba may have done. Kennedy's victory came with an agreement to dismantle the sites on Cuba, but a less-than-equivocal commitment from the United States to respect the territorial integrity of Cuba.

Nearly five months after the crisis of October 1962, the president queried McGeorge Bundy about why he was not informed of the crisis on October 15. Bundy replied:

You asked me the other night why I didn't call the evening of the 15th of October, when Ray Cline [Deputy Director of the CIA] reported the hard evidence of MRBM's in Cuba to me (at about 8:30 P.M.). I'm not sure I gave you a full answer, and you really need it for your memoirs—and perhaps even sooner if some reporter asks you. As I remember it, my thinking was like this:

1. This was very big news, and its validity would need to be demonstrated clearly to you and others before action could be taken. . . . The one obvious operational need was for more photography, and that was in hand.

2. It was a hell of a secret, and it must remain one until you had a chance to deal with it. . . .

3. On the other hand this was not something that could be dealt with on the phone except in the most limited and cryptic terms. . . .

4. Finally, I had heard that you were tired. . . .

5. So I decided that a quiet evening and a night of sleep were the best preparation you could have in the light of what could face you in the next days. I would, I think, decide the same again unless you tell me different.[14]

United States concerns about Soviet military actions in Cuba had emerged much earlier than October 15. On September 6 Theodore Sorensen made it clear to Ambassador Anatoly F. Dobrynin of the Soviet Union that the United States, as was evident from press speculation, had been concerned about Soviet military involvement in Cuba. Sorensen reported that Dobrynin said several times:

> They [Soviet Union] had done nothing new or extraordinary in Cuba—that the events causing all the excitement had been taking place somewhat gradually and quietly over a long period of time—and that he stood by his assurances that all of these steps were defensive in nature and did not represent any threat to the security of the United States. He neither contradicted nor confirmed my reference to large numbers of Soviet military personnel, electronic equipment and missile preparations.[15]

The Kennedy administration had been watching Cuba during the summer of 1962 as increasing arms supplies from the Soviet Union arrived in Cuba. It was not believed the Soviet Union would supply Cuba with surface-to-surface nuclear weapons, but the CIA was watching the situation with some consternation. Further worries were publicly aired to the extent that Congress passed a joint resolution on Cuba, approved on October 3, 1962. "[I]t was declared that the United States is determined to prevent by whatever means may be necessary, including the use of arms, the Marxist-Leninist regime in Cuba from extending, by force or the threat of force, its aggressive or subversive activities to any part of the hemisphere, and to prevent in Cuba the creation or use of an externally supported military capability endangering the security of the United States."[16]

This crisis over Cuba illustrated how Kennedy had matured in decision making and could orchestrate policy alternatives. An Executive Committee of the National Security Council was constituted to deal with the crisis over the thirteen days of the heightened problem, from October 16 to 28, meeting with a varied membership. At early meetings of the Executive Committee, the ambassador to the United Nations, Adlai Stevenson, and expert on the Soviet Union and former ambassador to the Soviet Union, Charles Bohlen, emphasized the importance of opening up diplomatic channels. They further emphasized the significance of diplomacy in a potential settlement. Dean Rusk and George Ball (under secretary of state) were largely cautious in their advice, although Rusk argued early on for a surgical strike; Robert McNamara, Robert Kennedy, and Theodore Sorensen were opponents of an air attack and favored the flexible blockade option; and General Maxwell Taylor (chairman, Joint Chiefs of Staff) emphasized military considerations throughout, arguing for a full invasion of Cuba. A quarantine did not exclude the future use of an air attack on Cuba. Whether or not John Kennedy was actually looking for clear advice or merely trying to build consensus from his advisers is unclear. The strategy became that of a quarantine of Cuba, and Kennedy informed the American public of the decision in a seventeen-minute speech on television on the evening of October 22 and enforced the naval interdiction in his presidential proclamation of October 23, stating:

> The forces under my command are ordered, beginning at 2.00 P.M. Greenwich time October 24, 1962, to interdict, subject to the instructions herein contained, the delivery of offensive weapons and associated materiel to Cuba. . . . The Secretary of Defense may make such regulations and issue such directives as he deems necessary to ensure the effectiveness of this order, including the designation, within a reasonable distance of Cuba, of prohibited or restricted zones and of prescribed routes.[17]

A B-52 bomber force loaded with nuclear bombs was put into the air, and the American people were warned that any nuclear missiles launched from Cuba against the Western hemisphere would lead to the United States retaliating against the Soviet Union.

It was when the Soviet ships stopped before the quarantine line that it was possible for the myth-creating rhetoric of Secretary Rusk to come into play. "We're eyeball to eyeball and the other fellow just blinked."[18] At the Cabinet meeting when it was announced that a number of Soviet ships had stopped or changed course, Rusk, sitting next to the president, made this comment to Bundy, sitting on his other side. It was a good enough comment to release to the press, although it sounded mildly triumphal and the crisis was not actually over. It was still necessary after the success of the quarantine line to get an agreement from the Soviet Union not to put missiles on Cuba and to get missiles removed from Cuba and the sites dismantled.

The event has provided considerable opportunity for modeling decision making and in particular investigating the rationality and irrationality of crisis management. It has also largely become an illustration of the use of clever and sober decision making. "When the Soviets sent two somewhat contradictory replies to his ultimatum, one hard and one more accommodating, Kennedy simply ignored the hard message and replied to the softer one. It worked. Khrushchev blinked, and in the memorable denouement, the Soviet ships turned and steamed away from Cuba."[19] United States ambassador-at-large and previous United States ambassador to the Soviet Union Llewellyn Thompson was on the Executive Committee and counseled that John Kennedy should respond to Khrushchev's more moderate letters and ignore the stern ones.[20] This approach was also promoted by Theodore Sorensen and Robert Kennedy.

The resolution of the crisis was clearly advanced by Robert Kennedy and his brother's trust in him. The president instructed Bobby to make it clear to

Soviet Ambassador Dobrynin on October 27 that once the crisis was resolved the president would remove Jupiter missiles (IRBMs) from Turkey. Theodore Sorensen, the unaccredited editor of Robert Kennedy's diary that became the posthumous memoir *Thirteen Days*, admitted in 1989 that he left out the references to the deal that would remove Jupiter missiles from Turkey.[21] This secret diplomacy was not to be publicly considered part of any deal. Dobrynin clearly believed it to be important in resolving the conflict and allowing Khrushchev to save face within the Soviet Presidium.

Academic and political interest has been strong since the crisis, and revelations have revealed that the Soviets had four times the number of military personnel in Cuba that the United States believed at the time. Kennedy-Khrushchev correspondence through November 1962 raised problems over Cuba, and the United States' commitments over Cuba were subject to clarification. Kennedy had not been as explicit over the future integrity of Cuba as sometimes portrayed. This provides the image of misinformation and miscommunication being evident over the Cuban missile crisis. Disagreements will persist as to whether or not the mistakes are substantial enough to alter the historical perspective of the Cuban missile crisis as a rather fine moment for the president.

It was, nevertheless, careful and confident decision making by the president. This was dovetailed with good communications and clear information provided for European allies, the Organization of American States, and the United Nations. The president kept President Charles de Gaulle of France, Chancellor Konrad Adenauer of West Germany, and Harold Macmillan, the prime minister of Great Britain, informed of his general actions.

The Kennedy administration had been concentrating on Berlin in the summer of 1962. In many ways the threat the United States perceived in Berlin from the Soviet Union also influenced the perception of the Cuban problem. Equally for the Soviet Union, European and Cuban issues were related and the deployment of missiles in Cuba was connected to broad strategic concerns. Yet the confrontation came over Cuba rather than Berlin. British ambassador to the United States David Ormsby-Gore recounted meeting Kennedy in the White House on the Sunday morning after Kennedy returned from Chicago. The president considered the repercussions of the Soviet Union "putting the squeeze on us [United States] in Berlin" and "nuclear war that week certainly was not excluded from his mind."[22] As the transcripts of Kennedy's taped conversations show, and Ernest May and Philip Zelikow conclude about the Executive Committee meetings, "Berlin was an omnipresent and dominating concern."[23]

The Kennedy presidency particularly illustrates the authority of the president in foreign policy matters, and the necessity for swift, decisive action under conditions of national security makes Congress an inferior partner to the president. The concentration of the deployment of nuclear weapons in the hands of the president, exhibited earlier by President Truman, had moved to new dimensions with larger nuclear devices and faster delivery systems. However masterly the action of John Kennedy in October 1962, the dangerous concentration of responsibility for nuclear weapons deployment in the hands of the president was very clear.

In cold war terms, the Cuban missile crisis occurs six years before the midway point of this period of history. Yet in some ways it *is* a midway point, since the use of nuclear weapons and a direct confrontation between the Soviet Union and the United States was never to be as evident again. A massive nuclear arms race continued and the United States and the Soviet Union embroiled themselves in separate conflicts around the world, but a direct cold war crisis of this magnitude would not be repeated. It is a defining moment of the cold war and, in clichéd historical terms, a watershed.

A positive outcome to the Kennedy-Khrushchev confrontation over Cuba was an initial softening of relations between the United States and the Soviet Union. The testing of nuclear weapons had been on the international agenda for a number of years, and scientists of the Pugwash movement had been recommending that new automatic seismic stations be installed. Khrushchev took up these developments with John Kennedy, and in a letter dated December 19 1962, noted, "It seems to me, Mr. President, that time has come now to put an end once and for all to nuclear tests. The moment for this is very, very appropriate. Left behind is a period of utmost acuteness and tension in the Carribean [sic]."[24] A nuclear test ban treaty was initialed in Moscow on July 25, 1963, by Nikita Khrushchev, Averell Harriman, and Lord Hailsham, and the next day President Kennedy announced to the American public that "Yesterday a shaft of light cut into the darkness. Negotiations were concluded in Moscow on a treaty to ban all nuclear tests in the atmosphere, in outer space and underwater. For the first time, an agreement has been reached on bringing the forces of nuclear destruction under international control—a goal first sought in 1946 when Bernard Baruch presented a comprehensive control plan to the United Nations."[25] Despite this major breakthrough and the signing of the treaty on October 7, 1963, the nuclear arms race moved on at an increasing pace. A nuclear test ban treaty did not prevent the expansion of the nuclear arsenals of the United States and the Soviet Union; it hoped to make any expansion safer for the world.

By the time of his death, John Kennedy was proud of the expansion and modernization of the nuclear power of the United States. In his undelivered speech on the day of his death, he was about to proclaim:

> In less than three years, we have increased by 50 percent the number of Polaris submarines scheduled to be in force by the next fiscal year, increased by more than 70 percent our total Polaris purchase program, increased by more than 75 percent our Minuteman purchase program, increased by 50 percent the portion of our strategic bombers on 15-minute alert, and increased by 100 percent the total number of nuclear weapons available in our strategic alert forces.[26]

Southeast Asia

"If it hadn't been for Cuba, we might be about to intervene in Laos."[27] According to Arthur Schlesinger Jr., the president made this off-the-cuff remark on May 3, 1961. Laos had witnessed the success of communist Pathet Lao guerrilla forces, a force supplied with weapons by the Soviet Union, although Kennedy had hoped that the Soviet Union would see the advantages of neutralization in Laos. The problem of Laos was temporarily resolved by the creation of a coalition government that incorporated the Pathet Lao.

Counterinsurgency tactics to fight the guerrillas in Laos captured the president's attention as important; having felt these tactics had some success in Malaya, Greece, and the Philippines. Counterinsurgency tactics were not as favorably looked upon by Kennedy's military advisers. A large invest-ment of time and money had been put into developing both conventional military tactics and also nuclear weapons in the United States. These were seen as more professional than the fad for counterinsurgency, which clearly put a different emphasis on the standing of the military.

Despite some opposition in the United States to counterinsurgency poli-cies, South Vietnam became a prime target for counterinsurgency tactics of the United States. The South Vietnamese government was grappling with Vietcong guerrilla movement, an organized force heavily supported by Ho Chi Minh's regime from North Vietnam. General Maxwell Taylor and Walt Rostow were sent to South Vietnam on a fact-finding mission (October 18 to November 2, 1961), and they rather optimistically believed that the military and political failings in South Vietnam could be reversed. Yet, strangely, Walt Rostow had warned the president about South Vietnamese president Ngo Dinh Diem's future as early as May 1961.

> Although we have no alternative except to support Diem now, he may be overthrown, as the accompanying cables suggest. If so, we should be prepared to move fast with the younger army types who may then emerge. Such a crisis is not to be sought, among other reasons because its outcome could not be predicted, but should it happen, we may be able to get more nearly the kind of military organization and perhaps even, the domestic political program we want in Viet-Nam but have been unable to get from Diem.[28]

The 16,200 military advisers that Kennedy supplied by 1963 to support South Vietnam fell short of a full military commitment, and the political support for Ngo Dinh Diem proved a disaster that led to a rather dramatic conclusion.

If the family autocracy of Ngo Dinh Diem was not enough for the United States to contend with, his insensitivity toward Vietnamese Buddhists gave Diem adverse international publicity that, he, in retrospect, could have done without. The secretary of state, Dean Rusk was informed by telegram on October 27:

> This morning about 10.00 am unidentified Vietnamese man with shaven head and dressed in civilian burned himself to death in front of Ministry of Finance building not far from Saigon Cathedral. Man arrived at scene on back of motorbike already soaked in gasoline, assumed Buddhist lotus position and set fire to himself.[29]

South Vietnamese generals moved further toward the position that Diem should be removed from office, and the American Embassy in Saigon felt it would be dangerous and inappropriate to intervene. Ambassador to South Vietnam Henry Cabot Lodge Jr. came to the conclusion that Diem should be replaced, and the Kennedy administration did not warn Diem of the impending coup d'état of November 1, 1963. John F. Kennedy, by all accounts, was upset at the news of the murder of Diem and his brother on November 2, and the resultant political turmoil in South Vietnam did not exactly assist the American cause.

John F. Kennedy clearly received conflicting advice on what should be done and what could be achieved in South Vietnam. Added to this was the confusion of how to deal with Hanoi against the clearer commitment to contain communism.

Other Initiatives

On a positive note, the president, early in his tenure, more clearly defined American attitudes toward Latin America in the Alliance for Progress program, an idea announced to Latin American diplomats in Washington, D.C. in March 1961.[30] This provided substantial economic aid for Latin America and supported humanitarian and national security objectives of the United States, as had earlier programs like the Marshall Plan for Western Europe in 1948. The Alliance for Progress program stood little chance of mirroring the success of the Marshall Plan, and Kennedy did not like the comparison. In reality, political instability in Latin America held up the kind of economic progress that appeared to be a faint prospect in the summer of 1961 when the Alliance for Progress was launched.

The Peace Corps was another idealistic invention that helped to capture the image of a youthful and idealistic administration in March 1961. Although it appeared to have a missionary zeal to sell American ideals abroad, under the directorship of R. Sargent Shriver, the president's brother-in-law, it attracted many youthful volunteers to go work in developing countries.

In the foreign policy arena, the record of John F. Kennedy is rather mixed and often exposed to the winds of academic fashion. There is a contrast between the image of a relatively youthful and dynamic president, an image promoted during his lifetime, and the hagiography that immediately followed his death, and the revisionist criticism amongst a number of historians that have found fault with most aspects of his life. Whether or not he was too reckless and lacked a moral compass to make his foreign policy judgments as well intentioned as he wished them to appear is still debated. The judgments made about Kennedy are almost as unsatisfactory as the incomplete nature and tenure of his presidency. He clearly continued the doctrine of containing the Soviet Union and communism, and had to live with the mutual mistrust that accompanied this policy. Alongside the policy of containment, the words of the president in June 1963 seemed to presage the era of détente.

What kind of peace do we seek? Not a *Pax Americana* enforced on the world by American weapons of war. Not the peace of the grave or the security of the slave. I am talking about genuine peace, the kind of peace that makes life on earth worth living, the kind that enables men and nations to grow and to hope and to build a better life for their children—not merely peace for Americans but peace for all men and women—not merely peace in our time but peace for all time.[31]

On October 22, 1963, George F. Kennan from the Institute for Advanced Study at Princeton University felt it necessary to write to the president.

I'm full of admiration, both as a historian and as a person with diplomatic experience, for the manner in which you have addressed yourself to the problems of foreign policy with which I am familiar. I don't think we have seen a better standard of statesmanship in the White House in the present century. I hope you will continue to be of good heart and allow yourself to be discouraged neither by the appalling pressures of your office nor by the obtuseness and obstruction you encounter in another branch of government. Please know that I and many others are deeply grateful for the courage and patience and perception with which you carry on.[32]

The president was assassinated one month later.

Notes

1. Words of Ophelia in W. Shakespeare, *The Tragedy of Hamlet, Prince of Denmark* (Chiswick, London: Folio Society, 1954), 60.

2. Kennedy's inaugural address, January 20, 1961, *Public Papers of the Presidents of the United States: John F. Kennedy, 1961,* Vol. 1 (Washington, D.C.: Government Printing Office, 1961), 1–3. Also, http://www.presidency.ucsb.edu/. Other sources for this speech include J. N. Giglio and S. G. Rabe, *Debating the Kennedy Presidency* (New York: Rowman & Littlefield Publishers, 2003), 169–172; and in M. Bose, *Shaping and Signaling Presidential Policy: The National Security Decision Making of Eisenhower and Kennedy* (College Station: Texas A&M University Press, 1998), 123–125.

3. *Time*, November 14, 1983, 43.

4. Ibid., 43.

5. A. M. Schlesinger Jr., *A Thousand Days* (Boston: Houghton Mifflin Company, 2002), 674.

6. Ibid., 289.

7. Ibid., 426.

8. Off-the-record briefing with the president, Palm Beach, Florida, December 29, 1961, Arthur M. Schlesinger Jr. Papers, White House Files, Box WH-66, 1961, John F. Kennedy Library (JFKL).

9. L. Chang and P. Kornblugh, eds, *The Cuban Missile Crisis, 1962: A National Archive Document Reader* (New York: New Press, 1998), 20.

10. Lord Harlech (William David Ormsby-Gore) interview, 1964, 7, JFKL.

11. "Remarks in the Rudolph Wilde Platz, Berlin, 26 June 1963," *Public Papers of the Presidents, John F. Kennedy*, http://www.presidency.ucsb.edu/.

12. Giglio and Rabe, *Debating the Kennedy Presidency*, 26–27.

13. *Public Papers of the Presidents, John F. Kennedy*, http://www.presidency.ucsb.edu/. The speech is briefly analyzed in L. Freedman, *Kennedy's War's: Berlin, Cuba, Laos and Vietnam* (Oxford: Oxford University Press, 2000), 268–269.

14. Memorandum for the President from McGeorge Bundy, March 4, 1963, Theodore C. Sorenson Papers, "Cuba" folder, Box 49, JFKL.

15. Memorandum for the files and Mr. Bundy and Mr. William R. Tyler (State Department), September 6, 1962, Theodore C. Sorensen Papers, "Cuba" folder, Box 48, JFKL.

16. This was used in the president's later proclamation on the "Interdiction of the Delivery of Offensive Weapons to Cuba," October 23, 1962, Theodore C. Sorensen Papers, "Cuba" folder, Box 48, JFKL.

17. Ibid.

18. Chang; Kornbluh, *The Cuban Missile Crisis, 1962*, 90. A useful account is also provided in T. J. Schoenbaum, *Waging Peace and War: Dean Rusk in the Truman, Kennedy and Johnson Years* (New York: Simon and Schuster, 1988), 319.

19. *Time*, November 14, 1983, 45.

20. D. Mayers, "JFK's Ambassadors and the Cold War," *Diplomacy & Statecraft* 11, 3 (November 2000), 190.

21. See J. Hershberg, "Anatomy of a Controversy: Anatoly F. Dobrynin's Meeting with Robert F. Kennedy, Saturday, 27 October 1962," *Cold War International History Project, Bulletin*, 5 (Spring 1995); B. J. Allyn, J. G. Blight, and D. A. Welch, eds., *Back to the Brink: Proceedings of the Moscow Conference on the Cuban Missile Crisis, 27–28 January 1989* (Lanham, Maryland: University Press of America, 1992); J. A. Nathan, ed., *The Cuban Missile Crisis Revisited* (New York: St. Martin's, 1992).

22. Lord Harlech interview, 1964, 13, JFKL.

23. E. P. May and P. D. Zelikow, eds., *The Kennedy Tapes: Inside the White House During the Cuban Missile Crisis* (Cambridge, Massachusetts: Harvard University Press, 1997), 668.

24. Khrushchev's letter to John Kennedy (in English), December 19, 1962, "Cuba–Missile Crisis–Khrushchev Correspondence" folder, President's Office Files, Box 115, JFKL.

25. A. Nevins, ed., *The Burden and the Glory* (Norwalk, Connecticut: Easton Press, 1988), 59.

26. Ibid., 273.

27. Schlesinger, *A Thousand Days*, 339.

28. Memorandum from W. W. Rostow to President Kennedy, May 10, 1961, National Security Files: Vietnam 1961–1963, microfilm, G. C. Herring, ed. (Frederick, Maryland: University Publication of America, 1987).

29. From acting consul, United States Embassy, Saigon to Secretary Rusk, October 27, 1963, ibid.

30. H. S. Parmet, *JFK: The Presidency of John F. Kennedy* (Norwalk, Connecticut: Easton Press, 1986), 97.

31. President John F. Kennedy's commencement address at American University in Washington, D.C., June 10, 1963, Nevins, *The Burden and the Glory*, 53–54.

32. A handwritten letter from George F. Kennan to John F. Kennedy, October 22, 1963, "George F. Kennan" folder, President's Office Files, Box 31, JFKL.

CHAPTER 6

Lyndon B. Johnson at War: Home and Abroad, 1963–1968

"The soldiers' music and the rite of war
Speak loudly for him.
Take up the bodies: such a sight as this
Becomes the field, but here shows much amiss."[1]
—*Act V, Scene II, The Tragedy of Hamlet,*
Prince of Denmark

Lyndon Baines Johnson wore his Texas origins on his sleeve. He would compare the problems of South Vietnam to those of Texas and sometimes to the situation at the Alamo. Johnson's homespun wisdom and brash style clearly disguised a thoughtful consideration of issues and policies. His own personal experience of the Depression made him seek a "Great Society" program for the disadvantaged in education, health care, and civil rights. However, Johnson's touch for the details of domestic politics strangely deserted him in the management of foreign policy. He prided himself in being a straight talker, although his rather strident outbursts were not restricted to senators, colleagues, and friends but also included visiting foreign dignitaries. Harold Wilson, the British prime minister, and Lester Bowles Pearson, the Canadian prime minister, were to separately receive some straight talking Johnson criticism when he believed they spoke out of turn about his escalation of the war in Vietnam. His trademark intimidation was holding friends or foes by the lapels of their coats or jackets.

The 1941 attack on Pearl Harbor influenced John F. Kennedy, Gerald R. Ford, and George H. W. Bush in their military careers and later decision making. This was also true of Lyndon Johnson, who, although in the United States Naval Reserve from June 1940, in quick response to the December 7, 1941, events became the first congressman to volunteer for active service; he reported for active duty two days later. President Roosevelt recalled members of Congress from active duty on July 16, 1942. Lyndon Johnson had seen active service by then and received the Silver Star medal for action during aerial combat over New Guinea.

If World War II was not enough foreign experience, John F. Kennedy used him as an emissary and fact finder by sending him to Europe, the Middle East, the Far East, Latin America, Africa, and Southeast Asia. In May 1961 Johnson visited South Vietnam on behalf of the president, and he would later deride subordinates who had not been to this trouble spot, by implication giving him superior knowledge and experience of the region.

Summit Diplomacy

Johnson's attempts at organizing or conducting summit diplomacy with the Soviet Union were extremely limited. Ambassador Dobrynin suggested that Chairman Khrushchev and President Johnson should meet in 1964, but political events in the Soviet Union prevented this. Nikita Khrushchev was ousted from office in 1964, and the United States expected the leadership change to be more hard-line and the new leaders to be committed to an orthodox communist ideology. In a period of collective rule, Leonid Ilyich Brezhnev became first secretary of the Communist Party of the Soviet Union: Aleksei Kosygin, prime minister of the Soviet Union; and Nikolai Podgorny, Soviet president. In reality, the escalation of the Vietnam War by Johnson soured United States-Soviet relations making summit diplomacy largely unpalatable.

President Johnson did meet with Aleksei Kosygin in June 1967 at Glassboro, New Jersey. The Middle East conflict was discussed, in addition to a North Vietnamese gesture to negotiate over Vietnam if the United States' bombing of Vietnam was halted. The results from this meeting never went beyond counterproposals being put forward. Any sense of progress in Soviet-United States rapprochement was then jettisoned with the invasion of Czechoslovakia by Warsaw Pact forces in August 1968. In fact, right up until the day before Soviet intervention in Czechoslovakia, Ambassador Dobrynin was encouraging President Johnson to announce a visit to Moscow for the first ten days of October. "There is no objections in Moscow—if the American side desires it—to an announcement in the nearest time about the coming visit of President Johnson to the Soviet Union."[2] The American side did not desire it.

Middle East

Before the Six Day War, the United States had attempted to establish good relations with Egypt (United Arab Republic), while still keeping the very good relationship they held with Israel. The Johnson administration did not overlook the sale of Soviet arms to the United Arab Republic and supplied both Israel and Jordan with advanced weapons. Johnson found it difficult to balance anti-Soviet policies and promote peaceful relations in the Middle East. He did not want to increase United States' arms sales in the volatile Middle East, but did want to counterbalance the supply of Soviet weapons to the United Arab Republic. Initially, the way around this dilemma was to meet Israeli requests for tanks by encouraging Western European allies to supply them instead of providing these from the United States. The issue became complicated by Jordan's request for tanks and fighter aircraft, where King Hussein was under pressure to take Soviet tanks and supersonic fighters, particularly if the United States did not provide them. Israel felt that if Jordan received arms from the United States, then so should Israel. Promises that Israeli requests would be looked at on a case-by-case basis, with concessions made in other areas including their nuclear program, did not satisfy them. According to NSC staff member Robert Komer, it prompted Averell Harriman, under secretary of state for political affairs, to say, "Even Soviets are less tough bargainers than Israelis."[3] This was probably the case, since not only did Jordan receive arms in 1965 but in 1966 Israel obtained forty-eight F-4s and Jordan thirty-six F-104s. The United States were particularly worried that at some future point in time, the aircraft sold to Israel might carry Israeli nuclear weapons, if they developed them. Further requests for arms sales from Jordan and Israel were reluctantly met by the United States in late 1966 and early 1967.

Latin America

For all the applause given to the Kennedy administration over the Cuban missile crisis, attitudes toward Castro did not appreciably change and continued into the Johnson administration. In December 1963 the CIA produced a status report showing that the intention of United States policy was to isolate Cuba from the Western hemisphere and "to exert maximum possible pressures, short of open and direct US military intervention, to prevent the consolidation and stabilization of the Castro-communist regime. The CIA covert action program is designed to support other governmental measures to proliferate and intensify the pressures on Castro to encourage dissident elements, particularly in the military, to carry out a coup and eliminate Castro and the Soviet presence in Cuba."[4] Covert and overt actions against Cuba were continued. The ostensible policy was to continue with the political, economic, and psychological isolation of Cuba from the rest of Latin America. Johnson did not want another pro-Soviet regime in Latin America.

As Warren Cohen points out, Johnson's reputation for being trustworthy and honest were tested over the Dominican Republic.[5] In 1965 Johnson sent United States Marines to support the loyalist military there, although the partiality of the action was much denied by the Johnson administration, and the communist influences within the rebel forces exaggerated. Initially,

under the useful umbrella argument of protecting United States nationals
and property, four hundred marines were dispensed to the Dominican
Republic. The deployment grew to over 20,000 service personnel being sent
to this Caribbean country, and was indicative of the policy of not allowing
another Cuban Revolution to develop in Latin America.[6]

In a book edited by H. W. Brands, a chapter called "Yankee, Go Home
and Take Me With You: Lyndon Johnson and the Dominican Republic" by
Peter Felten captures Johnson's policies in a country with a volatile political
situation.[7] The title of the chapter is marvelously ironic and derived from a
piece of graffiti scrawled on a wall in Santo Domingo, in the Dominican
Republic. Peter Felten summarized the success of Johnson in the Dominican
Republic as being due to a consistent policy; and of course, it was never to
be bedeviled with the same kind of domestic criticism within the United
States that became synonymous with Vietnam.

Vietnam: "A Dangerous Illusion"

"Let me acknowledge at the outset several personal premises: first, the
idea of a US military victory in Vietnam is a dangerous illusion."[8] This
memorandum from Townsend Hoopes to Clark Clifford on February 13,
1968, sums up the frightening dilemma that faced the Johnson administration and became acknowledged in the final year of his presidency.
Townsend Hoopes was a consultant for the NSC, and Clark Clifford was an
outside adviser to the president and one of the group of Johnson's "Wise
Men" before being made secretary of defense in 1968.

The nightmare of the Vietnam War for Americans has not just been confined to history books, but a generation of students is now growing up having been born after the Vietnam War ended for America, and the
dimensions of the war are being paraded in textbooks and feature films. The
dimensions of the war are recorded by most good textbooks, including that
"By the end of 1965 there were 184,000 American troops in Vietnam; in
1966 the troop level reached 385,000; and by 1969, the height of the American presence, 542,000. By the time the last American troops left in March
1973, 58,000 Americans had died and another 270,000 had been wounded.
The war had cost the American taxpayers $150 billion, . . . and divided the
country as no event in American history had since the Civil War."[9]

War was never formally declared on North Vietnam by the United States,
but in early August 1964 after two American destroyers (USS *Maddox* and
USS *Turner Joy*), purportedly in international waters, were allegedly fired
upon by North Vietnamese patrol boats, President Johnson persuaded Congress to pass the Gulf of Tonkin Resolution, which effectively by-passed the
issuing of a declaration of war. It stated "[t]hat the Congress approves and
supports the determination of the President, as Commander in Chief, to take
all necessary measures to repel any armed attack against the forces of the
United States and to prevent further aggression."[10] It can be argued that

Congress never intended to agree to a resolution that endorsed the intensive bombing of North Vietnam or the large escalation of the war undertaken by President Johnson.

The coordination of American policy toward Southeast Asia was clearly in the hands of President Johnson. In fact, the intimacy of the president with the problems in South and North Vietnam is also associated with the physical and mental toll that the war had on the president on a personal level. Through NSC meetings Johnson was kept informed of policy options. In 1964, fact-finding missions of secretary of state Dean Rusk, secretary of defense Robert McNamara, and chairman of the Joint Chiefs of Staff General Maxwell Taylor were instrumental in directing American commitments. The McNamara Report of March 1964 came in for some particular criticism in a memorandum from the Joint Chiefs of Staff to Secretary McNamara.

The Joint Chiefs of Staff do not believe that the recommended program in itself will be sufficient to turn the tide against the Viet Cong in South Vietnam without positive action being taken against the Hanoi Government at an early date. They have in mind the conduct of the kind of program designed to bring about cessation of DRV [Democratic Republic of Vietnam] support for operations in South Vietnam and Laos. . . . Such a program would not only deter the aggressive actions of the DRV but would be a source of encouragement to South Vietnam which should significantly facilitate the counterinsurgency program in that country. To increase our readiness for such actions, the US Government should establish at once the political and military bases in the United States and South Vietnam for offensive actions against the North and across the Laotian and Cambodian borders, including measures for the control of contraband traffic on the Mekong.[11]

On March 14, the president's special assistant for national security affairs, McGeorge Bundy, prepared Johnson for media questions about the importance of Vietnam.[12] Bundy acknowledged the rather strong commitment of the United States to South Vietnam going back over ten years, along with the perceived strategic importance of Southeast Asia. However, the emphasis Bundy put on fighting subversion and aggression was reminiscent of the Truman Doctrine.

The escalation of the war went through various stages of "Americanization," including: the "Rolling Thunder" bombing of North Vietnam in February 1965; combat troops sent to Da Nang in March 1965; increased combat operations; "search and destroy tactics"; the use of chemical weapons; and the replacement of dead American forces with new American soldiers. As Stephen Ambrose pointed out, it is unclear how United States bombing of the North would defeat the guerrilla tactics of the enemy, but it had the apparent virtue of saving American lives.[13] The bombing was designed to overcome the deficiencies and disadvantages of United States forces on the ground. Noam Chomsky's critique of the *Pentagon Papers* emphasized the impersonal language employed by the United States Department of Defense in its own history and explanation of the conflict in Vietnam.[14] Ironically the "body count" that was presented as a means for measuring success was to haunt the administration as the "body count" of United States service personnel became unbearable.

Intensive bombing of North Vietnam was the advice received by Johnson from most of his advisers. Support was given by Dean Rusk, Robert McNamara, McGeorge Bundy, Maxwell Taylor, General Westmorland, and General Earle Wheeler. The prospect of defeat seemed otherwise inevitable. Whether or not Johnson was given the advice he wanted has been speculated, but he certainly seemed seduced by the idea that bombing would aid a negotiation strategy. Opponents like George Ball, who did not see South Vietnam as vital to the United States security interests, were merely seen as playing the role of a Devil's advocate. The *Pentagon Papers* carry George Ball's memorandum to President Johnson on July 1, 1965 and warned:

> Once we suffer large casualties, we will have started a well-nigh irreversible process. Our involvement will be so great that we cannot– without national humiliation–stop short of achieving our complete objectives. *Of the two possibilities I think humiliation would be more likely than the achievement of our objectives–even after we have paid terrible costs.*[15]

In meetings about Vietnam on July 21, 1965, Robert McNamara presented his proposals for advancing the war by deploying more United States ground forces, getting Congress to authorize further increases in the armed forces, and gaining further appropriations. Armed forces would be increased by recruitment, draft, and an increase in the length of stay for those already in service (235,000 in Reserve and National Guard, 375,000 in the regular armed forces).[16] In summary, "We should increase our forces or get out."[17] Also he could not guarantee that the deployment of an additional 100,000 men in 1966 would actually be sufficient. The recommendations stood despite the rather ominous postscript.

George Ball was allowed to present alternative proposals. He felt Western forces could not wage war in the particular terrain of Vietnam or under the existing political atmosphere there. "It is like giving cobalt treatment to a terminal cancer case."[18] More obscurely, he recommended that the policy should be to let the government of South Vietnam "decide it doesn't want us."[19] Bundy supported the McNamara proposals and the president "regretted that we were embroiled in Vietnam. But we are there."[20] As NSC files show, the meeting clearly had moved against Ball.

> Mr. Bundy did not believe that Mr. Ball's "cancer analogy" was a good one. Immaturity and weakness, yes. A non-Communist society is struggling to be born. Before we take our decision to the American

people, Ambassador Taylor should go back to the GVN [Government of South Vietnam] and get greater, more positive assurances. There will be time to decide our policy won't work after we have given it a good try. (Mr. Ball disagreed here, feeling that the larger our commitment, the more difficult would be the decision to get out. "We won't get out; we'll double our bet and get lost in the rice paddies.")

Mr. Bundy felt that the kind of shift in US policy suggested by Mr. Ball would be "disastrous." He would rather maintain our present commitment and waffle through than withdraw. The country is in the mood to accept grim news.

Secretary Rusk emphasized that the nature and integrity of the US commitment was fundamental. It makes the US stance with the USSR creditable. It would be dangerous if the Communist leadership became convinced that we will not see this through. It is more important to convince the Communist leadership of this than to worry about the opinion of non-Communist countries.[21]

General Wheeler, Ambassador Lodge and Ambassador Unger agreed with Robert McNamara.

In 1970 Lyndon Johnson reflected on the decisions of 1965 with one of his biographers, Doris Kearns. It is never clear whether or not Johnson believed his own flamboyant rants, but his awareness of the historical context of his decision is interesting.

Yet everything I knew about history told me that if I got out of Vietnam and let Ho Chi Minh run through the streets of Saigon, then I'd be doing exactly what Chamberlain did in World War II. I'd be giving a fat reward to aggression. . . . I knew that Harry Truman and Dean Acheson had lost their effectiveness from the day that the Communists took over in China. . . . And I knew that all these problems taken together, were chickenshit compared with what might happen if we lost Vietnam.[22]

Throughout the period from 1965 to 1968, Lyndon Johnson and a substantial number of his advisers made continuous, optimistic forecasts that the war in Vietnam would soon be over, which also included statements that underestimated the size of American involvement that would be needed to effectively prosecute the war. Internally, the Johnson administration fretted over the depth of involvement and even the fact they had no ostensible policy about effectively ending the war, short of the Vietcong and North Vietnam capitulating. A significant amount of public opinion turned against Johnson's handling of the war, and anti-war protests in 1967 and 1968 added to the "bunker" mentality of the president. The anti-war protests on college campuses in the United States were quite moderate in 1965, but grew appreciably by 1967.

The anti-war activity within the United States had been further fueled in
1966 by the involvement of Congress and, specifically, the Senate Foreign
Relations Committee hearings investigating additional financial requests
from the president. The hearings were led by the Democratic Party senator William Fulbright of Arkansas and also televised within the United
States. Critics appearing before the committee argued for the withdrawal
of American forces, while defenders of the administration, including Dean
Rusk and Maxwell Taylor, received a forceful examination of their policies. President Johnson described the hearings as "a very, very disastrous
break."[23]

The State Department and White House advisers to the president made
extensive reviews of policy for 1967. They emphasized a range of policies,
having in mind Johnson's own ceilings on troop deployment and desire to
contain the aerial bombing of the North. The advice given included
"aggressive pacification and national reconciliation programs; promotion
of a popularly-based South Vietnamese Government and a land reform
scheme; reliance on the barrier to help reduce infiltration; the vigorous
pursuit of negotiating leads; continuation of the air war and the "spoiling
offensive" against main enemy forces; and improved management of the
war effort in Saigon."[24] Johnson's advisers were not predicting victory in
1967, but the majority did not warn that an acceptable conclusion to the
Vietnam War was not possible.

With the media coverage of the Vietcong Tet offensive of January 1968
(Tet was the date of the Vietnamese New Year), Johnson's credibility was
tested. The great irony was that American forces inflicted large losses on the
Vietcong who had penetrated deep into South Vietnam, occupied the city of
Hue, and temporarily occupied the American embassy in Saigon itself.
However, the depth of penetration of communist forces in South Vietnam
and public criticism within the United States made the Tet offensive appear
a victory for the Vietcong.

On March 30, 1968, Lyndon Johnson announced that he would not be
running for president in the November elections. His last nine months in the
White House were devoted to seeking progress toward peace in Vietnam,
but the war had consumed the best efforts of President Johnson.

Conclusion

Arthur Schlesinger Jr. points out, "Lyndon Johnson came to the Presidency with an old and honest belief in spacious presidential authority to
deploy force abroad in the service of American foreign policy."[25] In a similar point, George Herring felt to "some degree," Johnson "shared the yearn-
ing for military glory common to his generation."[26] Little did Johnson know
at the start of the war that this approach would also define his ignominious
policies toward Vietnam and hasten his departure from the political arena.
He managed to lose support for the war both at home and abroad. He lost

one of the major requirements for the commander in chief to prosecute a war: the respect of large sections of the American public.

Johnson had been fighting the cold war in Southeast Asia. For the president, he was merely continuing the containment policy that had been bequeathed by three previous presidents: Kennedy, Eisenhower, and Truman. If John Kennedy shares responsibilities for commitments to Vietnam, it may be because he sent his vice president to Vietnam and Johnson became a clear supporter of South Vietnam. As Robert Dallek points out, Johnson had become an evangelist for containing communism in South Vietnam.[27] Influencing President Kennedy and making your own decisions were clearly two different things. For Johnson the "domino theory" was very much alive during his tenure as president.

In terms of presidential decision making and the Vietnam War, Johnson was in many ways posing questions to and accepting answers from the "wrong" people. The Pentagon and the Joint Chiefs of Staff were liable to give military solutions to military and political problems. The *Pentagon Papers* are evidence of this. However, in Johnson's defense, if your doctor tells you that you are ill, you do not necessarily change your doctor. Johnson sought a range of advice and listened to the best available military and intelligence advice at his disposal. To use the cancer analogy of Ball, when a patient is diagnosed with such a severe disease, secondary confirmation is a good idea, and all the alternative or complimentary cures and treatments might also be outlined. Johnson was not without alternative advice on Vietnam. The NSC meetings show a number of alternative policies and suggestions, but they do clearly illustrate the very strong recommendations for escalation from the key advisers. Congress, the media, and student protests provided escalating voices of dissent outside the White House, and this gathered pace as policies unraveled in Vietnam. Whether or not containing communism in South Vietnam was an "incurable" situation is much debated. The attempted Johnson-administration cures in Southeast Asia ultimately proved to be as unpalatable within the United States as the diagnosed problem of communist expansion in Southeast Asia itself had been for Johnson.

If 1945 is considered the effective starting point of the cold war (and it often is) and 2001 is the end of the cold war, then 1968 is the chronological midway point of the cold war. Furthermore, it represents a low point in the Vietnam War for the United States and a low point for President Johnson. Richard Nixon was elected as the new president in November 1968, even though he represented an older Republican Party guard and held a decidedly cold war warrior reputation.

Notes

1. Words of Fortinbras in W. Shakespeare, *The Tragedy of Hamlet, Prince of Denmark* (Chiswick, London: Folio Society, 1954), 122.

2. A message written by Anatoly Dobrynin and delivered August 19, 1968. "Special Head of State Correspondence," Box 57, USSR–Presidential Correspondence, LBJ Library. Copy provided by John Wilson of the LBJ Library at the Conference of the Society for Historians of American Foreign Relations, University of Texas at Austin, June 2004.

3. *Foreign Relations of the United States (FRUS),* Vol. XVIII, *Arab-Israeli Dispute, 1964–1967* (Washington, D.C.: U.S. Government Printing Office, 2000), 371.

4. "Cuba–A Status Report," December 12, 1963, folder "Cuba," Box 48, Theodore Sorensen papers, JFKL.

5. W. I. Cohen, *The Cambridge History of American Foreign Relations,* Vol. IV, *America in the Age of Soviet Power, 1945–1991* (Cambridge: Cambridge University Press, 1993), 166.

6. Ibid., 166.

7. H. W. Brands, ed., *The Foreign Policies of Lyndon Johnson* (College Station, Texas: Texas A&M University Press, 1999).

8. In L. Berman, *Lyndon Johnson's War: The Road to Stalemate in Vietnam* (New York: W. W. Norton & Company, 1989), 216.

9. G. B. Tindall and D. E. Shi, *America: A Narrative History,* 3rd edition (New York: W. W. Norton & Company, 1992), 1358.

10. M. D. Gambone, *Documents of American Diplomacy: From the American Revolution to the Present* (Westport, Connecticut: Greenwood Press, 2002), 374.

11. "Memorandum from the Joint Chiefs of Staff to the Secretary of Defense (Robert McNamara)," March 14, 1964. A note on the source text indicates that McNamara saw this memorandum on April 2. *FRUS 1964,* Vol. 1, *Vietnam* (Washington, D.C: U.S. Government Printing Office, 1992), 82.

12. "Memorandum from the President's Special Assistant for National Security Affairs (Bundy) to the President." Ibid., 148–149.

13. S. E. Ambrose, *Rise to Globalism,* 3rd edition (Harmondsworth, Middlesex: Penguin, 1983), 288.

14. N. Chomsky, *The Backroom Boys* (Bungay, Suffolk: Fontana, 1973).

15. The emphasis is in the original. R. A. Strong, *Decisions and Dilemmas: Case Studies in Presidential Foreign Policy Making* (Englewood Cliffs, New Jersey: Prentice Hall, 1992), 107.

16. "Meetings on Vietnam, July 21, 1965," L. B. Johnson National Security Files, Vietnam, 1963–1969, [microform], G. C. Herring, general ed., R. E. Lester, project coordinator (Frederick, Maryland: University Publications of America, 1987).

17. Ibid.

18. Ibid.

19. Ibid.

20. Ibid.

21. Ibid.

22. D. Kearns, *Lyndon Johnson and the American Dream* (Norwalk, Connecticut: Easton Press, 1987), 252–253.

23. *FRUS, 1964-68,* Vol. IV, *1966* (Washington, D.C.: Government Printing Office, 1998), 205.

24. *FRUS,* Vol. IV, *Vietnam, 1966,* http://www.state.gov/. Volume Summary, Foreword, 8.

25. A. M. Schlesinger Jr., *The Imperial Presidency,* revised edition (Boston: Houghton Mifflin, 1989), 177.

26. G. C. Herring, "The Reluctant Warrior: Lyndon Johnson as Commander in Chief," in D. L. Anderson, ed., *Shadow on the White House: Presidents and the Vietnam War, 1945-1975* (Lawrence, Kansas: University of Kansas Press, 1993), 88.

27. R. Dallek, *John F. Kennedy: An Unfinished Life, 1917-1963* (London: Penguin Books, 2003), 354.

CHAPTER 7

Richard M. Nixon, Henry A. Kissinger, and the Search for Peace, 1969–1974

Are all thy conquests, glories, triumphs, spoils,
Shrunk to this little measure?[1]
—*Act III, Scene I, The Tragedy of Julius Caesar*

Although a slightly clumsy expression, a "Nixinger" form of foreign policy diplomacy is associated with the Richard Milhous Nixon presidency, as he became dependent on Dr. Henry Alfred Kissinger in the foreign policy arena. They were not entirely an odd couple, although the Quaker from Yorba Linda in California, history major at Whittier College, and lawyer does contrast with the German-born Jew and academic member of Harvard University who was to be the United States' fifty-sixth secretary of state. They were not entirely different since they shared a realism and pragmatism about foreign policy that helped to make them partners.

A person not at the heart of Nixon's foreign policy initiatives was his first secretary of state, William Rogers. Although holding this office until 1973, he was increasingly sidelined by Nixon's use of his assistant on national security affairs, Henry Kissinger. To the embarrassment of Rogers, he was kept out of the policy initiatives related to the United States rapprochement with China, secret diplomacy with Hanoi, and the arms control policies toward the Soviet Union.[2] Henry Kissinger replaced Rogers as secretary of state in September 1973 and lasted in this position until January 1977. Kissinger also retained his position as an assistant to the president on national security affairs until November 1975. Nixon's attitude toward William Rogers and Kissinger's comments on this is indicative of Nixon's attitude toward the State Department and the pique that Kissinger could display. Kissinger recounts in his memoir, *White House Years*, how he was not consulted on the appointment of Rogers and that Nixon considered Rogers's unfamiliarity with foreign policy a positive feature of the appointment.[3] Kissinger recounts, "Nixon said, Rogers was one of the toughest, most cold-eyed, self-centred, and ambitious men he had ever met. As a negotiator he would give the Soviets fits. And 'the little boys in the State Department' had better be careful because Rogers would brook no nonsense. Few Secretaries of State can have been selected because of their President's confidence in their ignorance of foreign policy."[4]

Background on Richard M. Nixon

By September 1942 Richard M. Nixon was commissioned in the United States Navy and soon after was sent to the Pacific. He served in the supply and legal services and by his own admission learned to play highly profitable poker. Like many of his generation, he returned to political life as a war veteran.

Nixon had unimpeachable anti-communist credentials. His national and international reputation was defined in congressional committees and as vice president. As a young congressman he was a member of the House Un-American Activities Committee. Through intensive investigation of the testimony of Whittaker Chambers, Nixon helped to expose the activities of Alger Hiss, a State Department official subsequently convicted of perjury. In 1947, Nixon went to Europe with a nineteen-member committee from Congress under the chairmanship of Christian Herter. It was to study problems related to foreign aid and the plan introduced by the secretary of state General George C. Marshall that would become the European Recovery Program. It was an interesting appointment since Nixon saw the Truman administration as soft on communism, a position he would exploit when the communist People's Republic of China was proclaimed in 1949. As one of his biographers, Jonathan Aitkin, pointed out, the public persona of Nixon, the young Republican was as "a ruthless, Red-baiting, Democrat hater."[5]

When Nixon was vice president, his position in August 1953 on the investigations of communists or communist sympathizers in public office was clear.

> Anyone who refuses to cooperate with a Congressional committee or with the courts or with any other law enforcement agency of this government in exposing a conspiracy to destroy America forfeits his right to work for the American government. . . . I believe that anybody who refuses to testify and to cooperate in exposing in the United States by that act disqualifies himself to teach the young people of America in any school, public or private, in this country.[6]

Like many vice presidents, Richard Nixon was used as an emissary and a replacement for the president on a number of foreign trips. From October 5, 1953, to December 14, 1953, the vice president and Mrs. Nixon undertook a goodwill trip to the Far East, southern Asia, Australia, New Zealand, Iran, and Libya. It was a very extensive trip and exposed Nixon to a number of foreign leaders. The shah of Iran, Reza Pahlavi; Prime Minister Nehru of India; President Sukarno of Indonesia; and Sir Robert Menzies, the Australian prime minister, were among leaders that met the United States vice president.

In February and March 1955, Richard Nixon visited Central America and the islands of the Caribbean, including Cuba, Guatemala, Mexico, Honduras, Nicaragua, Costa Rica, Panama, Puerto Rico, the Virgin Islands, the Dominican Republic, and Haiti. He addressed a number of regional economic issues and had direct meetings with Batista of Cuba, Cortines of Mexico, Armas of Guatemala, Figueres of Costa Rica, and Somoza of Nicaragua.

On July 1, 1956, the vice president and Mrs. Nixon left the United States for another trip to Asia and the Far East. He attended celebrations for the tenth anniversary of the independence of the Philippines and the second anniversary of the inauguration of Ngo Dinh Diem as president. In a speech in Manila he warned against neutralist policies toward communism. On the same trip he had discussions with Generalismo Jiang Jieshi of Taiwan, President Mirza of Pakistan, and Premier Songgram of Thailand.

On a trip to Africa in 1957, ostensibly to attend ceremonies to celebrate the independence of the Gold Coast, the British colony that became Ghana, Nixon unexpectedly met Martin Luther King Jr. but also made a friendship with Alec Douglas-Home, a future British foreign secretary and prime minister. Journalist Martin Walker spotted this useful connection.

Partly under Home's influence, Nixon came to the view that decolonisation should not proceed too fast and should involve safeguards for Western access to strategic minerals, particularly in southern Africa. This proved important in Nixon's presidency after 1969, when the US (and after 1970) the Heath government in Britain closely co-ordinated their policies towards Zimbabwe, South Africa and Portugal's colonies in Africa.[7]

The two most difficult trips that Richard Nixon made were to South America in April and May 1958 and the Soviet Union in July 1959. What was supposed to be a goodwill visit to Latin America caused major diplomatic problems and became controversial when Nixon encountered hostile demonstrations in Lima, Peru, on May 7 and 8, and in Caracas, Venezuela, on May 13. President Eisenhower responded by moving some United States forces in the Caribbean and made the point of meeting his vice president at the airport on his return to the United States. Nixon was accorded a hero's welcome on his return.

Another trip that ultimately turned favorable for Nixon was his official visit to the Soviet Union, opening the United States national exhibition at the Moscow Trade Fair. It became memorable for a "kitchen debate" between Premier Nikita Khrushchev and Nixon, where Nixon stood up for American capitalism and consumerism.

Background on Henry A. Kissinger

Henry Kissinger became a United States citizen in 1943, but despite this he was constitutionally restricted from being president of the United States. The Constitution restricts all immigrants to the United States from being president; Kissinger was no different and did not necessarily harbor any ill will about this. The reality is that over foreign policy issues, Henry Kissinger came to be more effective in diplomacy, and to some extent, in terms of political power, he was more relevant than the incumbent presidents he served. By the end of Richard Nixon's tenure, White House foreign policy was dominated by Henry Kissinger. It was Kissinger who was at the epicenter of foreign policy decision making.

Kissinger had two associations that might have excluded him from being a confidant of Richard Nixon. Although it was brief, he gave advice to the Kennedy administration in the first two years of Kennedy's presidency. Second, he supported and wrote speeches for Nelson Rockefeller's bid for the Republican Party presidential nomination in 1968. Kissinger was also the type of Harvard intellectual that Nixon sometimes disparaged, yet Kissinger had a background unlike the eastern seaboard elite by which the liberal Democratic Party were sometimes represented. It would appear that Kissinger's academic reputation overcame deficiencies since Nixon appointed him assistant to the president for national security affairs in January 1969. Kissinger clearly had resilience, the eye of an opportunist, and the desire for recognition.

Kissinger believed that there could be order in the international system. His published doctoral dissertation on the Concert of Europe, *A World Restored: Metternich, Castlereagh, and the Problems of Peace, 1812–22*, could almost be a template for his foreign policy approach.[8] George Ball, a former under secretary of state, went further in suggesting Kissinger and Nixon had medieval dynastic practices. Ball suggests that the White House was a court rather than a cabinet and the president a sovereign acting with or through his assistant for national security affairs, with ambassadors reduced to little more than messenger boys.[9]

Kissinger by 1973 was being referred to by much of the United States media as the second most powerful person in the United States. In foreign policy terms, although not constitutionally so, he may have been the most powerful individual. He was variously described, including as an international "Mr. Fixit" and a modern day Metternich.[10]

Vietnam War and the Nixon Doctrine

Henry Kissinger's view of President Nixon was that "No American President possessed a greater knowledge of international affairs."[11] Although both Nixon and Kissinger were extremely well-informed about foreign policy, it appears they were hazy about how this expertise should be deployed and had no exact strategy about how to end the war in Vietnam. However, both accepted the principle that United States power was preponderant and could be made credible for Western nations. Nixon famously and without any details promised "peace with honor" during the 1968 election campaign.

Richard Nixon began his presidency with a view that the Vietnam War could be helped through a policy of gradual "Vietnamization." This would allow for the withdrawal of United States ground troops. As Stephen Ambrose curtly remarked, "Ten months after taking office he announced that his secret plan to end the war was in fact a plan to keep it going, but with lower American casualties."[12] Jussi Hanhimäki begs the question "whether Kissinger (and Nixon) had missed a chance to conclude the Vietnam War when they first came into office, choosing to prolong the war by another four years at the cost of some 20,000 additional American (and countless Vietnamese) lives."[13]

The Nixon Doctrine or Guam Doctrine, as it was also known, meant the United States would not support developing countries with United States ground forces to combat communism. The United States under Nixon would continue to support Western European and Far Eastern allies, but would not sustain United States ground forces in Southeast Asia. This policy did not exclude heavy use of air power, although the intention was to train the army of the Republic of Vietnam more intensely and continue to supply them with military armaments. This did not prevent Nixon from intensifying the war, particularly by subjecting South Vietnam's neighbors Cambodia and Laos to intensive bombing. In many ways Nixon had set himself a paradox. To get the North Vietnamese to negotiate, he took the war into areas previously avoided. Nixon, after limiting his options, believed he had to find ways to oblige North Vietnam to accept a settlement that would allow the United States to save some face: the honor in "peace with honor."

Kissinger's announcements that "peace is at hand" in October 1972, coupled with separate détentes with the Soviet Union and China, helped Nixon win a landslide victory in the November 1972 presidential election. Peace in Vietnam could not be immediately or automatically delivered. Negotiations between Henry Kissinger and Le Duc Tho (special envoy for North Vietnam) continued into December 1972, punctuated by bombing of Hanoi and Haiphong in North Vietnam, to be followed by resumed peace talks in Paris. *Time* magazine reported:

First he [Nixon] ordered a new seeding of North Vietnamese harbors with mines. Then he launched the biggest, bloodiest air strikes ever aimed at the North. Nixon seemed determined to bomb Hanoi into a settlement that he is willing to accept. . . . Nixon also had an ultimatum of sorts . . . for South Vietnamese President Nguyen Van Thieu. Nixon sent Kissinger's deputy, General Alexander Haig, to Saigon with a letter for Thieu. It warned Thieu against making any diversionary peace demands of his own and told him to be prepared to sign any agreement reached between Washington and Hanoi.[14]

A peace agreement was signed on January 27, 1973. It was like some previous proposals, but assurances to the South Vietnamese that the United States would return with force if the agreements were violated appeared to convince President Thieu and the government in the South.

Henry Kissinger and Le Duc Tho received the Nobel Peace Prize for their diligence in working for the cause of peace. To the embarrassment of the Norwegian Nobel Committee, their choice was not greeted with universal approval, Le Duc Tho declined the award and Kissinger did not make the award ceremony due to a NATO meeting.[15]

Congress was to ban further bombing of Cambodia in 1973. With successful peace talks an American withdrawal and peace agreement was possible, and it was signed in early 1973. The excesses of the Vietnam War led the United States Congress to put restrictions on presidential authority over foreign policy by passing the War Powers Act.

For Nixon his authority as Commander in Chief conjoined with the principle of troop protection and the model of the missile crisis was all he needed. In his announcement of the incursion into Cambodia he compared himself to Kennedy who, "in his finest hour," had sat in the identical room in the White House and made "the great decision" that removed the missiles from Cuba. Later Nixon used the missile crisis to justify his failure to consult Congress over Cambodia.[16]

In the spirit of blaming someone else, Richard Nixon, in 1985, explained why South Vietnam surrendered on April 30, 1975, and why Soviet-built tanks had been allowed to roll into Saigon.

We won the war in Vietnam, but we lost the peace. All that we had achieved in twelve years of fighting was thrown away in a spasm of congressional irresponsibility. . . . First, it destroyed our ability to enforce the peace agreement, through legislation prohibiting the use of American military power in Indochina. Then it undercut South Vietnam's ability to defend itself, by drastically reducing our military aid.[17]

China and the Value of "Linkage"

Despite the problems of Indochina, other aspects of President Nixon's foreign policy brought about more cooperative relations between the United States and communist countries. An irony of the cold war was to be that after years of claiming that monolithic communism was a problem, it was the realization and impact of discord between the People's Republic of China and the Soviet Union, including border clashes in 1969, that helped produce détente.

Kissinger is seen at the heart of détente and the triangular diplomacy that played the Soviet Union and the Chinese People's Republic against one another, particularly in Southeast Asia. The Sino-Soviet split also allowed for this, and it also allowed for the joke that China was NATO's best ally. The relationship of the United States to China became tactically and strategically beneficial for the United States and consequentially NATO.

The United States softened its attitude toward China in 1969, reducing a number of barriers to trade. By 1971 Henry Kissinger had made two visits to Beijing to pave the way for the president's visit. Nixon's visit to China in 1972 defined a new development in relations between the United States and China, providing at least a symbolic change. If United States relations in Asia were reconstituted, then an American commitment to Southeast Asia could be reduced. Kissinger talked up the value of "linkage" as a doctrine, linking different objectives and policies together to get results. There was nothing very new about this, but it had a positive agenda, and the assumption that the United States was gaining concessions somewhere.

Soviet Union: Nixon, Brezhnev, and Cars

In 1968, President Nixon signed a treaty with the Soviet Union on the nonproliferation of nuclear weapons, and in 1972 he signed an interim agreement for the Strategic Arms Limitation Treaty (SALT I). The latter was produced in Moscow in May 1972, where a good working relationship with General Secretary Brezhnev facilitated the signing of the Anti-Ballistic Missile Treaty (ABM) and SALT I. Agreements to cooperate over health, environmental, and scientific areas were also made. This was as important for Nixon and Kissinger as the China visit, and the first visit of an American president to the Soviet capital city. Nixon's present to Brezhnev was a Cadillac car.

Next year the good relationship was to continue between Nixon and Brezhnev, and between June 18 and 25 in Washington D.C., Camp David, and the president's home in San Clemente, California, the two leaders had forty-seven hours of meetings. They signed nine agreements varying from principles on limiting nuclear weapons to further agricultural and scientific cooperation. They also both declared satisfaction with the Paris Agreement on Vietnam, signed in January 1973. Nixon gave Brezhnev a Lincoln Continental car as a present.

The final meeting of President Richard Nixon and General Secretary Brezhnev took place again in Moscow and in Brezhnev's villa at Oreanda on the Black Sea, shortly before Nixon resigned over the Watergate scandal. Nixon gave Brezhnev a sporty Chevrolet Monte Carlo car as a present at this summit meeting. That it was nearly half the price of the previous cars given by Nixon should not be seen as a slight; Brezhnev had requested this particular sporty car. It did allow *Time* magazine the opportunity to describe it as "The Chevrolet Summit of Modest Hopes."[18] Brezhnev and Nixon did agree to a further limit on ABM sites (i.e., one each), and limited the size of underground nuclear weapons tests, although this further test ban treaty was not ratified by the United States. The meeting really opened the way for further discussions that President Gerald Ford inherited. Nevertheless, Nixon had clearly taken advantage of the merits of summit diplomacy.

The Middle East and Defense Condition III

Despite the Vietnam War dominating United States foreign policy for a decade, it was the Middle East that often looked like it was escalating into a superpower confrontation. The Middle East, or more particularly the relationships between Israel and her Arab neighbors, appeared to resist political solutions. With United States military support of Israel, and the Soviet Union arming Egypt, Iraq and Syria, the situation appeared extremely volatile. Any attempt at "even-handedness" by the United States was a considerable struggle to maintain in the unstable circumstances of the Middle East.[19]

Gamal Abdul Nasser died in 1970 and his successor Anwar Sadat, although showing a disenchantment with the Soviet Union, exhibited a radical streak of his own. By 1972, Sadat ordered Soviet personnel out of Egypt. Sadat believed Egypt had been humiliated by Israel, but he also knew that Egypt did not have the military resources to defeat Israel. Egypt turned back to the Soviet Union and, along with Syria, received missiles and tanks that would facilitate an attack on Israel. With an oil embargo produced by Saudi Arabia, Egypt hoped that the United States would not act forcefully. It took the United States and Israel by some surprise when Sadat went to war on October 6, 1973, during the religious holiday of Yom Kippur. As Kissinger later realized, the Egyptians and Syrians lacked the military ability to gain territory by force, but they could change the political equilibrium in the Middle East: "The shock of war, he [Sadat] reasoned, would enable both sides, Israel as well as Egypt, to show a flexibility that was impossible while Israel considered itself militarily supreme and Egypt was paralyzed by national humiliation."[20] The Yom Kippur War can clearly be described as unexpected, so much so that President Nixon received a CIA report the day before that gave the following prediction for the Middle East: "The military preparations that have occurred do not indicate that any party intends to initiate hostilities."[21] Nixon's domestic preoccupation with the Watergate scandal was broken by necessary discussions about the Middle East conflict with Kissinger, Haig, and the National Security Council.

With the outbreak of the war, a considerable amount of cold war confusion followed. The United States provided military resources directly to Israel. Kissinger was taken by surprise when Brezhnev suggested a joint

Soviet-United States intervention in the conflict; if not, the Soviets would act alone. This potential Soviet unilateral action was unacceptable to the United States, and with considerable bravado United States armed forces were put on nuclear alert, Defense Condition III (Defense Condition II is an imminent attack, Defense Condition I is war). Nixon believed that the situation was the most serious since the Cuban missile crisis when President Kennedy had military forces on nuclear alert. Although Kennedy had used management skills in allowing the Executive Committee of the NSC to meet without him, not wishing to cause alarm and wanting to allow free discussion for a period of time, Nixon's intentions were not quite as clear. It appears more patently that Henry Kissinger was running foreign policy at this stage.

Alexander Haig notified Nixon of Brezhnev's stark proposal and Nixon authorized Kissinger to run a meeting, described by Kissinger.

> The proposed meeting started in the White House Situation Room, in the basement of the West Wing, with me in the chair, at 10:40 P.M. It went on with various interruptions until 2.00 A.M. early Thursday, October 25. Present were Secretary Schlesinger; Director of Central Intelligence William Colby; Chairman of the Joint Chiefs Admiral Moorer; presidential chief of staff Alexander Haig; Deputy Assistant to the President for National Security Affairs General Brent Scowcroft; Commander Jonathan T. Howe, my military assistant at the NSC; and me.[22]

As Kissinger further explained, although the authority of Nixon appears absent, "Admiral Moorer–at 11:41 P.M.–issued orders to all military commands to increase readiness to DefCon III. . . . At 11:55 P.M., the meeting approved a message to Sadat in Nixon's name reiterating our previous rejection of a joint U.S.-Soviet force."[23]

The strategy worked, United Nations peacekeeping forces were accepted, and the war brought to a close. Kissinger took advantage of the diplomatic opportunities and flew to Egypt to speak to Sadat in November 1973. However, the major success could be considered the Arab states agreeing to lift the oil embargo in March 1974.

The shuttle diplomacy of Henry Kissinger throughout the Middle East became legendary. In late April and May 1974, Kissinger spent thirty-four days shuttling between Jerusalem and Damascus, with additional trips to Saudi Arabia, Jordan, Cyprus, Algeria, and Egypt. He managed to travel 24,230 miles in this period, visiting Damascus thirteen times and Jerusalem sixteen times. It was not the longest absence of a secretary of state from the United States–secretary of state Robert Lansing had spent seven months at the Versailles Peace conference in 1919–but it was an incredible example of Kissinger's ambitious strategy for the Middle East.[24]

Nixon followed in the wake of Kissinger. Even in spite of the Watergate scandal at home, Nixon was acclaimed throughout the Middle East, receiving a tumultuous reception in Cairo and making very public but also sensitive visits to Israel, Saudi Arabia, Syria, and Jordan. It was a difficult balancing act by both Nixon and Kissinger to keep the Israeli and Arab nations even moderately satisfied.

Despite all of the international applause for Nixon, and Kissinger's visits to the Middle East, no immediate or substantial breakthroughs were made to the underlying causes of conflict. Kissinger introduced a coherent policy for the Middle East, but did little for the non-State actor, the Palestinians. A personal friendship between Kissinger and Anwar Sadat did help the peace process. However, substantial developments for the Middle East initiated by the United States would have to wait until President Jimmy Carter's Camp David accords in 1978.

Chile: An Overt or Covert American Policy?

John F. Kennedy had expressed humanitarian interest in Latin America in his Alliance for Progress program. It was also designed to help prevent the creation of a Castro-style Cuba in other Latin American countries. Covert operations were to continue toward Cuba after John Kennedy's death, but these were not confined to Cuba. The CIA also took a close inter-est in Chile and spent time and money developing propaganda techniques against the Marxist and Socialist Parties in Chile, often using propaganda to divide the left-wing groups. Between 1963 and 1973 the CIA spent approxi-mately $12,300,000 on propaganda for elections and disseminating propa-ganda and support for the mass media in Chile.[25]

In 1964, the CIA helped support the Christian Democratic candidate in the Chilean presidential elections. Money was spent to help defeat the Marxist candidate Salvador Allende. This approach by the United States continued into the Nixon administration and led to heightened activity for the 1970 election. Not only was the CIA interested in the result but multina-tional companies, most notably ITT (International Telephone and Tele-graph) through the connection of a previous director of the CIA, John McCone, also took a direct interest. Meetings took place between CIA and ITT representatives in Chile and the United States. Despite the expenditure of CIA and ITT funds, Allende won the presidential election in 1970. The Chilean Congress had to confirm the new president, and before this hap-pened, President Richard Nixon, Henry Kissinger, Richard Helms (director of the CIA), and John Mitchell (attorney general) had meetings about the plausibility of promoting a military coup in Chile. Under Nixon, the "40 Committee" determined how covert operations were organized and had a supervisory structure. In a section of his memoir on the years in the White House, Kissinger describes "The Coup That Never Was," pointing out a decision made by the 40 Committee on September 8, 1970: "Without real conviction we decided to instruct Ambassador Korry [United States ambas-sador to Chile] to prepare a 'cold-blooded assessment' of the likelihood and feasibility of a military coup and of the pros and cons involved in 'organizing an effective future Chilean opposition to Allende.'" [26]

Even with a "two-track" approach to stopping Allende from taking office, the collection of propaganda and covert operations under Track I was trumped by the more ambitious and secret Track II scheme to support a coup against Allende.[27] The coup did not materialize and Allende took office.

Salvador Allende's anti-American rhetoric was strong, and his control of the private sector in Chile was implemented. Copper mines and basic industries in Chile were nationalized, irrespective if foreign companies had interests in the industries. Chile began to default on a large number of her debts with overseas creditors, including foreign governments. "Falling domestic productivity and governmentally mandated increases in wages produced a spiralling inflation which, by 1973, exceeded 350 percent per annum."[28]

Allende was assassinated in September 1973, and Henry Kissinger is categorical about the lack of United States involvement. "It is the opposition he aroused within Chile that triggered the military coup of 1973, in the conception, planning and execution of which we played no role whatever."[29] Allende was followed by Augusto Pinochet and a military junta. A paradox is illuminated by Kissinger: "It is ironical that some of those who were vociferous in condemning what they called 'intervention' in Chile have been most insistent on governmental pressure against Allende's successors. The restrictions on American aid to Chile have been far more severe against the post-Allende government than during Allende's term of office."[30] The considerable difference between overt and covert operations appears to be lost on Kissinger, since he continued, "The measures have admittedly been overt but overtness does not change the inconsistency with the principle against outside intervention on which at least part of the assault on covert operations was based."[31] Henry Kissinger argued that criticism of covert operations has not served the national security of the United States.

War Powers Act: November 7, 1973

The War Powers Act that was passed by Congress on November 7, 1973, over the veto of President Nixon was to prove a controversial act. The War Powers Act, which is also known as the War Powers Resolution, required the president to "consult with Congress" if it appeared that United States armed forces were about to be involved in hostilities.[32] Unless Congress authorized otherwise, the president would have to terminate the use of United States armed forces within sixty days. One exception allowed the president to continue for a further thirty days, particularly when safety was an issue in extracting the armed forces from combat. This was a direct attempt by Congress to reassert its authority in the foreign policy arena in the wake of the Vietnam War.

Conclusions

Time magazine named Henry Kissinger and Richard Nixon Men of the Year for 1972. President Nixon's abuse of presidential power on the domestic political scene and his resignation have provided him with his own unique place in the history of the presidency. With revelations about the handling of the Vietnam War, the peace process, and the bombing of Cambodia the reputations of both Nixon and Kissinger as foreign policy experts have been sullied. Neither Nixon nor Kissinger stinted on producing their own accounts of events they were involved with or parading their expertise on foreign policy after leaving office in attempts to rehabilitate their reputations.

Of all of Henry Kissinger's books, including his memoirs, the most revealing may be his history of diplomacy, which has the simple and unfashionable title *Diplomacy.* It is also likely to be his book most used by undergraduate students. It is actually revealing about Kissinger's approach to foreign policy and history. It is the approach of a realist that emphasizes national interests, *realpolitik,* and power. This was exactly what Nixon and Kissinger pursued unabashedly in the White House. When Kissinger writes about Nixon's perception of the world, it appears that he is describing his own perspective. "Nixon sought to navigate according to a concept of America's national interest—repugnant as that idea was to many traditional idealists. If the major powers, including the United States, pursued their self-interests rationally and predictably, Nixon believed—in the spirit of the eighteenth-century Enlightenment—that an equilibrium would emerge from the clash of competing interests."[33] In summary, Nixon and Kissinger believed in balance of power to produce an international equilibrium.

It is noticeable that Kissinger appeared more comfortable with ideological opponents. Although a strange conclusion, Kissinger was disparaged more by Western European democracies or Japan than by totalitarian states. He appeared to have a dislike of dealing with the bureaucracies that accompanied the foreign policies of democratic states. Much of Western European diplomacy was pedantic and lacked the drama and originality required in cold war politics and crisis decision making.

The United States breakthroughs with both China and the Soviet Union are associated with Henry Kissinger, not the State Department or the NSC. The painstaking work undertaken by the State Department was overshadowed by the "back-channel" communications of Kissinger with Soviet diplomats that ultimately led to SALT I.[34] Kissinger's first visit to China was also made in secret. The State Department was reduced in importance under Nixon, and despite Kissinger becoming secretary of state this observation does not necessarily change. The secrecy and style of Nixon that worked well for détente became a pitfall in a domestic context. The pattern of secrecy, arrogance, and concerns for national security within the White House helped to bring about Nixon's fall from the presidency as the scandal of Watergate developed. As Nixon was wounded by Watergate, Kissinger became the voice of United States foreign policy.

As Robert Strong argued, it was difficult for Congress to influence foreign policy or play a significant and intelligent role if vital information was denied to Congress.[35] A number of reforms were introduced not only to weaken the president but to make Congress more effective. Nixon in his memoir was happy to blame Congress. "The war and the peace in Indochina that America had won at such cost over twelve years of sacrifice and fighting were lost within a matter of months once Congress refused to fulfill our obligations. And it is Congress that must bear the responsibility for the tragic results."[36] This attitude is one described by Warren Cohen as the "strong-state, weak-government paradigm."[37] Nixon and Kissinger were unable to act entirely the way they believed a powerful state like the United States should be able to act. The Nixon-Kissinger strategic approach to international relations was upset by democracy in their own country.

A summation and conclusion in Nixon's own words, tells us far more than Nixon might have ever imagined, "Christ, impeach the president on John Dean–John Dean's word," Richard Nixon blurted out to press secretary Ronald L. Ziegler on April 27, 1973.[38] This was followed by a remark cursing Charles Colson (presidential aide), followed by a ramble about Nixon's own status in the world. "[T]he press has got to realize that . . . whatever they think of me, they've got to realize I'm the only one at the present time in this whole wide blinking world that can do a Goddamn thing, you know. Keep it [the world] from blowing up."[39]

Notes

1. Words of Mark Anthony in W. Shakespeare, *The Tragedy of Julius Caesar* in *The Complete Oxford Shakespeare,* Vol. 111, *Tragedies* (London: BCA, 1987), 1104.

2. Obituary, *Guardian,* January 5, 2001.

3. H. A. Kissinger, *White House Years* (Boston: Little, Brown and Company, 1979), 26.

4. Ibid. A similar account is in J. Hoff, *Nixon Reconsidered* (New York: Basic Books, 1994), 148.

5. J. Aitken, *Nixon: A Life* (London: Weidenfeld and Nicolson, 1993), 194.

6. American Legion Convention, St. Louis, Missouri, August 31, 1953, Folder 1, Box 14, Richard M. Nixon's Pre-Presidential Papers, National Archives of the United States, Pacific Southwest Region, Laguna Niguel, California.

7. M. Walker, *Guardian,* April 25, 1994.

8. H. A. Kissinger, *A World Restored: Metternich, Castlereagh, and the Problems of Peace, 1812–22* (Boston: Houghton Mifflin, 1957).

9. G. W. Ball, *Diplomacy for a Crowded World* (Boston: Little, Brown and Company, 1976), 30.

10. *Time,* December 24, 1973.

11. H. A. Kissinger, *Diplomacy* (New York; Simon & Schuster, 1994), 704.

12. S. E. Ambrose, *Rise to Globalism,* 3rd edition (Harmondsworth, Middlesex: Penguin, 1983), 312.

13. J. Hanhimäki, *The Flawed Architect: Henry Kissinger and American Foreign Policy* (Oxford: Oxford University Press, 2004), xv.

14. *Time,* January 1, 1973.

15. J. Hanhimäki, *The Flawed Architect,* xiii–xiv.

16. A. M. Schlesinger Jr., *The Imperial Presidency,* revised edition (Boston: Houghton Mifflin, 1989), 187.

17. R. M. Nixon, *No More Vietnams* (New York: Avon Books, 1985), 165.

18. *Time,* July 8, 1974, 7.

19. J. E. Dougherty and R. L. Pfaltzgraff Jr., *American Foreign Policy: FDR to Reagan* (New York: Harper & Row, 1986), 263.

20. H. A. Kissinger, *Crisis: The Anatomy of Two Major Foreign Policy Crises* (New York: Simon & Schuster, 2003), 12.

21. Ibid., 13.

22. Ibid., 348.

23. Ibid., 350–351.

24. The itinerary of Kissinger was listed in *Time,* June 10, 1974, 23.

25. T. G. Paterson and D. Merrill, *Major Problems in American Foreign Relations,* Vol. II, *Since 1914* (Lexington, Massachusetts: D. C. Heath and Company, 1995) 61.

26. Kissinger, *White House Years,* 671.

27. S. M. Hersh, *Kissinger: The Price of Power* (London: Faber and Faber, 1983), 275–276.

28. Dougherty and Pfaltzgraff, *American Foreign Policy,* 272.

29. Kissinger, *White House Years,* 683.

30. Ibid., 658.

31. Ibid.

32. M. D. Gambone, ed., *Documents of American Diplomacy* (Westport, Connecticut: Greenwood Press, 2002), 396–401.

33. Kissinger, *Diplomacy,* 705.

34. R. A. Strong, *Decisions and Dilemmas: Case Studies in Presidential Foreign Policy Making* (Englewood Cliffs, New Jersey: Prentice Hall, 1992), 118.

35. Ibid., 97.

36. R. M. Nixon, *The Memoirs of Richard Nixon* (London: Arrow Books, 1978), 889.

37. W. I. Cohen, *The Cambridge History of American Foreign Relations,* Vol. IV, *America in the Age of Soviet Power, 1945–1991* (Cambridge: Cambridge University Press, 1993), 196.

38. John W. Dean III was counsel to the president and his testimony was crucial in revealing the nature of a cover-up in the White House. S. I. Kutler, *Abuse of Power: The New Nixon Tapes* (New York: Free Press, 1997), 349.

39. Ibid., 350.

CHAPTER 8

Gerald R. Ford: An Interregnum, 1974–1976

> I'm a Ford, not a Lincoln. My addresses will never be as eloquent as Mr. Lincoln's. But I will do my best to equal his brevity and his plain speaking.[1]
>
> – *Vice President Gerald R. Ford*

President Gerald R. Ford began chapter one of his memoir, *A Time to Heal*, with a quotation from Abraham Lincoln: "I know there is a God. I see the storm coming, and I know His hand is in it."[2] Lincoln, unlike Gerald Ford, was a great orator, an elected and assassinated president who oversaw victory in a tumultuous Civil War that rent the political and social fabric of the United States asunder. It would be unfair to compare Gerald Ford with Abraham Lincoln, or the Watergate scandal with the Civil War, or for that matter the Civil War with the Vietnam War. It is even unfair to compare Ford with Lincoln's successor, the seventeenth president of the United States, Andrew Johnson. Although both Gerald Ford and Andrew Johnson became presidents in dramatic circumstances, and both had to restore some faith in the American political process, it was Johnson who went one stage further than Richard Nixon and faced impeachment, and despite being acquitted, struggled to deal with a rather draconian reconstructionist Congress. In fairness to Gerald Ford, an interregnum of considerable healing was provided as the United States recovered from the Watergate scandal and the Vietnam War.

If the comparison is not too trite, was Gerald Ford more like an early Model T Ford car than the slick Lincoln Continental car also produced by the Ford Motor Company? The journalist Richard Reeves published a rather premature and critical study of Gerald Ford in 1975 that carried the title *A Ford, Not a Lincoln: The Decline of American Political Leadership*.[3] Ford's qualities that Reeves criticizes can be seen by others as virtues. Reeves writes, "His success was a triumph of lowest-common-denominator politics, the survival of the man without enemies, the least objectionable alternative."[4] He goes on to describe caution, perseverance, and ambition as if they are rather matter-of-fact human characteristics.[5] If President Ford was comfortable, unostentatious, reliable, and a little ordinary, that may also have been what the United States required in 1974. If Ford was homespun and patriotic, he could be compared to a number of presidents of the United States. Was President Ford sturdy and reliable in the foreign policy arena, rather than being charismatic and flamboyant?

Dr. Henry Kissinger has often provided a flattering portrait of President Ford, and Kissinger was undoubtedly happy that the strain of dealing with an embattled Nixon had passed to a calm man who would nevertheless also depend on him. Kissinger reminisces on the moment Ford became president: "But for that moment of near-despair I could think of no public figure better able to lead us in national renewal than this man so quintessentially American, of unquestioned integrity, at peace with himself, thoughtful and knowledgeable of national affairs and international responsibilities, calm and unafraid."[6]

The presidency of Gerald Ford saw the freedom of maneuver of the chief executive at an all-time low. This was partly due to the War Powers Act, but also an increased determination of Congress to control spending on foreign policy issues or countries they did not agree with. In this mood, Congress cut off military aid to Turkey after Turkey invaded Cyprus in July 1974. This made the president's policies in the Eastern Mediterranean and within NATO more difficult. Ford supported Turkey, seeing them as an important member of NATO and strategically important in the containment of communism in the region. Some Greek Cypriots made their cause worse by attacking the American Embassy in Nicosia, killing the American ambassador to Cyprus, Rodger Davies. John Greene has categorized the congressional reaction as taking an early opportunity to limit the Ford administration in foreign affairs.[7] Congress voted to stop military aid to Turkey, which Ford vetoed twice. The compromise legislation required a delayed embargo on Turkey. "The embargo finally went into effect on 5 February 1975. Turkey reacted by closing all U.S. military and intelligence facilities and all but one NATO air base on their territory. It was a major defeat for Ford, and one that he was unable to reverse. Despite repeated attempts to cajole Congress, the embargo was only slightly modified and not fully repealed until three years later, during the Carter administration."[8]

Détente with the Soviet Union was also problematic during the Ford presidential years. With inflation at home, support for the sale of wheat to the Soviet Union was lukewarm given that the reduced amount of wheat for domestic consumption contributed to price increases in wheat in the United States. Relations with the Soviet Union were also colored by human rights issues, including the restricted number of exit visas given to Soviet Jews wishing to emigrate to Israel. To make things worse, the secretary of defense, James Schlesinger, did not see eye to eye with President Ford or Secretary Kissinger over détente. With this background, Ford did well to negotiate a framework for a second Strategic Arms Limitation Treaty (SALT II) with General Secretary Brezhnev at Vladivostok in November 1974. Ford accepted the type of equal reductions in ceilings on strategic delivery vehicles and other armaments that Schlesinger had argued for. However, critics, including Schlesinger, the Pentagon, and a number of senators, argued that Ford was giving too much of American defense away cheaply. President Ford met again with Brezhnev, both before and after the Conference on Security and Cooperation in Europe (CSCE) from July 30 to August 2, 1975. Differences with the Soviet Union proved intractable, and Ford found he could satisfy neither Brezhnev nor Congress. The disagreements over cruise missiles and the Soviet Backfire bomber prevented a SALT II agreement. The United States believed that despite the Backfire bomber being designated a non-strategic weapon and only having medium-range capability, it could be modified to hit the United States. Disagreements remained unresolved as to whether or not cruise missiles needed to be restricted. "As the election drew nearer, Ford spoke less and less about the treaty; during the campaign, one could hardly tell that a treaty was before the Senate. Although Ford claimed in a 1988 interview that the passage of SALT II would have been 'guaranteed' in a second Ford administration, it did not happen in the first."[9] Despite the issue of Cyprus and difficulties over SALT II, the NATO alliance remained intact at the end of Ford's time in office.

During the thirty months that Gerald Ford would inhabit the White House, he was involved in serious refugee foreign policy crises in Indochina and the Middle East: Da Nang, Phnom Penh, Saigon, and the *Mayaguez* problems of Indochina in 1975, and the evacuation of America citizens from Lebanon in 1976.

President Ford never believed that the War Powers Act was appropriate to the crises he faced in the Middle East and Indochina. He did not believe that the War Powers Act was applicable when the evacuation of American citizens was a major part of the crisis. More than this, he did not believe or "concede that the resolution was equally binding on the president on constitutional grounds."[10] However, he did attempt to keep Congress informed during foreign policy crises, and this was largely done through his Congressional Relations staff in the White House. On a practical front, the information given to Congress often went through a number of drafts, and congressional leaders were not always available to receive the information. Equally pertinent, Ford recounted:

In the interests of absolute accuracy, a summary of actions that I proposed to take or had taken was drafted by the National Security Council staff. This summary was reviewed by senior officials at the departments

of State and Defense and by me at the White House. This careful attention to detail was absolutely essential. But let me assure you it was also
time-consuming for senior officials who were at the same time acting as
my advisers in a fast-moving international situation.[11]

Foreign Policy Credentials

In April 1942 Gerald Ford joined the United States Naval Reserve and
was sent to the United States Naval Academy at Annapolis, Maryland, for
one month of training. At the end of this training he was transferred as a
lieutenant j.g. to the United States Navy Pre-Flight School at Chapel Hill,
North Carolina. His duties included instructing cadets in sports, but also in
seamanship, military drill, and elementary ordnance and gunnery. It was
while here that he sought active service at sea and was subsequently posted
to the light aircraft carrier, USS *Monterey*. As a result he participated in
actions in the Gilbert Islands, Bismarck Archipelago, Marshall Islands,
Aitape and Humboldt Bay, Marianas Islands, Western Carolines, Western
New Guinea, and the Leyte Gulf.

In February 1946, I received my Navy discharge as a lieutenant commander and returned to Michigan. . . . Before the war, I'd been an iso-
lationist. Indeed, while at Yale, I had expressed the view that the U.S.
ought to avoid "entangling alliances" abroad. But now I had become
an ardent internationalist. My wartime experiences had given me an
entirely new perspective. The U.S., I was convinced, could no longer
stick its head in the sand like an ostrich. Our military unpreparedness
before World War II had only encouraged the Germans and Japanese. In the future, I felt, the U.S. had to be strong. Never again could
we allow our military to be anything but the best. [12]

This extract from Gerald R. Ford's memoir reflects the ideological importance of World War II on the thirty-two-year-old Ford in February 1946.
Given these rather strong views about military preparedness, it is ironic
that when Gerald Ford inherited the presidency he had to oversee the final
withdrawal of American troops from South Vietnam and the ending of a
war in Indochina that America fought and lost.

Undergraduate and postgraduate history students still debate the question
of whether or not America could have won the war in Vietnam, and Gerald
Ford was honest in his memoir in admitting that he felt that congressional
support, "Vietnamization" of the war, popular support in South Vietnam,
and adequate use of American forces had not been achieved. As the war
dragged out, Ford like others had to admit that the assumptions underlying
the American commitment were faulty and for the United States the "damage it caused this country both domestically and internationally was truly
staggering."[13]

If President Ford can be seen as slightly naïve in his approach of what went wrong in South Vietnam, his assumptions that the Paris peace accords of January 1973 would be adhered to by the North Vietnamese is stretching the naïveté further. Of course the United States did not respond effectively when the accords were violated by the North Vietnamese; the consequences of Watergate and the redress required by Congress over many issues, a picture largely presented by Gerald Ford, partially accounts for this. By the time the War Powers Act was passed by Congress in November 1973, Congress was in no mood to throw considerable amounts of good money after bad. The War Powers Act was passed over the veto of President Nixon, and Gerald Ford had voted in Congress against the legislation. Ford voiced his opposition to the resolution while president and also after leaving office.

In 1975, the situation in South Vietnam became desperate as President Ford recounts for the fiscal year:

> I requested a total of $1.4 billion in military aid for South Vietnam and Cambodia. Congress authorized $1 billion but appropriated only $700 million. From the time I became President, I urged Congress to supply additional aid to prevent the collapse of both nations. "With adequate United States military assistance, they can hold their own," I said. "We cannot turn our backs on these embattled countries." If we did not stand up to aggression, I told the Congressional leadership, we would lose our credibility around the world. Their reaction was mixed.[14]

In early April 1975, the United States participated in transporting refugees from Da Nang to safer spots in southern areas of South Vietnam. The president used the military to ostensibly protect the evacuation of Americans. On the CBS evening news, anchorman Walter Cronkite highlighted the confusion surrounding the authority of the president.

> The question about the President's authority to use troops for an evacuation involves the War Powers Act. . . . That law says the President may use troops if it becomes necessary because of an attack on the United States, its territories or possessions, or its armed forces. But the law says nothing about the protection of Americans overseas, neither authorizing the use of troops nor expressly forbidding it, for that matter. Spokesmen in the offices of some Senators who backed the law concede that this is a murky area.[15]

On April 4, 1975, Jack Marsh, counselor to the president, informed the president via Donald Rumsfeld that under Section 4A (2) of the War Powers Act (Public Law 93-148) the speaker of the House of Representatives and the president pro tempore of the Senate should be informed of the action to assist refugees from Da Nang and other seaports in Vietnamese waters. The

Counselor's Office at the White House, the Department of Defense, and the State Department concurred in their view that this was necessary, and they all contributed to the draft letter that was prepared for the president whereby he would fulfill his obligations to Congress. President Ford informed Congress that he had introduced United States naval vessels into Vietnamese waters to provide humanitarian relief, which he believed would take several weeks.

The secretary of state, Henry Kissinger, who was in Palm Springs, California, gave a press conference on April 5, 1975, but this largely addressed the deteriorating military position in South Vietnam. Pointing out that the North Vietnamese were in violation of Article 7 of the Paris accords, Kissinger appeared to be closing an imaginary door after the proverbial horse had bolted. The North Vietnamese were in the South in large numbers and given the large losses of military equipment by South Vietnam, Congress was in no mood to send additional supplies. Kissinger wished to point out the guilty party.

> Under the Paris accords, North Vietnam was not permitted to infiltrate or to add any additional forces to those it already had in South Vietnam. At that time, it had something like 80,000 to 100,000 people in South Vietnam. Today, it has closer to 400,000 in South Vietnam.
>
> Under the Paris accords, North Vietnam was not permitted to introduce new equipment except through JCCS checkpoints and in replacement on a one-to-one basis for equipment that had been lost, damaged and destroyed.
>
> The North Vietnamese never even permitted the establishment of these checkpoints and totally disregarded the agreement. This is what brought about the change in the military situation which was compounded by the fact that the South Vietnamese Army inventories were running down while the North Vietnamese inventories were increasing. This is the objective structure of what happened in the last two years.[16]

The refugee situation was acerbated by the fact that South Vietnamese divisions often moved families and dependents with them. Thus in any retreat, families needed to be protected alongside soldiers. It was thus possible to present both strategic and humanitarian arguments to justify further aid to South Vietnam.

Fall of Saigon

Throughout 1975 the military situation worsened in Southeast Asia for the South Vietnamese government. By April there were still approximately six thousand Americans in South Vietnam, largely in the vicinity of Saigon. Also in April, Khmer Rouge troops seized control of Cambodia.[17] Gerald

Ford, first with the use of advisers Henry Kissinger, General Brent Scowcroft, and Vice President Nelson Rockefeller, and later with the NSC, made some difficult decisions about the evacuation of, by then, about a thousand American personnel from Saigon. Initially because of bombing of the airport and then refugees swamping the runways, the decision was taken to evacuate Americans by helicopter from the roof of the American Embassy in Saigon. As Ford recounts, "Choppers were standing by on the decks of U.S. Navy ships steaming off the coast, and just before midnight I ordered the final evacuation. Over the next sixteen hours we managed to rescue 6,500 U.S. and South Vietnamese personnel without sustaining significant casualties."[18] An additional number (as many as one hundred and twenty thousand) of South Vietnamese fled across the borders out of South Vietnam, and the number of refugees would rise.

As a consequence of the War Powers Act, the president was required to inform Congress of action in Southeast Asia in April. On the morning of April 29, 1975, White House staff members telephoned senators—sometimes twice—and various responses were received. Senator Mansfield replied, "Oh Lord—thanks for calling," and Senator Sparkman answered, "Thanks for letting me know; I'll be relieved when we get the last American out."[19] However, given the Easter recess and the emergency need for humanitarian assistance, Ford acted without full consultation, indicative of how legislation cannot easily prescribe foreign policy decision making. On April 30, 1975, President Ford notified Senator James O. Eastland, president pro tempore of the Senate.

> In accordance with my desire to keep the Congress fully informed on this matter, and taking note of the provision of section 4 of the War Powers Resolution (Public Law 93–148), I wish to report to you that at about 1.00 A.M. EDT, April 29, 1975, U.S. forces entered South Vietnam airspace. A force of 70 evacuation helicopters and 865 Marines evacuated about 1400 U.S. citizens, together with approximately 5500 third country nationals and South Vietnamese, from landing zones in the vicinity of the U.S. Embassy, Saigon, and the Defense Attache Office at Tan Son Nhut Airfield.[20]

Mayaguez Crisis

With the ignominious final withdrawal of Americans from Cambodia and South Vietnam, Gerald Ford was to find it difficult to stand firm in the foreign policy arena. Where would the new lines of what was acceptable and unacceptable in the treatment of America abroad be drawn? It was not long before this was tested. An American merchant ship, SS *Mayaguez*, en route from Hong Kong to Thailand, was seized by Cambodian (Khmer Rouge) gunboats some sixty-five miles off the Cambodian coast in international waters. The situation had a vague historical parallel in the *Pueblo* incident of

1968, in which an intelligence ship of the U.S. Navy was seized by North Korea. Amid some humiliation for the United States, the negotiations for the crew of the *Pueblo* had lasted nearly a year.

President Ford held four meetings of the NSC in the immediate days following the seizure of the *Mayaguez* one on May 12, two on May 13, and another on May 14. At all four meetings were President Ford; Nelson Rockefeller, the vice president; James Schlesinger, secretary of defense; General David Jones, acting chairman of the Joint Chiefs of Staff; William Colby, CIA director; Robert Ingersoll, deputy secretary of state; William Clements, deputy secretary of defense; Donald Rumsfeld, assistant to the president; General Brent Scowcroft, deputy assistant for the national security agency; and Richard Smyser, a senior staff member. Counselors at a number of the meetings included John Marsh, Robert Hartmann, and Philip Buchen. Admiral James Holloway, chief of naval operations, was only at the fourth meeting. Henry Kissinger, both secretary of state and assistant to the president for national security affairs at the time, was at all but the third meeting. Kissinger kept a speaking engagement in St Louis, Missouri, and thus missed the third meeting. This was the approach that Gerald Ford wished to cultivate; routine appointments would be kept when possible. On the day the *Mayaguez* was recaptured, the president spent thirty minutes with the dentist; met with Michigan businessmen; held a session with the prime minister of the Netherlands (one hour); met with businessmen from Nassau County, New York; and held a formal state dinner for the prime minister of the Netherlands that lasted three hours.[21] This prevented the White House from being an isolated "bunker" for decisions and allowed for some relatively calm deliberation. Nevertheless, when time is a crucial factor in decision making, long hours have to be devoted to the problem. Press secretary Ron Nessen recounts:

> I arrived at the White House shortly before 6 A.M. on the second morning of the *Mayaguez* crisis because the TV networks needed fresh information for their early morning news shows. I found Scowcroft asleep on the couch in Kissinger's office. His assistant, Marine Lieutenant Colonel Robert C. "Bud" McFarland, was asleep in a chair in his cubbyhole office. Spread out on his desk was a map on which he had plotted the movements of the *Mayaguez* during the night by monitoring radio reports from the reconnaissance pilots circling overhead.[22]

The decision to act and the method of the action—using marines to rescue the thirty-nine merchant seamen held captive and also launching air strikes against a number of Cambodian military installations—was decided at the fourth meeting. The president was also mindful of his legal position, and the crisis was a further significant test of the War Powers Act and the complicated congressional-executive relationship.

Under the provisions of the War Powers Act, I was required to consult with Congress before sending U.S. troops into action. The afternoon before, at my direction, White House aides had contacted twenty-one Congressional leaders to inform them of my plans to prevent the ship and her crew from being transferred to the mainland. Now at the conclusion of this final meeting of the NSC, I asked Jack Marsh to spread the word that I wanted to see the bipartisan leaders of Congress.[23]

The three-day foreign policy ordeal was brought to an end for Ford and the crew members of the *Mayaguez.* Whether or not it was a successful conclusion is a debatable point, particularly since the American forces suffered forty-one fatal casualties, which is more than the number of crew members originally seized. Ford was also to discover that not all orders are carried out precisely. Two of four air strikes that were ordered did not take place.

The first strike never took place, although we were told it had been "completed." The Navy jets dropped their bombs into the sea. . . . What is harder for me to understand is why the fourth air strike—and I had specifically ordered four—was never carried out. I hadn't told anyone to cancel that attack. Apparently, someone had, and I was anxious to find out who had contravened my authority. The explanations I received from the Pentagon were not satisfactory at all, and direct answers kept eluding me.[24]

Ford appeared in a live television broadcast to announce the success of recovering the crew of the *Mayaguez.*

Hugh Sidey of *Time* magazine interviewed the president on May 16, 1975, with the intention of taking a personal look at President Ford's thinking during the crisis. Sidey pressed the president on why he did not try to negotiate for the hostages after they had been taken. Ford replied, "Because I didn't think it worked in the case of the *Pueblo* and we were dealing with a government that, by its recent actions, had shown a very abnormal attitude toward its own people and I could imagine how they might treat Americans."[25] The president also reiterated his strong opinion that notification to Congress was enough to satisfy the War Powers Act. Furthermore, the White House did not believe that the action had been in breach of the Cooper-Church Amendment of 1971, which had prohibited the use of U.S. ground combat troops in Cambodia. The president believed he had the constitutional authority to save American lives and protect American vessels from illegal seizure.

Based on telephone and telegram communications received by the White House by 10:00 A.M. Friday, May 16, 1975, Ford's forceful actions commanded a considerable amount of support. The White House received 5,068 telegrams in favor of the action and 336 against, plus 3,062 telephone calls in favor and 192 calls against.[26]

Lebanon

In the presidential election year of 1976 with Ronald Reagan contesting the Republican Party nomination of Gerald R. Ford, the primaries were temporarily obscured by events in Lebanon. On June 16, the U.S. ambassador to Lebanon, Francis E. Meloy Jr.; the counselor for economic affairs in the American Embassy in Beirut, Robert Olaf Waring; and their Lebanese chauffeur, Zohair Moghrabi, were kidnapped and murdered. Some 1,400 America citizens were living in Lebanon, and Ford, two days after the assassination, orchestrated the evacuation of 263 Americans and Europeans who opted to leave.[27] John Robert Greene describes this mission: "With a speed unprecedented among Ford's advisers, the decision was made to evacuate the U.S. nationals by sea."[28] This was a policy decision that was made difficult because it relied on some cooperation from Palestinian guerrillas to allow the evacuation. Also, given the primary elections in the United States, it was an action that was criticized for being politically motivated. It was, nevertheless, an evacuation that was carried out successfully with unarmed American landing craft, although Beirut subsequently degenerated into an even greater war zone. Ford's intervention appeared swift and timely.

Conclusion

With the advent of a post-Watergate presidency and the ending of the Vietnam War, the United States recognized that it was not going to play the kind of role that President Harry S. Truman or a relatively young naval lieutenant Gerald R. Ford expected and then witnessed in the early post–World War II years. The global policing role of the United States was curtailed under President Ford. Congress helped to see to that, although Ford held firm in a defense of presidential powers. In retirement he reflected on this. "The role of the president in these critical situations is clearly defined by the traditions, if not by the laws. As commander-in-chief and chairman of the National Security Council, my job as any president's job was to concentrate on resolving the crises, as expeditiously and as successfully as possible. As you might expect, it's a full-time job."[29] In criticism of the War Powers Act, Ford concluded:

> When a crisis breaks it is impossible to draw Congress into the decision-making process in an effective way. It's impractical to ask them to be as well-versed in the fast breaking developments as the president, the National Security Council, the Joint Chiefs of Staff, who deal with foreign policy and national security situations every hour of every day. . . . There is absolutely no way American foreign policy can be made or military operations commanded by 535 members of Congress on Capitol Hill, even if they all happen to be on Capitol Hill when they are needed.[30]

When notifying Congress of action that appeared related to the War Powers Act, President Ford invariably commented, "The operation was ordered and conducted pursuant to the President's Constitutional executive power and his authority as Commander-in-Chief of U.S. Armed forces."[31] In some ways Gerald Ford as the president of the United States appeared to be more "impotent" than "imperial." He did not create a Kennedy-style "New Frontiers" strategy or develop a new form of détente, but neither will he be castigated for escalating the Vietnam War or being involved in an "Irangate-style scandal. It is sometimes argued that great statesmen are an aberration from the norm. Gerald Ford, in trying to restore the United States to some form of normal, stable political behavior, was unlikely to stand out. However, Ford had to make difficult foreign policy decisions, and saving American lives while South Vietnam inevitably fell to communists can be trumpeted as a considerable achievement.

Notes

1. G. R. Ford, December 6, 1973, an excerpt from the text of Ford's swearing-in ceremony and his address to Congress on being made vice president. As reported in the *New York Times*, December 7, 1973, 27.

2. G. R. Ford, *A Time to Heal* (Norwalk, Connecticut: Easton Press, 1987), 1.

3. R. Reeves, *A Ford, Not a Lincoln: The Decline of American Political Leadership* (London: Hutchinson of London, 1975).

4. Ibid., 16.

5. Ibid., 17.

6. H. Kissinger, *Years of Upheaval* (London: Weidenfeld and Nicolson and Joseph, 1982), 1212.

7. J. R. Greene, *The Presidency of Gerald R. Ford* (Lawrence, Kansas: University of Kansas Press, 1995), 118.

8. Ibid., 119.

9. Ibid., 126.

10. G. R. Ford, *The War Powers Resolution*, Alfred M. Landon lectures on public issues (Manhattan, Kansas: Kansas State University, 1978), 9. Also available at http://www.ford.utexas.edu/library/speeches/770411.htm.

11. Ibid., 9.

12. Ford, *A Time to Heal*, 61.

13. Ibid., 249.

14. Ibid., 250.

15. April 3, 1975, folder "Evacuation of Vietnamese Refugees," Box 122, John Marsh Files, 1974–1977, Gerald R. Ford Library.

16. Henry A. Kissinger, press conference, The International Hotel, Palm Springs, California, April 5, 1975, folder "Evacuation of Vietnamese Refugees," Box 122, John Marsh Files, 1974–1977, Gerald R. Ford Library.

17. Ford, *A Time to Heal*, 252.

18. Ibid., 256.

19. April 29, 1975, folder "Evacuation of Vietnamese Refugees," Box 122, John Marsh Files, 1974–1977, Gerald R. Ford Library.

20. President Ford to Senator James O. Eastland, April 30, 1975, folder "Final Evacuation of Saigon," Box 122, John Marsh Files, Gerald R. Ford Library.

21. Memorandum from Dick Cheney to Peter Roussel, July 1, 1975, folder "*Mayaguez* Crisis," Box 9, Richard Cheney Files, Gerald R. Ford Library.

22. R. Nessen, *It Sure Looks Different from the Inside* (Chicago: Playboy Press, 1978), 121.

23. Ford, *A Time to Heal,* 280–281.

24. Ibid., 284.

25. Hugh Sidey interview, May 16, 1975, folder "*Mayaguez*–Media Interviews," Box 14, Ron Nessen Papers, Gerald R. Ford Library.

26. Updated reaction to *Mayaguez,* May 16, 1975, folder "*Mayaguez*–Telephone calls and telegrams," Ron Nessen Papers, Gerald R. Ford Library.

27. Greene, *Presidency of Gerald R. Ford,* 169.

28. Ibid., 169.

29. Ford, *The War Powers Resolution,* 9.

30. Ibid., 10.

31. President Ford to Senator James O. Eastland, April 30, 1975, folder "Final Evacuation of Saigon," Box 122, John Marsh Files, Gerald R. Ford Library.

CHAPTER 9

Jimmy Carter: Prisoner in the Rose Garden, 1977–1980

> The Norwegian Nobel Committee has decided to award the Nobel Peace Prize for 2002 to Jimmy Carter, for his decades of untiring effort to find peaceful solutions to international conflicts, to advance democracy and human rights, and to promote economic and social development.[1]
> —*Norwegian Nobel Prize Committee, Oslo, October 11, 2002*

Not only were a human rights and an ethical foreign policy at the heart of James "Jimmy" Earl Carter's ambitions as president, but also the idea that more conservative, defense-minded administrators in Washington, D.C. could also be controlled. He was clearly a post-Vietnam, post-Watergate president, carrying the hopes of an electorate that morality could be firmly applied to domestic and foreign policy.

Jimmy Carter's tenure as a peanut farmer and a one-term governor of Georgia did not appear to qualify him in the foreign policy arena, although his navy career gave him military credentials. From the Naval Academy at Annapolis (no previous Annapolis graduate had become commander in chief of the United States) he went to cruise the Caribbean and North Sea. Although he joined the navy in 1942, World War II was not the major reason Jimmy Carter sought a navy career; he had harbored feelings about joining the United States Navy since childhood. An influential uncle was captured on the island of Guam by the Japanese shortly after Pearl Harbor, but the Japanese attack on Pearl Harbor was not the same turning point for Carter as it was for presidents Gerald R. Ford and George H. W. Bush. During the early cold war and until October 1953, he was a submarine officer aboard the USS *Pomfret*, a posting that included naval experience on and off mainland China in 1948, an experience that allowed him to observe the events of the civil war.

In 1975 Jimmy Carter published *Why Not the Best?* and although this auto-biography dealt with his early life, naval career, and political success in Georgia, it also concluded by emphasizing morality and trustworthiness.[2] Moral issues were influential in his presidential election campaign, and he also addressed human rights in his inaugural address in January 1977. This created high expectations for a new style of foreign policy for the United States. Carter went on to create a Bureau of Human Affairs in the State Department. The principles inherent to the administration were that human needs and civil liberties would be emphasized. He offered a populist approach and the promise of self-respect in foreign policy.

Carter understood an essential paradox of this moralistic approach to for-eign policy, but felt he could avoid it: "I was familiar with the widely accepted arguments that we had to choose between idealism and realism, or between morality and the exertion of power; but I rejected those claims. To me, the demonstration of American idealism was a practical and realistic approach to foreign affairs, and moral principles were the best foundation for the exertion of American power and influence."[3] Carter hoped to draw on the idealism promoted by presidents Thomas Jefferson and Woodrow Wilson. However, as Coral Bell has pointed out, Woodrow Wilson may be good currency in the United States, but outside the United States some asso-ciate him with "high-minded ineffectiveness."[4] A high moral position can also be associated with naiveté. One biographer noted that Carter "might agree with his national security adviser [Brzezinski] that he needed to be Truman before he could be Wilson."[5]

The post–World War II agenda of containment of the Soviet Union and China was not abandoned, but a pacific approach to reduce military spending and control the proliferation of nuclear weapons was clearly evi-dent. This would have strategic merit, but it was also the product of Carter's strong Christian beliefs. Carter wanted ethics and morality to be strong considerations for United States foreign policy. In theory, the United States would avoid supporting brutal dictatorships, irrespective of how anti-communist they might be. In this regard weapons and economic aid were restricted from Uruguay, Ethiopia, and Argentina. It was rela-tively easy to criticize the violations of an internationally isolated South Africa, but more difficult to advance Soviet-United States relations while condemning the Soviet Union for human rights violations.

A new-look foreign policy and a Democratic Party president who was considered inexperienced by many political pundits required an administra-tion that reflected experience and enthusiasm for the president's ideas. Cyrus Vance was a family friend and had been secretary of the army under John F. Kennedy and deputy defense secretary under President Lyndon Johnson, and he was appointed secretary of state by Carter. In a parallel to the appointment of Henry Kissinger (although no one could exactly compare with Henry Kissinger), Carter made the Polish-born academic Zbigniew Brzezinski his national security adviser. Unlike Vance and Young, Brzezinski had a more hawkish approach to foreign policy and emphasized geopolitical interests. Carter describes him: "Zbig was astute in his analyses, particularly knowledgeable about broad historical trends affecting the industrialized nations, and a firm believer in a strong defense for our country and in the enhancement of freedom and democratic principles both here and abroad. His proposals were innovative and often provocative, and I agreed with them—most of the time."[6]

As Brzezinski's advice was given more importance by Carter, Vance's opinions and influence were consequentially reduced. Although the secretary of state's reports were delivered to Carter with his newspaper, the president's first scheduled meeting in the Oval Office each morning was with Brzezinski. This led to the joke in Washington, D.C. that for Vance to influence the president he would need to get in the shower with him. Jimmy Carter later acknowledged the friction, recounting how Vance would complain to him, reacting to news stories attributed to Brzezinski. "Almost without exception, Zbig had been speaking with my approval and in consonance with my established and known policy. The underlying State Department objection was that Brzezinski had spoken at all."[7]

Andrew Young of Georgia, a supporter of the new liberal agenda, was appointed United States ambassador to the United Nations. Carter felt he was appointing a sincere voice that would be welcomed in the developing world. Young was an outspoken voice, but his downfall and resignation in 1979 resulted from meeting Palestine Liberation Organization representatives in his apartment in New York. Although Young believed this was in his capacity as president of the United Nations Security Council, he was accused of breaking United States understandings with Israel; but more obviously he had embarrassed the State Department and White House by not keeping them fully informed of his actions. The president replaced him with Donald McHenry.

The working style of President Carter had to adapt to the pressure of work. In general he preferred briefings in writing; then he could mull over them at any time of day. The mountain of paperwork led Carter to arrange a speed-reading course for himself and his aides. It reminded Carter of his time as a novice submarine officer when he had to master extremely difficult things at short notice.[8]

One of President Carter's role models was Harry S. Truman, and to Carter's surprise he realized he was faced with many of the same international problems experienced by Truman. In 1977 the problems of the Middle East, Poland, China, oil, and Soviet interference outside its borders were evident and would also have been very familiar to Harry Truman when he was president. Carter, of course, had a much larger nuclear arsenal to consider and some thirty years of cold war historical baggage to contend with.

Another role model for Jimmy Carter was Admiral Hyman Rickover, and the president believed he had learned a considerable amount from him when he was a submarine officer and Rickover was a captain. Rickover was a noted authoritarian and became an important influence on Carter. As Jimmy Carter acknowledged, "I'm an engineer at heart, and I like to understand details of things that are directly my responsibility. I like to delegate administration to others."[9]

Whereas John F. Kennedy's Roman Catholicism almost proved to be an obstacle to his candidacy for president, Jimmy Carter's faith and Southern Baptist beliefs were an asset in a post-Watergate period. It gave him an optimism and belief that all things were possible, and it drove Carter to look for reconciliation in problems. At least for a short period of time, the Democratic Party and the United States public accepted humility and tolerance as political virtues. These virtues would be tested during Carter's presidency.

Jimmy Carter, largely a novice to foreign policy issues, attempted to bring his own style and approach to the issues of strategic arms limitations, the Panama Canal treaties, and Middle East problems. The ratification of the Panama Canal treaties took up a lot of the president's time, but he was very pleased to reconcile a problem that gave him credit in Latin America and appeared to be morally right.

An influence on Carter's presidency was the Trilateral Commission, an international group privately funded by David Rockefeller, the chairman of Chase Manhattan Bank and brother of President Ford's vice president, Nelson Rockefeller. The commission emphasized the relationships between Europe, Japan, and the United States. Cyrus Vance, Andrew Young, and Zbigniew Brzezinski were all members of the commission. "Brzezinski later recalled meeting Carter at early Trilateral Commission sessions, held shortly after Carter's election to the Georgia state-house."[10] The influence of this group was a new way of looking at international relationships, acknowledged by "trilateralism." This view questioned United States hegemony in the world, saw interdependence within the triangle as necessary, and believed a degree of international cooperation was required on the part of the United States. The argument that the United States would be well served by cooperation suited Jimmy Carter's own optimism.

Middle East: Triumph

Success in the Middle East does not have an obvious barometer, but getting Israel and Arab nations to simultaneously take peace initiatives seriously could be a useful measure. The Carter administration accepted that Egyptian president Anwar Sadat had an honest desire to see peace brokered in the Middle East. Jimmy Carter was happy to be the "helpful fixer" or "honest broker," and, as an American president, he had the influence with Israel to have this taken seriously. Egypt and Saudi Arabia were "softened" in their attitudes toward Israel by large arms sales from the United States.

At some risk to his own political reputation, Jimmy Carter invited Menachem Begin, the Israeli prime minister, and President Sadat to a summit at Camp David in September 1978. Sadat had already made the historic trip to Jerusalem and the Israeli Knesset in November 1977. It was still a brave decision for President Carter to look for a breakthrough in Egyptian-Israeli relations that might last. Carter recounts "I went to Camp David with all my maps, briefing books, notes, summaries of past negotiations, and my annotated Bible, which I predicted–accurately, as it turned out–would be needed in my discussions with Prime Minister Begin. Before it was all over, I would also have mastered major portions of a good dictionary and thesaurus, and would have become an amateur semanticist as well."[11] The words that Carter had to clarify with his dictionary included *sovereignty, rights,* and *autonomy*.[12]

> Again our problems were manifested in the use of different phrases. To us and the Egyptians, it was "West Bank"; to Begin it was "Judea and Samaria." To us, it was "Palestinians" or "Palestinian people"; to Begin, it was "Palestinian Arabs." We finally decided to use our language in the Egyptian and English texts and to use his words in the Hebrew text, and that I would either write Begin a public letter or add a footnote to explain the difference.[13]

The president was to hold the position of a referee rather than just a host, and he managed to appropriately outline the areas that exhibited signs of agreement and warn against the prospect of failure.

This intense Camp David summit led to a "Framework for Peace," and in March 1979 the previously unthinkable: an Israeli-Egyptian peace treaty. It clearly did not address a large number of Palestinian questions, or satisfy other Arab nations, but it produced an enduring definition of acceptable relations between Egypt and Israel. The radical departure from the past had required a new flexibility from Egypt and Israel, but it also required determination and organization from the Carter administration.

Middle East: Disaster

A human rights policy by President Carter was never clearly applied to Iran; even the rhetoric employed by the president regarding Iran appeared different than for other countries. It was very difficult to put the breaks on years of United States support for the Iranian regime, despite the use of secret police and torture in Iran, and opponents of the regime often being sent into exile. Not only did Carter not try to get Mohammad Reza Pahlavi, the shah of Iran, to democratize Iran in any haste, Carter visited the shah and publicly described Iran as an "island of stability."[14] The shah was not pressed hard on liberalization, partly because CIA bases in northern Iran were rather useful for monitoring the Soviet Union, particularly Soviet Central Asia.

Before the shah met President Carter for the first time at the White House in November 1977, the shah had made eleven previous official visits to the United States.[15] The 1977 visit was memorable mostly for the police's deployment of tear gas that accidentally wafted into the White House garden, disturbing the reception and embarrassing the president and shah as they tried to hold back their tears. Carter's official return visit to Teheran was to be remembered differently; Carter was seen as being far too gracious toward the shah. Not only did Carter make the remark about Iran being an "island of stability" in the region, he continued, "We have no other nation on earth who is closer to us in planning our mutual security. We have no other nation with whom we have closer consultation on regional problems that concern us both. And there is no leader with whom I have a deeper sense of personal gratitude and personal friendship."[16]

Despite the support of the United States, the shah was overthrown and he fled the country in January 1979. Every American president since World War II had hailed the shah of Iran as a friend of the United States. Not only had the shah provided useful opposition to the Soviet Union, but Iran under the shah did not support the 1973–1974 oil embargo against the West.

In January 1979 the shah fled Iran. He had been encouraged by the United States to leave on the grounds that the Bakhtiar government might survive the opposition from the Ayatollah Khomeini. The shah fled to Egypt and then Morocco, David Rockefeller helped to provide a temporary stay in the Bahamas, and the shah and his family then moved to Mexico. David Rockefeller, Henry Kissinger, and John McCloy helped to look for schools in the United States for the children of the shah. In October, the shah's illness was made apparent and his medical records presented to David Newsom, the under secretary of state for political affairs. Under these medical circumstances he was admitted to the United States to be treated for cancer.

Carter has been criticized by David Rockefeller and Henry Kissinger for his vacillating decision making over the exile of the shah of Iran. In reviewing the writing of Cyrus Vance and President Carter, Rockefeller came to the conclusion

Neither President Carter nor Secretary Vance mention that having decided to bar his entry, they asked private citizens to deliver the "official" message. They also leave unanswered why, over the course of the next seven months, they refused to provide any official assistance to the Shah or to have any official communication with him, while they indirectly sent word to him on a number of occasions that they hoped to admit him to the United States in the not-too-distant future.[17]

The Carter administration was not courageous enough to say they had abandoned the shah. In the *Washington Post* on November 29, 1979, Henry Kissinger reminded the American public of Carter's previous and rather glowing public support for the shah. Carter had created enemies for befriending the shah and different enemies for apparently relinquishing that friendship.

It was on Sunday, November 4 1979, that President Carter learned from Brzezinski that the United States embassy in Teheran had been overrun by militants. It would become apparent that the Iranian militants were holding sixty-six Americans and wanted the shah returned to Iran in exchange for the hostages. The situation was to become a torment for Carter. "I would walk in the White House gardens early in the morning and lie awake at night, trying to think of additional steps I could take to gain their freedom without sacrificing the honor and security of our nation."[18]

It was two days after the seizure of hostages that the Carter White House began deliberations on a possible rescue mission. The president quickly used his authority to ban demonstrations on federal property and expel Iranian students from the country. "A pattern of meetings to deal with the crisis became established: At least once each day my top advisers—the Vice President, Secretaries of State, Defense, and Treasury, Attorney General, National Security Adviser, members of the Joint Chiefs of Staff, my Press Secretary, Legal Counsel, Director of the Central Intelligence Agency, and others as necessary—met in the Situation Room at the White House to discuss Iran."[19]

It was a controversial although successful decision of Carter's not to campaign in the Democratic Party primary elections while the hostage crisis was continuing. Vice president Fritz Mondale and Rosalynn Carter campaigned on behalf of the president. Over time the president's dedication to his difficult task of dealing with the hostages made him look captive in the White House. Carter did spend Thanksgiving at Camp David, but this was only to have a crisis decision-making session with his key advisers. Thirteen hostages released on November 19 and 20 had not alleviated the gloom.

The issue of Soviet intervention in Afghanistan also was to occupy the president's foreign policy decision making, but it was not until April 1980 that Carter opted for a rescue plan for the remaining hostages in Teheran. Diplomacy had not produced the results Carter had hoped for, and at the NSC meeting on April 11, the outline of a rescue plan for the hostages was presented and the available options prioritized. On April 15 at an NSC meeting, Cyrus Vance voiced his opposition to a rescue plan. The plan was audacious. It involved eight helicopters flying six hundred miles from the Gulf of Oman. They would liaise in the desert in Iran with six C-130 aircraft. The helicopters and rescue team would hide in a remote mountainous area. Carter explains what should have happened next.

The next night, provided everything went well and I decided the rescue mission should proceed, the trucks our agents had purchased would be removed from a warehouse on the outskirts of Tehran, driven to a point near the mountain hiding place, and used to carry the rescue team into the city. At a prearranged time, the rescue team would simultaneously enter the foreign-ministry building and the compound, overpower the guards, and free the American hostages. Guided by radio communications and prearranged schedules, the helicopters would land at the sites, picking up our people and carrying them to an abandoned airstrip near the city. From there, two C-141's would fly all the Americans to safety across the desert area of Saudi Arabia. The helicopters would be left in Iran. I planned to notify the Saudis only after the rescue mission was completed.[20]

The rescue mission was not launched until April 24, but after the failure of three helicopters it had to be aborted. While withdrawing, a helicopter hit the front of a C-130 aircraft, causing eight casualties. Despite the War Powers Act the relationship of the president as commander in chief to Congress, and what and when he should inform Congress of his actions was still very fuzzy. Carter had sought the advice of Senator Robert Byrd on how to inform Congress. A difference could be drawn between the consultation requirement of the War Powers Act for a military engagement and the type of covert rescue operation that the president was undertaking in Iran. Carter later confessed, "I had planned on calling in a few members of the House and Senate early Friday morning, before the rescue team began its move into Tehran, in accordance with Bob Byrd's suggestion and Lloyd Cutler's advice. But I never got around to that."[21] A direct consequence of the aborted rescue mission was that Carter had to find himself a new secretary of state. Cyrus Vance resigned in protest and was replaced with the Democratic Party stalwart Senator Edmund S. Muskie.

Much work had to be done with Iran to repair the damage caused by the military operation to release the hostages. The crisis did not end with the death of the shah in a military hospital in Egypt on July 27, 1980, or with the outbreak of the Iran-Iraq war in September. Algerian intermediaries helped to present United States proposals to Iran that included a deal to release Iranian assets, which added up to billions of dollars frozen in American banks. Continuous diplomatic work was pursued with political and financial arrangements until the hostages were released, and this occurred when Carter was no longer president: The hostages were freed on January 20, 1981, the day Ronald Reagan was inaugurated. It was day 444 of the hostage crisis.

The Soviet Union, SALT II, and Afghanistan

Carter inherited the problem of SALT II, a potential treaty that had languished during the presidential election of 1976. The new president hoped to incorporate into a treaty what had been agreed between President Ford and General Secretary Brezhnev at Vladivostok in 1974, and also embark on proposals for a SALT III. Give that the SALT II Treaty was never ratified, the fact that Carter and Brezhnev signed the treaty in Vienna in June 1979 becomes a footnote of history. Perhaps it should not be forgotten that both discussed other issues, including human rights, the Middle East, Afghanistan, Africa, and China. Whatever trust Carter had in Brezhnev was to be severely tested. It became difficult for the United States Senate to accept SALT II due to the Soviet Union's invasion of Afghanistan in late 1979 when the Soviets undertook a large airlift of Soviet troops into Afghanistan on December 27. Although Carter hoped the United States and the Soviet Union would continue to honor the strategic arms agreement, this became an even more controversial domestic issue when the governor of California, Ronald Reagan, in his bid to be president, denounced SALT II and promised substantial increases in the nuclear arsenal of the United States.

Perhaps one of the best summaries of United States relations with the Soviet Union was captured in President Carter's diary entry for November 7, 1977. "At the Cabinet meeting this morning Zbig made an interesting comment that under Lenin the Soviet Union was like a religious revival, under Stalin like a prison, under Khrushchev like a circus, and under Brezhnev like the U.S. Post Office."[22]

Despite the Soviet Union's claim that they intervened in Afghanistan because of an invitation from Afghan leaders, the president of Afghanistan, Hafizullah Amin, was assassinated at the time of the invasion. Jimmy Carter recorded in his diary on December 27, 1979: "The Soviets have begun to move their forces in to overthrow the existing government . . . 215 flights in the last 24 hours or so. They've moved in a couple of regiments and now have maybe a total of 8,000 or 10,000 people in Afghanistan–both advisers and military. We consider this to be an extremely serious development."[23]

This was a galling development for Carter, since he had believed Soviet-United States relations were improving. This expansion of Soviet interests could lead to a deterioration in the region that incorporated Iran, Pakistan, and the Persian Gulf. Clearly, Carter had two major crises with the hostage situation in Iran and the Soviet occupation of Afghanistan. President Carter's retaliation against the Soviet Union became itself rather controversial within the United States. A grain embargo against the Soviet Union and a refusal to send United States athletes to the 1980 Olympic Games in Moscow appeared also to punish American citizens. The shipment of seventeen million tons of grain to the Soviet Union was canceled. To stop this embargo from hurting United States farmers, taxpayers' money would need to be used to buy grain to stop the price from becoming too depressed in the United States. Another problem arose regarding how to stop other nation-states from supplying the Soviet Union. Argentina had been criticized for its human rights record; why should it agree to the United States grain embargo? Fortunately, Argentina had little excess grain, but it exposed the weakness of the moralistic approach to foreign policy. Looking for condemnation from the United Nations even had problems when seeking support from countries that had been accused of human rights violations.

Conclusions

The citation from the Norwegian Nobel Prize Committee that was used at the beginning of this chapter went on to say, "During his presidency (1977–1981), Carter's mediation was a vital contribution to the Camp David Accords between Israel and Egypt, in itself a great enough achievement to qualify for the Nobel Peace Prize."[24] This award, offered since 1901, was only granted to two other presidents, Theodore Roosevelt in 1906 and Woodrow Wilson in 1919. Historian Douglas Brinkley noted that some supporters or even some of those that thought kindly toward Carter believed it might have done much for the reinterpretation of Carter's presidency had this prize been granted earlier.[25] Jimmy Carter did not share the earlier prize given in 1978 to President Sadat and Prime Minister Begin for progressing peace between Egypt and Israel, although a strong case could be made for it. Other opportunities to reward Carter were also missed by the Nobel Prize Committee. Yet Jimmy Carter takes considerable credit for the Camp David Accords, and the belated award may do much to revise the historical interpretations of the Carter presidency.

In terms of decision making, Carter ruminated over advice rather than making immediate decisions. He wished to analyze all the papers and details presented to him before making decisions. Even despite improvement in methods after embarking on a speed-reading course, the volume of work would remain problematic. Carter was a micromanager of policy and the details that accompanied policies. In essence, he was conscientious and failed to delegate enough foreign policy work to subordinates.

Carter became associated with weaknesses in defense, and, rather strangely, weaknesses because of Soviet aggression in Afghanistan. Clearly Carter was not responsible for Soviet aggression, but the punishments that Carter orchestrated did not appear to fit the crime perpetrated by the Soviet Union. The cold war was not over, and Carter's responses to the Soviet Union lacked mechanisms and policies to help progress toward that end.

Carter can be accused of not being attentive enough to the Vance-Brzezinski divergence of ideas and practices. Was it Vance or Brzezinski running foreign policy for Carter? Neither President Nixon nor President Ford had to address this type of question as long as they employed Henry Kissinger. By the time Vance resigned, the appointment of Muskie was too late to restore harmony to Carter's foreign policy team. Muskie would have to play catch up with the experienced and entrenched Brzezinski.

Until the summer of 1979, Carter did not appoint a chief of staff. He encouraged a collegiality among his staff, but the competition among his staff in expressing the needs of different departments pulled him in different directions. His staff would not simply be lieutenants reporting to a captain, and the White House was not a submarine, although with the advent of the hostage crisis Carter unfortunately made the White House feel almost as claustrophobic as a submarine.

The temporary hospitalization of the shah of Iran in the United States caused a disaster for Carter. The hostage crisis began in November 1979 and kept the Carter administration rather impotent until the end in January 1981. An attempted military solution led to a disaster in the desert in April 1980. Cyrus Vance showed his displeasure with the operation by resigning as secretary of state. Carter effectively imprisoned himself in the White House and, euphemistically, the Rose Garden of the White House, a strategy that ultimately helped his Republican Party opponent, Ronald Reagan, in the 1980 presidential elections. An unattractive conclusion for Carter and democracy is that Iran determined the outcome of the American presidential election of November 1980. In fairness, Carter's noble strategy of publicly making his work to release the hostages his main priority backfired.

Carter's first two years in office showed many foreign policy breakthroughs. A normalization of diplomatic relations with China was negotiated, an Israeli-Egyptian accord was achieved, and the Panama Canal treaties were ratified. He had managed to set an agenda that was fresh when he launched a discussion of human rights. The last two years of his tenure as president had a number of contrasting problems: the failure to have SALT II ratified, the hostage crisis in Iran, and poor relations with the Soviet Union as a consequence of the Soviet intervention in Afghanistan. The most significant change in the pattern of United States foreign policy under Carter was the decline in détente. Soviet-American relations could, as a consequence, be addressed in different terms by Carter's successor, President Ronald Reagan.

Notes

1. J. Carter, *The Nobel Peace Prize Lecture* (New York: Simon & Schuster, 2002), x.

2. J. Carter, *Why Not the Best?* (Eastbourne: Kingsway Publications, 1977).

3. J. Carter, *Keeping Faith* (Norwalk, Connecticut: Easton Press, 1982), 143.

4. C. Bell, "From Carter to Reagan," *Foreign Affairs: America and the World* 63, 3 (1985), 493.

5. E. C. Hargrove, *Jimmy Carter as President* (Baton Rouge: Louisiana State University Press, 1988), 112.

6. Carter, *Keeping Faith*, 51.

7. Ibid., 53.

8. Ibid., 57.

9. Hargrove, *Carter as President*, 6.

10. J. Dumbrell, *The Carter Presidency* (Manchester: Manchester University Press, 1995), 111.

11. Hargrove, *Carter as President*, 322.

12. Ibid., 377.

13. Ibid., 387.

14. R. A. Strong, *Working in the World: Jimmy Carter and the Making of American Foreign Policy* (Baton Rouge: Louisiana State University Press, 2000), 61.

15. Ibid., 51.

16. Ibid., 61.
17. D. Rockefeller, *Memoirs* (New York: Random House, 2002), 373.
18. Carter, *Keeping Faith*, 459.
19. Ibid., 462.
20. Ibid., 510.
21. Ibid., 518.
22. Ibid., 223.
23. Ibid., 471.
24. Carter, *Nobel Peace Prize Lecture*, x.
25. D. Brinkley, "The Rising Stock of Jimmy Carter: The 'Hands on' Legacy of Our Thirty-ninth President," *Diplomatic History* 20, 4 (Fall 1996), 510. Also, D. Brinkley, *The Unfinished Presidency* (New York: Penguin Books, 1998), 27.

CHAPTER 10

Ronald Reagan, Star Wars, and the Evil Empire, 1981–1988

It reminds me of the little joke about the Kremlin. There was a
break-in in the Kremlin one night, and someone stole next year's
election results.[1]

—Ronald Reagan

Cold War Pedigree

During the 1980 presidential election, Ronald Wilson Reagan promised
to restore the military strength of the United States by rearmament, and he
evoked cold war imagery to help his cause. He appeared to have the same
anti-communist Republican Party roots as Richard Nixon. This contrasted
with the approach of Jimmy Carter, although both Carter and Reagan could
be seen as lacking foreign policy experience before becoming president.
The new president was a former Hollywood actor, Screen Actors Guild
president, and governor of California who intended to evoke patriotism and
conservatism for his benefit. Not only was Ronald Reagan consistent in his
career in arguing for free enterprise and small government, but also in his
anti-Soviet and anti-communist rhetoric.

Lieutenant Ronald Reagan did not see active service overseas during
World War II because of poor eyesight. He did, however, make training
films for the United States Army Air Force. In 1943 he was promoted to
captain and concluded his active duty in December 1945, having been
involved in a unit that produced over four hundred training films.

As president of the Screen Actors Guild he had to address the issue of
communist infiltration of Hollywood, although he is not associated with the

McCarthyite witch-hunts that took place. At Republican Party fund raising events, including the campaigns of Barry Goldwater and Richard M. Nixon, Reagan developed a reputation for being fervently anti-communist. He was fifty-five years old when he became governor of California in 1966, and he was sixty-nine years old by the time he became president, making him the oldest person to become president. He had few foreign policy credentials, but his conservatism was unshaken. As the president stated about his first trip to meet General Secretary Gorbachev in 1985, "Who would have guessed it? Here I was, the great anti-communist, heading off for a meeting with the leader of the evil empire."[2]

The New Cold War

The Reagan strategy toward the Soviet Union was to be openly critical of the Soviet political system and Soviet domestic and foreign policies. This harkened back to an earlier period of containment and evoked the image of a new cold war and post-détente. Carter's difficulties with the Soviet Union allowed for an ideological opposition to the Soviet Union from Reagan.

Like Carter, Ronald Reagan held a broad vision, albeit a very different one, of what he wanted, and he had to rely on the experience of his chosen administrators to deliver it. The previous emphasis under Carter for a North-South dialogue and approach was replaced with a return to the East-West dichotomy. Reagan's new secretary of state was the powerful figure General Alexander M. Haig, chief of staff to Richard Nixon from 1973–1974 and NATO's Supreme Allied Commander from 1974–1979. Haig rather swiftly showed a determination to have the State Department play a very strong role in foreign policy and downgraded the influence of the NSC and the national security adviser, the academic Richard Allen. Allen also had a link to Nixon, having been a foreign policy adviser to Nixon before his election in 1968, but he was passed over for national security adviser when Nixon chose Henry Kissinger for the position.

Caspar Weinberger became the secretary of defense, and although he had a cost-cutting reputation having been director of the Organization of Management and Budget under Nixon, he was empowered to build up the military arsenal of the United States. He held the office of secretary of defense until 1987.

Alongside Richard Allen, Jeane J. Kirkpatrick, the United States ambassador to the United Nations and a former professor of political science at Georgetown University, argued for an "America first" approach to foreign policy, a unilateralist policy that would also emphasize the importance of Latin America and the Pacific rim for the United States. In contrast Haig and the vice president, George H. W. Bush, argued for a prominent "North Atlantic" foreign policy. This latter more prudent approach had a tendency to prevail with the president.

Ending the Cold War

On April 24, 1981, Ronald Reagan handwrote a letter to General Secretary Brezhnev, ending the so-called United States grain embargo on the Soviet Union. "It is in this spirit, in the spirit of helping the people of both our nations, that I have, lifted the grain embargo. Perhaps this decision will contribute to creating the circumstances which will lead to the meaningful and constructive dialogue which will assist us in fulfilling our joint obligation to find lasting peace."[3]

During his election campaign Reagan had promised to remove the grain embargo, and he did so. According to Jack F. Matlock Jr., United States ambassador to the Soviet Union, Haig disagreed with the president on this decision. "At Haig's direction, the State Department drafted a replacement letter designed to stress that a grain embargo did not mean that the United States considered the Soviet intervention in Afghanistan acceptable. Reagan insisted on sending his personal appeal too, and both letters were finally delivered at the same time."[4] Reagan's memoir account is less than flattering to Alexander Haig. "As I was to learn over the next year, he didn't even want me as the president to be involved in setting foreign policy–he regarded it as his turf. He didn't want to carry out the president's foreign policy; he wanted to formulate it and carry it out himself."[5]

Matlock also describes Reagan's appointment of George Shultz as the replacement for Secretary of State Haig as being a consequence of Haig behaving like President Reagan's "vicar," a description that Haig had presented of himself.[6] The resignation of Haig is also associated with his disenchantment with the degree of influence he was having on policies and his failure to avert war between Britain and Argentina over the Falkland Islands in the South Atlantic. Clearly the Reagan administration did not unite behind Haig, and he footnotes his problems with Jeane Kirkpatrick. "That Mrs. Kirkpatrick chose to keep on pushing her own view should not be taken to suggest that she had departed from honorable practice, because the concept of closing ranks had no meaning to the President's aides. The necessity of speaking with one voice on foreign policy . . . simply never took hold among Reagan's advisers."[7]

Despite the personal nature of the handwritten letter from Ronald Reagan, Brezhnev gave it a frosty reply. Reagan's personal diplomacy was not going to be the obvious key to immediately unlocking a difficult relationship with the Soviet Union.

Ronald Reagan wanted to negotiate with the Soviet Union from a position of strategic, military, economic, and intelligence-gathering strength. United States military bases were set up in Saudi Arabia, Oman, Kenya, and Somalia. Defense spending was substantially increased and investment put into the MX IBM missiles and the older B-1 bomber. Further investment was also made in the CIA under Director William Casey. This did not run entirely smoothly since Congress temporarily declined to support the MX program, and in May 1983 confirmed a nuclear freeze. However, an early success in October 1981 was congressional approval for an extensive arms sale to Saudi Arabia that included five Airborne Warning and Control System aircraft (AWACS), more simply known as early-warning aircraft. This sale was achieved despite the criticism from lobbyists for the United States Jewish community.

Support from European allies in NATO was not entirely smooth because of a strong peace movement in Western Europe. The stationing of Cruise and Pershing-2 missiles in Western Europe caused considerable opposition, but Reagan had strong support from the governments of the United Kingdom and the German Federal Republic.

At Geneva in November 1981, Ronald Reagan put forward his "zero option" policy. The delivery of Pershing-2 and Cruise missiles in Western Europe would be canceled as long as the Soviet Union dismantled SS-20 missiles. However, this program was set back by Alexander Haig's resignation as secretary of state, and the imposition of military law in Poland. George Shultz, another old hand from the Nixon administration, was appointed as the new secretary of state, and further cooperation with Western Europe was promoted.

Leonid Ilyich Brezhnev died in November 1982 and was replaced by Yuri Vladimirovich Andropov. Brezhnev's funeral was attended by Vice President Bush rather than President Reagan. Andropov only lived until February 1984, when he was replaced by Konstantin Chernenko, who in turn died in March 1985 to be replaced by Mikhail Sergeevich Gorbachev. Gorbachev was to prove a contrast to the older generation of Soviet leaders who had passed from office in a relatively short period of time.

On March 23, 1983, while Andropov was still in office, Reagan announced his Strategic Defense Initiative (SDI), or what was to become more commonly known and misunderstood as "Star Wars." It was never an impenetrable missile-defense system, but even a defense system that could potentially combat ICBMs was in theory a serious problem for the strategically minded Soviet leaders. Reagan would effectively talk up the effectiveness of SDI as a space-based shield to intercept missiles. In his inaugural address of January 21, 1985, he continued this promotion, "I have approved a research program to find, if we can, a security shield that will destroy nuclear missiles before they reach their target. It wouldn't kill people; it would destroy weapons. It wouldn't militarize space; it would help demilitarize the arsenals of Earth. It would render nuclear weapons obsolete."[8] What became important over time was less the technical feasibility of SDI as much as how seriously the Soviet Union believed in it; clearly Reagan's rhetoric scared them. At the very least the president was promising to outspend the Soviet Union in new defensive-missile technology.

Reagan's ideological counteroffensive had also been promoted earlier in the month of March. At the Annual Convention of the National Association of Evangelicals in Orlando, Florida, Reagan announced, "I urge you to

beware the temptation of pride—the temptation of blithely declaring your-
selves above it all—and label both sides equally at fault, to ignore the facts of
history and the aggressive impulses of an evil empire, to simply call the arms
race a giant misunderstanding and thereby remove yourself from the struggles between right and wrong and good and evil."[9]

Foreign policy has a tendency to throw up unpredictable events, and 1983
was no different. In September 1983 a South Korean civilian aircraft was shot
down by the Soviet Union, killing 269 passengers, including United States
congressman Lawrence McDonald. Although the aircraft had strayed into
Soviet airspace, the United States Congress, president, and public opinion
presented anti-Soviet rhetoric. Support for the MX missile and the B-1
bomber grew in Congress, and Reagan even sent troops to the island of
Grenada to combat Marxist rebels.

With the stationing of Cruise and Pershing-2 missiles in Western Europe,
the Soviet Union walked out of the Strategic Arms Reduction Talks
(START) in Geneva in December 1983. Reagan's hard-line defense
approach was running into problems. By 1985, however, the United States
was able to negotiate with the Soviet Union from a position of considerable
military strength. Also, relations with the Soviet Union improved enormously after 1985 when Mikhail Gorbachev launched substantial reforms.
The domestic reforms, which included perestroika (restructuring) and glas-
nost (openness), had ramifications throughout Eastern Europe. These ostensibly domestic changes had even wider foreign policy implications as the
Soviet Union moved politically closer to Western democracies and developed a less threatening military posture. The old guard figure of Soviet foreign policy, Andrei Gromyko, was replaced with the more compliant
Eduard Shevardnadze by Gorbachev in mid-1985.

The Regan administration emphasized the importance of defense expenditure in ending the cold war. The military build-up by the United States
proved particularly difficult for the Soviet Union to counter without putting
increasing burdens on their own economy and civilian population. In
Reagan's State of the Union address in 1985, the president promoted a
defense against Soviet-supported activities in what was to become known as
the "Reagan doctrine," proclaiming rather boldly "Support for freedom
fighters is self-defense."[10]

General Secretary Gorbachev and President Ronald Reagan met
November 19–21, 1985, in Switzerland and discussed four main issues:
arms control, human rights, regional conflict, and bilateral matters. The
"fireside" discussions on mutual defense issues saw some symmetry in both
parties calling for fifty percent reductions in offensive nuclear weapons.
President Reagan tried to make the most of the issue of Soviet human rights
violations, the Soviet troops in Afghanistan, and the problems evident in
Nicaragua, Cambodia, Angola, and Ethiopia. In the spirit of cooperation,
Gorbachev and President Reagan agreed to continuing meeting in the following years.

At Reykjavik from October 10–12, 1986, Gorbachev and Reagan discussed general issues similar to those of Geneva in the previous year. In principle, the two leaders agreed to a fifty percent reduction in strategic offensive nuclear arms, to a level of 6,000 warheads on a specific number of delivery systems. However, by the final day all was not well, and Gorbachev linked progress on the Intermediate-range Nuclear Forces Treaty (INF Treaty) and START to restrictions on the United States SDI. However, President Reagan would not bargain with SDI and no joint statement on progress was possible.

Reagan was not to let up on his criticism of the Soviet Union or the political and social conditions in Eastern Europe. In almost as memorable a way as President John F. Kennedy before him, Reagan went to West Berlin and spoke out against the Soviet Union. After attending an economic summit in Vienna, Reagan went to Berlin on June 12, 1987, for a speaking engagement at the Brandenburg Gate, a dividing position between East and West Berlin. In what was to prove mildly prophetic within three years, Reagan enjoined, "General Secretary Gorbachev, if you seek peace, if you seek prosperity for the Soviet Union and Eastern Europe, if you seek liberalization: Come here to this gate! Mr. Gorbachev, open this gate! Mr. Gorbachev, tear down this wall!"[11]

By December 1987 in Washington, D.C., General Secretary Gorbachev and President Reagan were ready to sign a treaty on the reduction and limitation of strategic offensive arms. It was an implementation of the fifty percent reduction in these categories of arms, as discussed at Reykjavik. The agenda was similar to Reykjavik, and a very frank discussion of human rights took place. The United States secretary of state, George Shultz, and the Soviet foreign minister, Eduard Shevardnadze, signed agreements to improve air services between the Soviet Union and the United States. At the formal signing of the INF agreement by Gorbachev and Reagan in the East Room of the White House, Reagan reminded Gorbachev of a Russian maxim "Dovorey no provorey—trust, but verify." With some humor, Gorbachev was quick to remind the president that he said that at every meeting, and Reagan was quick to reply, "I like it."[12]

The long-standing arrangement for President Reagan to visit Moscow in 1988 was fulfilled from May 29 to June 1, 1988. The previous organizational work on nuclear arms reduction came to fruition in that Reagan and Gorbachev signed ratification documents for the INF Treaty, which the Supreme Soviet of the Soviet Union and the United States Senate had previously approved. The treaty required the destruction of intermediate-range missiles of the United States and the Soviet Union, the first time an entire class of nuclear weapons had been banned.[13] Additional progress was made on START. Shultz and Shevardnadze managed to achieve understandings in several separate areas, including two on arms control: the Joint Verification Agreement on nuclear testing and the Agreement of Advanced Notification of Strategic Ballistic Missile Launches.

As a footnote to the Gorbachev-Reagan relationship, it may be worth noting that they did meet again on Governor's Island in New York harbor on December 7, 1988. Both were visiting New York City for a United Nations session. Progress on the four major issues of arms control, bilateral concerns, human rights, and regional conflicts was reviewed. More significantly, in principle the cold war ended with the Reagan administration. The Bush administration would have to oversee the ultimate demise of the cold war— and this was not a simple task—but the START I agreement was signed by Gorbachev and President Bush in 1991. Reagan's strategy toward the Soviet Union was successful, but he was also fortunate that the Soviet Union was in a far worse economic position than the United States. Reagan's domestic and international standing was advanced enormously because of his success with the Soviet Union. This success was considerably tempered by certain difficulties in the Middle East and Central America.

Lebanon and Libya

Reagan, like his two immediate predecessors, objected to the constitutionality of the War Powers Act and believed it put too many restrictions on him as commander in chief. The act had been rather clumsy for the *Mayaguez* crisis under Ford and the hostage rescue mission under Carter, so the first major use of the 1973 act was over Lebanon. In September 1983, Congress took a strong interest in the president's decision to send U.S. Marines to Lebanon. In compliance with the act, on August 31, 1983 President Reagan notified Congress that marines were involved in hostilities, two days after two marines had been killed in Beirut. He was notified of the sixty-day rule. An agreement between Reagan and Congress allowed United States troops to be kept in Lebanon for an extended eighteen months, although they were restricted to Beirut and participation as an international force.

The situation for United States forces in Lebanon worsened when a terrorist attack on October 23 killed 241 United States military personnel at the United States Marine headquarters in Beirut and prompted some Democrats in the House of Representatives to seek amendments to the agreement with the president. It was defeated in a vote of 153 to 274.

Even by the unpredictable standards of Colonel Qaddafi of Libya, 1986 was to see him testing the limits of Western resolve. The United States would not adhere to the territorial waters claimed by Libya in the Gulf of Sidra. The United States launched a measured reply against Libya after surface-to-air missiles were launched by Libya against United States aircraft flying from aircraft carriers. As a consequence of some tit-for-tat activity, the United States increased intelligence surveillance of Libya. Further, as a consequence, the United States linked Libya with the bombing of a discotheque in West Berlin. It was a popular venue for United States servicemen, and although only two people were immediately killed by the bombing, some fifty servicemen from the United States were injured. Reagan recalled his response:

> Now that the American oil workers were out of Libya, I knew we had to do something about the crackpot in Tripoli. "He's not only a barbarian, he's flaky," I said at the time. I felt we had no alternative but a military response: As a matter of self-defense, any nation victimized by terrorism has an inherent right to respond with force to deter new acts of terror. I felt we must show Qaddafi that there was a price he would have to pay for that kind of behaviour, that we wouldn't let him get away with it. So I asked the Joint Chiefs of Staff for a plan: What can we do that would send the right signal to Qaddafi without harming innocent people?[14]

The exact response was to bomb the military headquarters and intelligence center of Libya's terrorist structure, but it was apparently not an assassination attempt on the life of Qaddafi. If success can be measured by these matters, seventy percent of the telephone calls received in the twenty-four hours after the event were in favor of the president's action.[15] However, one of the missiles had gone off target and hit a civilian neighborhood, and two United States servicemen were shot down and killed by the Libyans. It was a decisive action by President Reagan, particularly since the French and Italian governments would not allow the United States F-111 bombers that originated in military bases in the United Kingdom to fly across their air space. The refusal annoyed Reagan, but it did not stop him.

Central America

Civil war pervaded much of Central America, but the United States successfully supported incumbent regimes in Honduras, Guatemala, and El Salvador. Considerable unrest developed in both El Salvador and Nicaragua, and these problems occupied the attention of the Reagan administration. In El Salvador a combination of money, military training, and CIA advice kept leftist forces from overthrowing the government of President José Napoleon Duarte. Nicaragua provided a different scenario in that the leftist Sandinistas held power and the United States funded the opposition, the Contras, who were fighting to overthrow the Sandinistas. As Walter LaFeber effectively points out, "Bitter disputes erupted within the Reagan administration between State Department area experts, who believed that Sandinista power could be better (and certainly more cheaply) contained through diplomatic negotiations, and other civilians—especially in the Pentagon and the White House—who favored escalating the fighting."[16] The confusion continued with Congress cutting military aid to the Contras and attempting to tie aid to the advancement of human rights. The funding of the Contras was a problem that would be revisited by the president in a different form with the Iran-Contra scandal.

It was the island of Grenada that saw the direct intervention of United States troops to oppose a Cuban-backed government in October 1983. Cuban soldiers were on the island, and Cuban workers were also detected building a large airfield in Grenada that had military implications for the United States–Soviet reconnaissance airplanes would be able to land there. With a left-wing faction in office in Grenada and the Cuban connection, Reagan ordered an invasion of Grenada. A joint Senate and House of Representatives bipartisan agreement triggered the War Powers Act, and within one week of six thousand troops arriving in Grenada, the sixty-day rule was invoked. Reagan's second problem was the British. Despite very harmonious relations between Ronald Reagan and Margaret Thatcher, the British prime minister, she had to rather sternly remind him that Grenada was part of the Commonwealth.

In "Operation Urgent Fury" United States forces overcame the Grenadian and Cuban resistance. This adventure helped to further the career of United States deputy commander Norman Schwarzkopf. It also represented what political scientist Andrew Busch described as "the first time that a Communist country was liberated by U.S. troops and the first major use of force by the U.S. since Vietnam. The strategic and psychological balance in the Caribbean was altered favorably, and for the first time in recent memory, it was more dangerous to be America's enemy than her friend."[17]

The Iran-Contra Affair

The Iran-Contra scandal began in 1985 when the Reagan administration was informed that moderates within the Iranian regime wished to establish better relations with the United States. This appeared to be because of the anticipation by some Iranians that the Ayatollah Khomeini would not live much longer and new diplomatic opportunities would emerge. For a shipment of arms to Iran, the moderates would intervene with pro-Iranian Hezbollah guerrillas in Lebanon to help gain the release of six American hostages being held there. The normal procedure for arms sales was for the State and Defense Departments to handle the details, notifying Congress of sales. One of the hostages, William Buckley, a CIA officer in Beirut, was executed by his captors in 1985. Three hostages were released after Israel shipped United States arms to Iran, and in November 1986 it was first publicly revealed in an Arabic-language Lebanese magazine that the United States was exchanging arms for hostages. The way arms had been shipped to Iran was in violation of the Arms Export Control Act, and a failure to notify Congress of the covert activity was in breach of the Intelligence Oversight Act.

Lieutenant Colonel Oliver L. North, a NSC staff member and a marine officer, diverted some of the money from the arms sales to the Contras in

Nicaragua who were fighting the Soviet-allied Sandinista government. If an arms-for-hostages deal was not embarrassing enough, North had contravened a congressional ban against such funding of the Contras. In late 1982, Congressman Edward P. Boland, a Democrat from Massachusetts and chairman of the House Intelligence Committee, introduced a ban on the United States aiding insurgent groups attempting to overthrow the Sandinista government in Nicaragua. The president signed a version of the Boland Amendment in October 1984 that stated "no funds available to the Central Intelligence Agency, the Department of Defense, or any other agency or entity of the United States involved in intelligence activities may be obligated or expended for the purpose or which would have the effect of supporting, directly or indirectly, military or paramilitary operations in Nicaragua by any nation, group, organization, movement or individual."[18] North was rather brazen in testifying before the House and Senate select committees investigating the Iran-Contra affair, declaring that he had a choice between "lies and lives."[19] He also took the line that "I was authorized to do everything that I did," and this put Admiral John Poindexter, assistant to the president for national security affairs since December 1985, in a vulnerable position.[20]

Poindexter and Oliver North left office as a consequence of the investigations; North was fired and Poindexter resigned. Both were found guilty of destroying documents. North's testimony to a congressional committee implicated the director of the CIA, William Casey, in having full knowledge of North's activities. However, Casey never testified due to his untimely death during the investigations. Ronald Reagan survived the scandal by denying all knowledge of the illegal activity, and neither President Reagan nor Vice President Bush was called to testify before Congress. The president admitted serious mistakes were made by his administration regarding Nicaragua and Iran.

Ronald Reagan acknowledged in his memoir that Caspar Weinberger and George Shultz never got along with each other very well, and there were often policy conflicts between them. However, Reagan is magnanimous in acknowledging that they agreed in their opposition to the proposal of selling arms to Iran and warned him against it.[21] They were also clearly opposed to any link between arms sales and negotiating for hostages. This partly explains how the State Department and Department of Defense were sidelined as staff of the NSC took up the issue.

Equally revealing and somewhat mystifying is Reagan's acknowledgment that he approved the sale of TOW (tube-launched, optically-tracked, wire command-link guided) anti-tank missiles to Iran at an NSC meeting on January 7, 1986, but he does not link this to negotiations for hostages. Why then were the missiles being sold to Iran via Israel? Yet Reagan is unequivocal: "I did not think of the operation (and never have) as an 'arms-for-hostage' deal, because it wasn't."[22]

A number of investigations had been set in motion by the Iran-Contra events, including the creation of the three-man Tower Commission to investigate the NSC's operations that were at the heart of events. The commission included the Republican senator John Towers; former secretary of state Edmund S. Muskie; and Brent Scowcroft, a former national security adviser for President Ford. The report criticized the president for the ineffectual way he managed the NSC and the loss of institutional process in the pursuit of a particular policy aim. Reagan had allowed the NSC staff to become policy operators rather than researchers and advisers.

In commenting on presidential decision making, General Brent Scowcroft addressed the position of Ronald Reagan.

> I think that one of the President's major problems in the Iran-contra affair is how long it took him finally to understand how significant it really was. When we first talked to him he was convinced that his only real problem was the possible diversion of funds. . . . President Reagan had come into office declaring he was going to make American stand tall again, that no longer were we going to kowtow to terrorists and hostage takers. Those words struck a very resonant chord. He adopted a position that was not only right, but was also very popular. Then he turned on that policy in secret and did the very opposite. That was the most damaging aspect of the Iranian issue.[23]

The Iran-Contra affair illustrated a major weakness of Ronald Reagan's decision-making approach. In collecting together experienced people with like-minded views, Reagan produced a coherent team of administrators. However, in allowing his staff to create the substantial policy details, a command of what was being produced and introduced could easily be lost, as subordinates took on excessive levels of responsibility.

The Reagan decision-making style was a great contrast to his predecessor's style. Carter involved himself in the details of policy decisions. Reagan sought short memoranda that he would often have verbally delivered to him, on which he could then pronounce. This allowed for a manageable workday, not unlike Eisenhower's work practices, and, like Eisenhower, Ronald Reagan received some criticism for his approach but also considerable support for being comfortable with the presidency. Eisenhower is now largely seen as an activist president, but Reagan has left the impression of being unassertive with his staff. The Iran-Contra scandal left the impression that Reagan, in his final years as president, had been disengaged and uninformed and to some extent easily manipulated. Reagan's hands-off style of management that worked well in the early years of his presidency was heavily criticized as a consequence of the Iran-Contra affair.

At the end of Reagan's time as president, the constitutional relationship between Congress and the White House over some aspects of foreign policy responsibility was still unclear. Like his predecessors, Reagan had not accepted the constitutionality of the War Powers Act in limiting the commander in chief. In addition, the authority and working practices of the NSC had been brought into disrepute by the Iran-Contra scandal. Donald T. Regan, the president's secretary of treasury and later his chief of staff, captured the recent historical context of Ronald Reagan as a president and a decision maker.

Another President would almost certainly have had his own ideas on the mechanics of policy, but Reagan did not trouble himself with such minutiae. His preoccupation was with what might be called 'the outer Presidency.' He was content to let others cope with the inner details of running the Administration. In this he was the antithesis of most recent Presidents. Kennedy might call up a minor bureaucrat to check on a detail; Johnson might twist a senator's arm; Nixon might discuss the tiniest details of China policy with his staff; Carter might micromanage a commando raid on the Iranian desert from his desk in the Oval Office. But Reagan chose his aides and then followed their advice almost without question. He trusted his lieutenants to act on his intentions, rather than on his spoken instructions, and though he sometimes asked what some of his visible Cabinet officers were doing with their departments, he seldom spontaneously called for a detailed status report. The degree of trust involved in this method of leadership must be unprecedented in modern American history.[24]

Notes

1. Ronald Reagan, "Interview with Editors of the Hearst Corporation," October 30, 1984, Ronald Reagan Presidential Library, http://www.reagan.utexas.edu/resource/speeches/1984/103084q.htm.

2. R. Reagan, *Speaking My Mind* (New York: Simon and Schuster, 1989), 247.

3. A copy of this letter was provided by Nancy Kegan Smith, director of the Presidential Materials Staff, National Archives and Records Administration, Washington, D.C. The full text of the letter appears in R. Reagan, *An American Life* (New York: Simon and Schuster, 1990), 272–273.

4. J. F. Matlock Jr., *Reagan and Gorbachev: How the Cold War Ended* (New York: Random House, 2004), 21.

5. Reagan, *An American Life*, 270.

6. Matlock, *Reagan and Gorbachev*, 25.

7. A. M. Haig Jr., *Caveat: Realism, Reagan, and Foreign Policy* (New York: Macmillan Publishing Company, 1984), 269.

8. "Inaugural Address," January 21, 1985, Ronald Reagan Presidential Library, http://www.reagan.utexas.edu/resource/speeches/1985/12185a.htm.

9. *Public Papers of the President, Ronald Reagan, 1983* (Washington D.C.: U.S. Government Printing Office, 1984), March 8, 1983, 363.

10. Quotation from the State of the Union address in A. E. Busch, "Ronald Reagan and the Defeat of the Soviet Empire," *Presidential Studies Quarterly* 27, 3 (Summer 1997), 437.

11. Reagan, *An American Life*, 683.

12. Reagan, *Speaking My Mind*, 325–326.

13. D. Mervin, *Ronald Reagan and the American Presidency* (London: Longman, 1990), 161.

14. Reagan, *An American Life*, 518.

15. Ibid., 520.

16. W. LaFeber, *The American Age: United States Foreign Policy at Home and Abroad*, 2nd edition (New York: W. W. Norton & Company, 1994), 721.

17. Mervin, *Reagan and the American Presidency*, 459.

18. R. A. Strong, *Decisions and Dilemmas: Case Studies in Presidential Foreign Policy Making* (Englewood Cliffs, New Jersey: Prentice Hall, 1992), 173.

19. *Iran–Contra Puzzle* (Washington, D.C.: Congressional Quarterly Inc., 1987).

20. *Time*, July 20, 1987.

21. Reagan, *An American Life*, 512.

22. Ibid., 516.

23. General Brent Scowcroft was assistant to the president for national security affairs under President Ford, but also a member of the Tower Commission, chairman of the President's Advisory Committee on Strategic Forces, and a member of the President's Advisory Committee on Arms Control. See K. W. Thompson, editor, *The Ford Presidency* (New York: University Press of America, 1988).

24. D. T. Regan, *For the Record* (New York: Harcourt Brace Jovanovich, Publishers, 1988), 267–268.

CHAPTER 11

George H. W. Bush and the End of the Cold War, 1989–1991

> The challenge of presidential leadership in foreign affairs is not to listen to consensus, but to forge it at home and abroad.[1]
>
> —*George H. W. Bush*

It was very appropriate that President George Herbert Walker Bush should read a eulogy at the National Cathedral in Washington, D.C. on June 11, 2004, for the man he had served as vice president and succeeded as president. It was equally appropriate that George H. W. Bush should have opened his remarks with a reference to Franklin D. Roosevelt. Roosevelt worked with the Soviet Union to resolve the problems of World War II and set a post-war agenda that was only eventually resolved when George H. W. Bush oversaw the ending of the cold war, benefiting from the work achieved by President Reagan and his presidential predecessors. All of the presidents since Roosevelt had to deal with various crises against the background of the cold war. Not all crises were related to the cold war, but they took place in an international cold war environment. The different approaches to the various crises that these very different presidents and personalities had to contend with were met with mixed fortunes.

Europe and Latin America would dominate the first year of the presidency of George H. W. Bush, with the destruction of the Berlin Wall in Germany and the fall of the Manuel Noriega regime in Panama. Furthermore, the move to considerable cooperation between the superpowers was advanced through the Malta summit on December 2 and 3, 1989–although George Bush was reluctant to call it a summit, hoping that this would reduce the expectations from it.

It would be nice to attach some symmetry to the cold war, as if the cold war spans Malta to Malta conferences, but the Yalta conference in 1945 is a more obvious starting point, and the Malta conference of 1989 was only the prelude to the end of the cold war. President Roosevelt met Winston Churchill onboard ships off Newfoundland in 1941 and Malta in 1945 to discuss World War II and what the structure of the post-war world would look like. The 1945 Malta meeting was a prelude to the Yalta Big Three conference, a conference to which some responsibility has been attributed for starting the cold war. Forty-four years later, in the first shipboard presidential summit since Roosevelt, President Bush met with President Mikhail Gorbachev onboard a ship off Malta. It may be even rather too neat to describe the cold war as from Yalta to Malta, yet in diplomatic terms some observations on both as being instrumental in the rise and fall of the cold war are respectively sound.

Military and Diplomatic Background

George H. W. Bush belongs to a generation that distinguished themselves in active service during World War II, and to his credit he did not look for advancement because of it. As president he often had his speechwriters exclude his own military achievements in speeches to servicemen. Yet, George H. W. Bush enlisted in the U.S. Navy Reserve in 1942, on his eighteenth birthday, as a seaman second class. On receipt of his flying wings, he became the youngest pilot in the U.S. Navy at that time. Like so many of his generation he had been profoundly affected by the events of December 7, 1941, and he enlisted at the first opportunity. Bush was on active service from August 1942 until September 1945, a service mostly confined to the Pacific area, flying torpedo bombers from the USS *San Jacinto*. Film footage exists of his dramatic rescue from the Pacific Ocean after his airplane had been struck by flack, where he spent two hours alone in the water, his two crew members not surviving. For his exploits in destroying enemy communications on the island of Chici Jima he was honored with the award of the Distinguished Flying Cross. Subsequently he was also awarded the Navy Air Medal with two stars. President Bush's record is considerable, justified on the back of having flown fifty-eight combat missions.

The formal political career of Bush began in 1966 when he was elected to the House of Representatives from the 7th District in Texas. His foreign policy credentials were advanced when he became ambassador to the United Nations during the Nixon presidency. Holding this office from 1971 to 1973, he went on to become the chief of the U.S. Liaison Office in the People's Republic of China in October 1974. As noted in the chapter on President Ford, George Bush served as the director of the Central Intelligence Agency from 1976, and is the only former director of the CIA to become president of the United States. Also, as discussed in chapter 10, Bush served as a two-term vice president, and was a close confidante of President Reagan. With these credentials, and with the exception of the Iran-Contra scandal, it is not unduly surprising that he obtained the presidency, or for that matter was to oversee the end of the cold war. Being a one-term president and not taking direct responsibility for Reagan's foreign policy achievements puts George Bush in the shadow of Ronald Reagan. This may be unfair to Bush given the support he provided to Ford and Reagan, having coordinated Reagan's activities to combat terrorism and having visited seventy-four countries as vice president. President Bush's previous diplomatic tenure and work as vice president allowed him to cultivate close personal relationships with a number of foreign leaders.

On becoming president, George Bush did not see himself as a micro-manager of foreign policy, although he did surround himself with a trusted group of advisers, expecting recommendations from a number of quarters, including the NSC and cabinet. On January 30, 1989, in National Security Directive 1 the president made his methods clear. "Along with its subordinate bodies, the NSC will be my principal means for coordinating Executive departments and agencies in the development and implementation of national security policy."[2] From his own experience as director of the CIA, he did not make the CIA director of cabinet rank, believing the director should be above politics and be concerned with just intelligence matters.[3] However, this did not prevent Bush from calling in his director of the CIA, William Webster, and his successor, Robert Gates, for important advice.

The president's normal daily routine included an 8:00 A.M. national security briefing in the Oval Office, which was largely an intelligence briefing on events around the world. Having already scanned about seven newspapers, the president was ready for the larger national security meetings. Bush adopted a hands-on and centralized approach to foreign policy decision making and avoided the more detached approach of President Reagan.

Panama

Panama as a problem came to the fore during the Panamanian elections of May 1989. Despite the presence of international observers, widespread fraud led to the continuation of the dictatorship of Manuel Antonio Noriega. Although at one time on the payroll of the CIA, he was more closely associated with drug trafficking and human rights violations. However, as R. A. Strong has pointed out, "Just as the Carter administration had overlooked Panamanian problems in the interests of getting the canal treaties ratified, the Reagan administration ignored obvious threats to Panamanian democracy in the interests of promoting democracy elsewhere in Central America."[4] The years of difficult presidential association with Noriega and senatorial criticism of Noriega made the decision to intervene easier.

Ten years after the 1989 Panamanian election, George Bush was to reflect on Panama.

During Reagan's presidency, George Shultz and President Reagan had favored a deal to get Noriega to leave Panama peacefully. Indeed, the USA had tried to find asylum for him in Spain and elsewhere.

I will never forget the meeting in the lovely Yellow Room upstairs in the President's residence in May of 1988. This was the only time I differed in front of the others with President Reagan. I told him, seconded by Jim Baker, that it would be very bad to cut a deal with Noriega, letting him get asylum and escape punishment for his drug activities.[5]

As president, George Bush refused to recognize any Panamanian government controlled by General Noriega and set the target of removing him from office. This policy turned into a major military intervention when, at 1:00 a.m. on December 20, 1989, 22,000 forces of the United States invaded Panama in operation "Just Cause." It was an unusual occupation, which was made militarily easier for the Bush administration since more than fifty percent of the troops were already in Panama. The decision appears to have been made on December 17 with the crucial inner circle of advisers James Baker, secretary of state; Dan Quayle, vice president; John Sununu, White House chief of staff; Brent Scowcroft, national security adviser; Robert Gates, deputy national security adviser; Dick Cheney, secretary of defense; Colin Powell, chairman of the Joint Chiefs of Staff; Marlin Fitzwater, press secretary; and also Lieutenant General Thomas Kelly. President Bush and Colin Powell agreed on the need for an invasion.[6] The night before the invasion, President Bush telephoned a number of members of Congress to tell them of his plans, but this was not effectively an attempt to carry out the obligations of the War Powers Act, since no direct approval was sought from Congress. The Panamanian action did not cause a breach in relations between the president and Congress, and Congress appeared reluctant to fully investigate the consequences of the president's actions over Panama.

A rather bizarre set of circumstances developed as Noriega obtained refuge in the papal embassy. With some normal persuasion combined with American forces playing excessively loud music outside, Noriega surrendered. It had been a rather swift, and despite casualties, a successful engagement of force by President Bush as commander in chief.

The Persian Gulf War

On Thursday, August 2, 1990, Iraq invaded Kuwait, a country that had approximately ten percent of the world's oil supplies. Saddam Hussein, the military dictator of Iraq, was likened to Adolf Hitler by President Bush, and clearly the Bush administration believed appeasement was not the answer and that Iraq's blatant aggression had to be opposed.[7] The NSC defined four principles to guide the strategy of United States policy: complete and unconditional withdrawal of all Iraqi forces from Kuwait; the reinstatement of Kuwait's legitimate government and consequentially the elimination of the regime installed by Iraq; the creation of stability and military security for the Persian Gulf; and the protection of American citizens.[8] With strong determination the United States implemented diplomatic, economic, and energy policies aimed to weaken the position of Iraq. In a multilateral move and with the support of the United Nations under Article 51 of the Charter and subsequent resolutions, two multinational forces were coordinated: the Multinational Force for Saudi Arabia (MNFSA) and the Multinational Force to Enforce Sanctions (MNFES). The latter was designed to enforce sanctions against Iraq and to achieve the withdrawal of Iraqi forces from Kuwait. The United States encouraged the Soviet Union to provide "lift support" within Saudi Arabia, but to participate in MNFSA only as the Saudi government directed.

The first operation of United States forces within a United Nations coalition was called "Operation Desert Shield," and this incorporated additional military support from the United Kingdom, Egypt, Morocco, United Arab Emirates, Qatar, and Oman. Ostensibly this was to protect Saudi Arabia after Iraq invaded Kuwait. By January 1991 the United Nations coalition of forces, dominated by a majority of United States forces, shifted to "Operation Desert Storm." This operation had the ambitious policy of liberating Kuwait and was commanded by General H. Norman Schwarzkopf.

Famous investigative journalist and author Bob Woodward, in *The Commanders*, provided a study of United States military decision making between President Bush's inauguration and the implementation of "Operation Desert Storm" in January 1991.[9] It is essentially a study of the importance of the secretary of defense, Dick Cheney, and the chairman of the Joint Chiefs of Staff, Colin Powell, in dealing with a number of international issues and organizing the Gulf War with their commander in chief. It was mildly embarrassing to the president, since Colin Powell was depicted as having reservations about military action. White House staff also complained that the Department of Defense had leaked too much information to the author of *The Commanders* and reporters.[10]

Both the United Nations and the United States Congress passed resolutions authorizing action to assist Kuwait. The United Nations used language incorporating "all necessary means" and Congress further specified the "use of military force."[11] The vote in the House of Representatives was substantially behind the resolution, 250 votes to 183; but the vote was much closer in the Senate, with 52 senators behind the resolution and 47 against. On Tuesday January 15 "At 10:30 a.m. Bush met in the Oval Office with his inner council: Quayle, Baker, Cheney, Scowcroft, Powell, Sununu and Gates. Bush had the two-page draft of the top-secret National Security Directive (NSD) before him. . . . The President signed it."[12] The order to execute "Operation Desert Storm" under certain provisions was signed later in the day by Cheney and Powell and sent to Schwarzkopf.

Although it was a war against Iraq that was directed by the United States, it had United Nations support with twenty-eight nations contributing to the allied forces (sixteen sending ground forces), with particularly strong support from the British, and financial support from Germany and Japan. The forty-two day war was considered successful in that it achieved the main objective of liberating Kuwait. Since the conflict had the support of the Soviet Union, despite internal Soviet conflicts, and this was the first time since World War II that responsibility for this type of international action was shared with the Soviet Union, it provided further evidence that new international alignments were possible.

Cold War Thaw and Meltdown

The Bush administration adopted a five-part agenda toward the Soviet Union and concluding the cold war.[13] It was an attempt to move beyond the difficulties associated with détente and to emphasize much more than arms control—but also to include arms control and defense programs as part of the negotiation package. First, both bilateral and multilateral arms control discussions were encouraged. Second, regional conflicts, particularly in Central America where the Soviet Union might have influence on "clients," were to be debated, with the hope that a "new thinking" would extend beyond the Soviet Union and help resolve difficulties in trouble spots.[14] Third, the human rights problems within the Soviet Union would continue to be addressed by the United States. Fourth, commercial, cultural, and scientific exchanges with the Soviet Union would be encouraged. Last, global and transnational problems gave opportunities for cooperation, particularly environmental topics and the problem of international terrorism. This agenda provided in all a rather cautious approach by President Bush toward the Soviet Union.

Although serious problems would continue between the Soviet Union and the United States after 1989, it was this year that saw Soviet control of Eastern European satellites disappear and the Berlin Wall opened. Further domestic changes would take place in the Soviet Union, and diplomatic and military arrangements would have to be made between the United States and the Soviet Union before the cold war was declared over.

> Of course, leadership has a constant companion: responsibility. And our responsibility is to look ahead and grasp the promise of the future. I said recently that we're at the end of an era and the beginning of another. And I noted that in regard to the Soviet Union, our policy is to move beyond containment. For forty years, the seeds of democracy in Eastern Europe lay dormant, buried under the frozen tundra of the Cold War. And for forty years, the world has waited for the Cold War to end. And decade after decade, time after time, the flowering human spirit withered from the chill of conflict and oppression; and again, the

world waited. But the passion for freedom cannot be denied forever. The world has waited long enough. The time is right. Let Europe be whole and free.[15]

President Bush's comments, made in Germany in May 1989, recognized the changes in Eastern Europe, and in December further negotiations were held aboard ships off Malta to advance the ending of the cold war. It advanced the personal relationship between Bush and Gorbachev and produced the first joint press conference in United States-Soviet relations. It had little else of substance, but the verbal commitments to ending the character of the cold war held true. Although some American congressmen wanted a reduction in NATO expenditure by the United States, Bush was aware of his multilateral commitments and would not address these on a unilateral basis with Gorbachev.

The United States Information Agency did a survey of eighty-five newspapers and broadcasting reports from twenty-five countries relating to the Malta summit meeting. West European commentaries clearly believed the cold war was coming to an end, but was not yet over.

President Bush's warm remarks about President Gorbachev and his reform efforts were well-received by the foreign media and observers gave advice on how to help advance *perestroika*. The *Financial Times* saw one of the President's "main tasks at the Malta mini-summit being to give Mr Gorbachev a great enough sense of security to carry on with his good works." Brussels' independent *Le Soir* felt the Administration "was seeking to create a stable international atmosphere." The centrist *Ottawa Citizen* declared, "Help Gorbachev out" and Moscow's Government-owned *Izvestia* called for a "resolute and rapid expansion of economic cooperation."[16]

Good relations were to continue into a summit in Washington, D.C. in May 1990. Although there were not the same detailed briefings as before the Malta summit, Condoleezza Rice (director for Soviet and East European affairs in the NSC) organized separate one-hour briefings for the president on Soviet internal affairs, the Soviet economy, arms control, Soviet policy toward Germany, and the outcome of a ministerial meeting with Eduard Shevardnadze.[17] The Washington, D.C. summit was the second of five bilateral summits between President Bush and President Gorbachev. Discussions were built around the topics of Europe, arms control, and Soviet internal developments, and both statesmen agreed to the end of chemical weapons production. As Condoleezza Rice announced unofficially in a press conference, the intention was to put signatures to agreements that had been negotiated over years.[18]

In July 1991 Bush and Gorbachev signed START and in November joined with other countries to limit the non-nuclear armaments of the Warsaw Pact and NATO. The meeting in Paris in November 1991 acknowledged the end of the cold war. On Christmas day 1991, Mikhail Gorbachev resigned as president of the Soviet Union and the Soviet red flag was lowered from the Kremlin to be replaced by the flag of a democratic Russia. President Bush recognized twelve republics of the former Soviet Union.

Summary

All presidents of the United States, from Franklin Delano Roosevelt to George Herbert Walker Bush, held summit meetings with political leaders of the Soviet Union. President Johnson had limited direct personal contact with his respective counterpart in the Soviet Union as his presidency was swamped by the Vietnam War. All ten presidents, from Roosevelt to Bush, were tested in their role as commander in chief.

The growth of the United States as an economic power has been closely related to the diplomatic and military strength of this superpower. The constitutional power of the president, as the representative of the United States abroad and as commander in chief of the armed forces, became measurably more significant as the United States became a leading world power. The president has, with bureaucratic management aside, overall control of military strategy for his country. Not only have presidents controlled military resources at home, but they have undertaken significant initiatives overseas. American presidents have been directly behind the policies of the United States during World War II, the Korean War, the Vietnam War and the Gulf War. John F. Kennedy learned a salutary lesson over the Bay of Pigs invasion, and President Johnson suffered failures in Vietnam that led ultimately to the United States losing its first war.

Other substantial initiatives have been pursued by presidents. Richard Nixon was instrumental in forming a détente with the People's Republic of China. Jimmy Carter helped to conclude a peace settlement between Israel and Egypt. John F. Kennedy initiated a test ban treaty. Richard Nixon, Gerald Ford, Jimmy Carter, and Ronald Reagan undertook to make advances with the Soviet Union in strategic arms limitations. And Ronald Reagan took an active role in Central America and the Middle East. Failures in Vietnam and Iran have been partially obscured by the positive outcome of the cold war.

With the exception of President Carter, all other presidents between 1945 and 1991 have evoked appeasement as a weakness. Truman, Johnson, Nixon, Ford, Reagan, and Bush were happy at times to draw upon the weakness of appeasing Nazi Germany in the 1930s. It was felt to be wrong to appease communist aggression, and consequentially an active strategy against communism was initiated in Berlin, Korea, Cuba, Southeast Asia, Chile, Central America, and Afghanistan. John F. Kennedy's attitude toward Soviet missiles in Cuba was indicative of this anti-appeasement approach. "The 1930s taught us a clear lesson: aggressive conduct, if allowed to go unchecked, ultimately leads to war."[19] In a similar vein, although with reference to action against Iraq, President Bush wrote on December 31, 1990, to his children, George, Jeb (John Ellis), Neil, Marvin, and Doro (Dorothy), "How many lives might have been saved if appeasement had given way to force earlier on in the late 30s or earliest 40s? How many Jews might have been spared the gas chambers, or how many Polish patriots might be alive today? I look at today's crisis as 'good' vs. 'evil.' Yes, it is that clear."[20]

The foreign policy power of presidents since 1945 has clearly been dependent on the personalities of the incumbent president. Actions of various presidents have been modified by the incumbent's interpretation of his role as commander in chief, and, from November 1973, with considerations of the War Powers Act. However, descriptions or classification of presidents as active or passive can be misleading since presidents are often reacting to unique foreign policy crises and at times may have, through good diplomacy, forestalled serious crises from developing. Furthermore, the instruments of foreign policy action have changed as technology has given presidents different choices and made comparisons more difficult. What has been true for all ten cold war presidents is that unforeseen international events have meant for each "Times of heroism are generally times of terror. . . . But whoso is heroic will always find crisis to try his edge."[21]

Notes

1. President George H. W. Bush was a full one-term president until January 1993. The quotation comes from G. H. W. Bush and B. Scowcroft, *A World Transformed* (New York: Alfred A. Knopf, 1998), 566.

2. "Organization of the National Security Council System," January 30, 1989, National Security Directive 1, Bush Presidential Records, George Bush Presidential Library, http://bushlibrary.tamu.edu/research/directives.html.

3. Bush and Scowcroft, *A World Transformed*, 21.

4. R. A. Strong, *Decisions and Dilemmas: Case Studies in Presidential Foreign Policy Making* (Englewood Cliffs, New Jersey: Prentice Hall, 1992), 203.

5. G. H. W. Bush's remarks at the Fall Leadership Conference of the Center for the Study of the Presidency at Texas A&M University, October 23, 1999. J. McGrath, ed., *George Bush in His Own Words* (New York: Scribner, 2001), 309.

6. Strong, *Decisions and Dilemmas*, 208.

7. W. LaFeber, *America, Russia, and the Cold War 1945–1996*, 8th edition (New York: McGraw-Hill, 1977), 341.

8. National Security Directive 45, August 20, 1990, Bush Presidential Records, George Bush Presidential Library, http://bushlibrary.tamu.edu/research/directives.html.

9. B. Woodward, *The Commanders* (New York: Simon & Schuster, 1991).

10. M. Fitzwater, *Call the Briefing! A Memoir of Ten Years in the White House with Presidents Reagan and Bush* (United States: Xlibris Corporation, 2000), 233.

11. Woodward, *The Commanders*, 362.

12. Ibid., 366.

13. "Gist," November 1989, a quick reference aid on U.S. foreign relations, edited by Harriet Culley (Washington D.C.: Bureau of Public Affairs, Department of State, 1989). Photocopy held in Sean Walsh Files, "Presidential Overseas Travel Notebooks File," OA 7938 WHORM: Bush Presidential Records, White House Staff and Office Files, George Bush Presidential Library.

14. Ibid

15. G. H. W. Bush's remarks at the Rheingoldhalle to the citizens of Mainz, Federal Republic of Germany, May 31, 1989. Ibid., 39.

16. "Foreign Media Reaction," November 29, 1989, ID# 094180, FO005-03, WHORM: Subject File, Bush Presidential Records, George Bush Presidential Library.

17. Memorandum to Brent Scowcroft from Condleezza Rice, "Briefings for the President," Condoleezza Rice Files, OA/IDCFO717, WHORM: Bush Presidential Records, White House Staff and Office Files, George Bush Presidential Library.

18. "Background Briefing by Senior Administration Official," the Briefing Room, the White House, May 29, 1990, ibid.

19. "Report to the American People," October 22, 1962, *Public Papers of the Presidents of the United States, John F. Kennedy, 1962* (Washington, D.C.: U.S. Government Printing Office, 1963), 807.

20. Bush and Scowcroft, *A World Transformed*, 435.

21. R. W. Emerson, *Essays, First Series* (Boston: Houghton, Mifflin and Company, 1883), 246–247.

Selected Bibliography

Listed here are the main published sources used in the production of this text. It provides a breakdown of useful sources for the study of individual presidents of the United States and their foreign policies. Primary sources from a number of presidential libraries have been used in the text, and the exact sources used can be found in the notes and acknowledgments. The presidential libraries provide exceptional resources for detailed academic research and the Web sites for these libraries have direct sources of information and a selection of available documents and photographs.

General Works: Books and Articles

Ambrose, Stephen E., and Douglas Brinkley. "The Presidency and Foreign Policy." *Foreign Affairs* 70, 5 (Winter 1991/1992).

———. *Rise to Globalism: American Foreign Policy Since 1938*. 8th ed. Middlesex: Penguin Books, 1997.

Anderson, David L., ed. *Shadow on the White House: Presidents and the Vietnam War, 1945–1975*. Lawrence: University Press of Kansas, 1993.

Andrew, Christopher. *For the President's Eyes Only: Secret Intelligence and the American Presidency from Washington to Bush*. London: Harper Collins, 1995.

Bohlen, Charles E. *Witness to History: 1929–1969*. New York: Norton, 1973.

Bose, Meena. *Shaping and Signaling Presidential Policy: The National Security Decision Making of Eisenhower and Kennedy*. College Station: Texas A&M University Press, 1998.

Boyle, Peter G. *American-Soviet Relations. From the Russian Revolution to the Fall of Communism*. London: Routledge, 1993.

Caraley, Demetrios. *The President's War Powers: From the Federalists to Reagan*. New York: Academy of Political Science, 1984.

Cohen, Warren I. *The Cambridge History of American Foreign Relations*. Vol. IV, *America in the Age of Soviet Power, 1945–1999*. Cambridge: Cambridge University Press, 1993.

Coker, Christopher. *Reflections on American Foreign Policy Since 1945.* London: Pinter Publishers, 1989.

Craig, Gordon. A., and Alexander L. George. *Force and Statecraft: Diplomatic Problems of Our Time.* New York: Oxford University Press, 1990.

Dallek, Robert. *Hail to the Chief: The Making and Unmaking of American Presidents.* New York: Hyperion, 1996.

Dobrynin, Anatoly. *In Confidence: Moscow's Ambassador to America's Six Cold War Presidents (1962–1986).* New York: Times Books, 1995.

Dougherty, James E., and Robert L. Pfaltzgraff Jr. *American Foreign Policy: FDR to Reagan.* New York: Harper & Row, 1986.

Gaddis, John L. "The Rise, Fall and Future of Détente." *Foreign Affairs* 62, 2 (Winter 1983/1984).

———. *Strategies of Containment: A Critical Appraisal of Post-war American National Security Policy.* Oxford: Oxford University Press, 1982.

———. *The United States and the Origins of the Cold War, 1941–1947.* New York: Columbia University Press, 1972.

Gambone, Michael, D., ed. *Documents of American Diplomacy.* Westport, Connecticut: Greenwood Press, 2002.

Gardner, Lloyd. C. *Architects of Illusion: Men and Ideas in American Foreign Policy, 1941–1949.* Chicago: Quadrangle, 1970.

———. *A Covenant with Power: America and World Order from Wilson to Reagan.* London: Macmillan, 1984.

Gates, Robert M. *From the Shadows: The Ultimate Insider's Story of Five Presidents and How They Won the Cold War.* New York: Simon and Schuster, 1996.

Gromyko, Andrei. *Memoirs.* New York: Doubleday, 1989.

Hyland, William. *Mortal Rivals: Superpower Relations from Nixon to Reagan.* New York: Random House, 1987.

LaFeber, Walter. *The American Age: United States Foreign Policy at Home and Abroad.* 2nd ed. New York: W. W. Norton & Company, 1994.

———. *America, Russia and the Cold War, 1945–1996.* New York: McGraw-Hill, 1997.

Kennedy, Paul. *The Rise and Fall of the Great Powers: Economic Change and Military Conflict from 1500 to 2000.* London: Unwin Hyman, 1988.

Kissinger, Henry A. *American Foreign Policy.* New York: Norton, 1977.

McMahon, Robert J. *Major Problems in the History of the Vietnam War.* 2nd ed. Lexington, Massachusetts: D. C. Heath and Company, 1995.

Morris, Richard B., and Jeffery B. Morris. *Great Presidential Decisions: State Papers that Changed the Course of History from Washington to Reagan.* Norwalk, Connecticut: Easton Press, 1992.

Newmann, William. "Causes of Change in National Security Processes: Carter, Reagan, and Bush Decision Making on Arms Control." *Presidential Studies Quarterly* 31, 1 (March 2001).

Neustadt, Richard. *Presidential Power and the Modern Presidents: The Politics of Leadership from Roosevelt to Reagan.* New York: Free Press, 1991.

Paterson, Thomas G. *Meeting the Communist Threat: Truman to Reagan.* Oxford: Oxford University Press, 1989.

———, and D. Merrill. *Major Problems in American Foreign Relations.* Vol. II, *Since 1914.* 4th ed. Lexington, Massachusetts, 1995.

Schick, Frank. L., Renee Schick, and Mark Carroll. *Records of the Presidency: Presidential Papers from Washington to Reagan.* Phoenix, Arizona: Oryx Press, 1989.

Schlesinger, Arthur Jr. *The Imperial Presidency.* Boston: Houghton Mifflin, 1989.

Schoenbaum, Thomas J. *Waging Peace and War: Dean Rusk in the Truman, Kennedy, and Johnson Years.* New York: Simon and Schuster, 1988.

Siracusa, Joseph M. "The 'New' Cold War History and the Origins of the Cold War." *Australian Journal of Politics and History* 47, 1 (2001).

Spanier, John. *American Foreign Policy Since World War II.* Washington, D.C: CQ Press, 1988.

———, and Eric M. Uslaner. *How American Foreign Policy Is Made.* New York: Praeger Publishers, 1974.

Stern, Paula. *Water's Edge: Domestic Politics and the Making of American Foreign Policy.* Westport, Connecticut: Greenwood Press, 1979

Strong, Robert A. *Decisions and Dilemmas: Case Studies in Presidential Foreign Policy Making.* Englewood Cliffs, New Jersey: Prentice Hall, 1992.

Stuckey, Mary E. *Strategic Failures in the Modern Presidency.* Cresskill, New Jersey: Hampton Press, 1996.

Tindall, George B., and David E. Shi. *America: A Narrative History.* New York: W. W. Norton and Company, 1992.

Yergin, Daniel. *Shattered Peace: The Origins of the Cold War and the National Security State.* Boston: Houghton Mifflin, 1977.

Presidency of Franklin D. Roosevelt

Franklin D. Roosevelt Presidential Library
4079 Albany Post Road
Hyde Park, New York, 12538
http://www.fdrlibrary.marist.edu/index.html.

Published Documents

Foreign Relations of the United States: The Conferences at Malta and Yalta. Washington, D.C.: U.S. Government Printing Office, 1955.

Roosevelt, Elliott, ed. *Roosevelt Letters: Being the Personal Correspondence of Franklin Delano Roosevelt.* Vol. 3, *1928–1945.* London: Harrap, 1952.

Stalin's Correspondence with Roosevelt and Truman, 1941–1945. New York: Capricorn Books, 1965.

Vandenberg, Arthur H., ed. *Private Papers of Senator Vandenberg.* Boston: Houghton Mifflin Company, 1952.

Memoirs

Grew, Joseph C. *Turbulent Era.* Vol. II. Boston: Houghton Mifflin Company, 1952.

Harriman, W. Averell, and Eli Abel. *Special Envoy to Churchill and Stalin 1941–1946.* London: Hutchinson, 1975.

Leahy, William D. *I Was There.* New York: McGraw Hill, 1950.

Stettinius, Edward R. *Roosevelt and the Russians: The Yalta Conference.* London: Jonathan Cape, 1950.

Books

Bishop, Jim. *FDR's Last Year.* New York: Morrow, 1974.

Black, Conrad. *Franklin Delano Roosevelt: Champion of Freedom.* London: Wiedenfield & Nicolson, 2003.

Brundu Olla, Paola. *Yalta: Un Mito Che Resiste.* Roma: Edizioni Dell'Ateneo, 1988.

Clemens, Diane S. *Yalta.* New York: Oxford University Press, 1970.

Dallek, Robert. *The American Style of Foreign Policy.* New York: Oxford University Press, 1983.

———. *Franklin D. Roosevelt and American Foreign Policy, 1932–1945.* Oxford: Oxford University Press, 1979.

Dickinson, Matthew J., *Bitter Harvest: FDR, Presidential Power and the Growth of the Presidential Branch.* New York: Cambridge University Press, 1997.

Divine, Robert A. *Roosevelt and World War II.* Baltimore: The Johns Hopkins Press, 1969.

Dobson, Alan P. *U.S. Wartime Aid to Britain, 1940–1946.* London: Croom Helm, 1986.

Feis, Herbert. *The Atomic Bomb and the End of World War II.* Princeton, New Jersey: Princeton University Press, 1966.

———. *Churchill–Roosevelt–Stalin: The War They Waged and the Peace They Sought.* Princeton, New Jersey; Princeton University Press, 1967.

Ferrell, Robert H. *The Dying President: Franklin D. Roosevelt, 1944–1945.* Columbia: University of Missouri Press, 1998.

Gunther, John. *Roosevelt in Retrospect: A Profile in History.* London: Hamilton, 1950.

Hoopes, Townsend, and Douglas Brinkley. *FDR and the Creation of the U.N.* New Haven, Connecticut: Yale University Press, 1997.

Kimball, Warren F. *Forged in War: Roosevelt, Churchill and the Second World War.* New York: W. Morrow, 1997.

Larrabee, Eric. *Commander in Chief: Franklin Delano Roosevelt, His Lieutenants, and Their War.* New York: Simon & Shuster Inc., 1987.

Lowenheim, Francis L., Harold D. Langley, and Manfred Jonas, eds. *Roosevelt and Churchill: Their Secret Wartime Correspondence.* London: Barrie and Jenkins, 1975.

MacGregor Burns, James. *Roosevelt: The Soldier of Freedom 1940–1945.* London: Weidenfeld and Nicolson, 1971.

Morgan, Ted. *FDR: A Biography.* New York: Simon & Schuster, 1985.

Nisbet, Robert. *Roosevelt and Stalin: The Failed Courtship.* Washington, D.C.: Regnery Gateway, 1988.

Sherwood, Robert E. *Roosevelt and Hopkins: An Intimate History.* New York: Harper & Brothers, 1948.

Stafford, David. *Roosevelt and Churchill: Men of Secrets.* London: Little, Brown and Company, 1999.

Theoharis, Athan G. *The Yalta Myths: An Issue in U.S. Politics, 1945–1955.* Columbia: University of Missouri Press, 1970.

Underhill, Robert *FDR and Harry: Unparalleled Lives.* Westport, Connecticut: Praeger, 1996.

Presidency of Harry S. Truman

Harry S. Truman Library and Museum
500 W. US Hwy. 24
Independence, Missouri, 64050
http://www.trumanlibrary.org/.

Published Documents

Ferrell, Robert H., ed. *Dear Bess: The Letters from Harry to Bess Truman, 1910-1959.* New York: Norton, 1983.

——. *Off the Record: The Private Papers of Harry S. Truman.* Norwalk, Connecticut: Easton Press, 1989, first published 1980.

Foreign Relations of the United States, 1945 volumes. Washington, D.C.: U.S. Government Printing Office, (1967-1969); 1946 volumes, (1967-1972); 1947 volumes (1972-1988); 1948 volumes (1972-1976); 1949 volumes (1974-1989); 1950 volumes (1976-1981); 1951 volumes (1978-1983); 1952-1954 volumes (1979-1992).

Hoag, Gary, Paul Kesaris, and Robert E. Lester. *President Harry S. Truman's Office Files, 1945-1953.* Microfilm. Frederick, Maryland: University Publications of America, 1989.

Kesaris, P., ed. *Map Room Messages of President Truman.* Microfilm. Frederick, Maryland: University Publications of America, 1980.

Public Papers of the Presidents of the United States: Harry S. Truman, 1945-1953. Vols. 1–8. Washington D.C.: U.S. Government Printing Office, 1961-1966.

Smith, Jean E, ed. *Papers of General Lucius D. Clay: Germany, 1945-1949.* Vol. 2. Bloomington: Indiana University Press, 1974.

Neal, Steve, ed. *Eleanor and Harry: The Correspondence of Eleanor Roosevelt and Harry S. Truman.* New York: Scribner, 2002.

Memoirs and Diaries

Acheson, Dean. *Present at the Creation.* New York: Norton, 1969.

Baruch, Bernard M. *The Public Years.* New York: Holt, Rinehart & Winston, 1960.

Byrnes, James F. *All in One Lifetime.* New York: Harper and Brothers, 1958.

——. *Speaking Frankly.* New York: Harper & Brothers, 1947.

Ferrell, Robert. H. ed. *Truman in the White House: The Diary of Eben A. Ayers.* Columbia: University of Missouri Press, 1991.

Kennan, George F. *Memoirs.* Vol. 1, *1925-1950.* Vol. 2, *1950-1963.* Boston: Little, Brown and Company, 1967-1972.

MacArthur, Douglas. *Reminiscences.* New York: McGraw-Hill, 1964.

Smith, Walter Bedell. *My Three Years in Moscow.* New York: J. B. Lippincott Company, 1950.

Truman, Harry S. *Memoirs.* Vol. 1, *1945, Year of Decisions.* Suffolk: Hodder and Stoughton, 1955.

——. *Memoirs.* Vol. 2, *Years of Trial and Hope.* London: Hodder and Stoughton, 1956.

Books

Alperovitz, Gar. *Atomic Diplomacy: Hiroshima and Potsdam.* New York: Simon and Schuster, 1965.

——. *The Decision to Use the Atomic Bomb and the Architecture of an American Myth.* New York: Alfred A. Knopf, 1995.

Bernstein, Barton J., ed. *Politics and Policies of the Truman Administration.* Chicago: Quadrangle, 1970.

Brinkley, Douglas, ed. *Dean Acheson and the Making of U.S. Foreign Policy.* New York: St. Martin's Press, 1993.

Cohen, Michael J. *Truman and Israel.* Berkeley: University of California Press, 1990.

Donovan, Robert J. *Conflict and Crisis: The Presidency of Harry S. Truman, 1945–1948.* New York: Norton, 1977.

Feis, Herbert. *From Trust to Terror: The Onset of the Cold War, 1945–1950.* New York: Norton, 1970.

Ferrell, Robert H. *Harry S. Truman: A Life.* Norwalk, Connecticut: Easton Press, 1994.

Gimble, John. *The American Occupation of Germany.* Stanford: Stanford University Press, 1968.

———. *The Origins of the Marshall Plan.* Stanford: Stanford University Press, 1976.

Gormly, James L. *The Collapse of the Grand Alliance, 1945–1948.* Baton Rouge: Louisiana State University Press, 1987.

Hamby, Alonzo I. *Man of the People: A Life of Harry S Truman.* New York: Oxford University Press, 1995.

Isaacson, Walter, and Evan Thomas. *The Wise Men: Six Friends and the World They Made.* New York: Simon & Schuster, 1986.

Jones, Joseph M. *The Fifteen Weeks.* New York: Viking, 1955.

Leffler, Melvyn P. *A Preponderance of Power: National Security, the Truman Administration and the Cold War.* Stanford: Stanford University Press, 1992.

McCullough, David. *Truman.* New York: Simon & Schuster, 1992.

Miscamble, Wilson. D. *George F. Kennan and the Making of American Foreign Policy.* Princeton, New Jersey: Princeton University Press, 1992.

Ovendale, Ritchie. *The English-speaking Alliance: Britain, the United States, the Dominions and the Cold War 1945–1951.* London, Allen & Unwin, 1985.

Schlaim, Avi. *The United States and the Berlin Blockade, 1948–1949; A Study in Crisis Decision Making.* Berkeley: University of California Press, 1983.

Smith, Gaddis. *Dean Acheson.* Vol. 16, *American Secretaries of State and Their Diplomacy.* Ferrell, Robert. H., and Samuel F. Bemis, eds. New York: Cooper Square Publishers, 1972.

Articles

Bernstein, Barton. J. "Seizing the Contested Terrain of Early Nuclear History: Stimson, Conant, and Their Allies Explain the Decision to Use the Atomic Bomb." *Diplomatic History* 17, 1 (Winter 1993).

———. "Writing, Righting, or Wronging the Historical Record—President Truman's Letter on his Atomic Bomb Decision." *Diplomatic History* 16, 1 (Winter 1992).

Boyer, Paul. "Hiroshima in American Memory." *Diplomatic History* 19, 2, (Spring 1995).

Dingman, Roger V. "Atomic Diplomacy During the Korean War." *International Security* 13 (Winter 1988–1989).

Foot, Rosemary. "Making Known the Unknown War: Policy Analysis of the Korean Conflict in the Last Decade." *Diplomatic History* 15, 3 (Summer 1991).

Gaddis, John. L. "Was the Truman Doctrine a Real Turning Point?" *Foreign Affairs* 52 (1973–1974).

Hamby, Alonzo L. "An American Democrat: A Reevaluation of the Personality of Harry S. Truman." *American Political Science Review* 106 (1991).

Kohn, Richard H. "History and the Culture Wars: The Case of the Smithsonian Institution's Enola Gay Exhibition." *Journal of American History* 82, 3 (December 1995).

Longevall, Fredrik. "A Critique of Containment." *Diplomatic History* 28, 4 (September 2004).

Ovendale, Ritchie. "Britain, the U.S.A. and the European Cold War, 1945–8." *History* 67 (1982).

Schlesinger Jr., Arthur M. "Origins of the Cold War." *Foreign Affairs* 46 (1967–1968).

Siracusa, Joseph M. "The 'New' Cold War History and the Origins of the Cold War." *Australian Journal of Politics and History* 47, 1 (2001).

Walker, J. Samuel. "The Decision to Use the Atomic Bomb: A Historiographical Update." *Diplomatic History* 14, 1 (Winter 1990).

——. "History, Collective Memory, and the Decision to Use the Bomb." *Diplomatic History* 19, 2 (Spring 1995).

Wright, C. Ben. "Mr 'X' and Containment." *Slavic Review* 35 (March 1976).

Presidency of Dwight D. Eisenhower

Dwight D. Eisenhower Library and Museum
200 Southeast Fourth Street
Abilene, Kansas 67410
http://www.eisenhower.utexas.edu/.

Published Documents

Boyle, Peter G., ed. *Churchill-Eisenhower Correspondence.* Chapel Hill: University of North Carolina Press, 1990.

Eisenhower, J. S. D., ed. *Letters to Mamie.* New York: Doubleday and Co., 1978.

Foreign Relations of the United States, 1952–1954 volumes. Washington, D.C.: U.S. Government Printing Office (1979–1992); 1955–1957 volumes (1986–1998); 1958–1960 volumes (1986–1998).

Galambos, Louis, and Daun Van Ee, eds. *Papers of Dwight D. Eisenhower.* Baltimore: The Johns Hopkins University Press, 1996.

Public Papers of the Presidents of the United States: Dwight D. Eisenhower. Vol. 1–8. Washington, D.C.: U.S. Government Printing Office, 1958–1961.

Memoirs and Diaries

Brownell, Herbert, and John P. Burke. *Advising Ike: The Memoirs of Attorney General Herbert Brownell.* Lawrence: University Press of Kansas, 1993.

Donovan, Robert J., *Eisenhower: The Inside Story.* New York: Harper and Brothers, 1956.

Eisenhower, Dwight D. *Mandate for Change, 1953–1956: The White House Years.* New York: Doubleday & Co., 1963.

——. *Peace With Justice: Selected Addresses.* New York: Columbia University Press, 1961.

——. *Waging Peace, 1956–1961: The White House Years.* New York: Doubleday & Co., 1965.

Ferrell, Robert H., ed. *The Eisenhower Diaries.* New York: W. W. Norton & Co., 1981.

Books

Allen, C. *Eisenhower and the Mass Media.* Chapel Hill: University of North Carolina Press, 1993.

Alteras, Isaac. *Eisenhower and Israel: US-Israeli Relations, 1953–1960.* Gainesville: University Press of Florida, 1993.

Ambrose, Stephen. E., *Eisenhower*. Vol. 2, *The President*. New York: Simon and Shuster, 1984.

——, and Bischof, Gunter., eds. *Eisenhower: A Centenary Assessment*. Baton Rouge: Louisiana State University Press, 1995.

Anderson, David. L. *Trapped by Success: The Eisenhower Administration and Vietnam, 1953–1961*. New York; Columbia University Press, 1991.

Beal, John R. *John Foster Dulles: A Biography*. New York: Harper & Brothers, 1957.

Beschloss, Michael R., *Mayday: Eisenhower, Khrushchev, and the U-2 Affair*. New York: Harper and Row, 1986.

Brendon, Piers. *Ike: His Life and Times*. New York: Harper & Row Publishers, 1986.

Briggs, Philip J. *Making American Foreign Policy: President-Congress Relations from the Second World War to Vietnam*. Lanham, Maryland: University Press of America, 1991.

Broadwater, Jeff. *Eisenhower and the Anti-Communist Crusade*. Chapel Hill: University of North Carolina Press, 1992.

Burke, Robert F. *Dwight D. Eisenhower: Hero and Politician*. Boston: Twayne Publishers, 1986.

Coblentz, G., and Roscoe Drummond. *Duel at the Brink*. New York: Doubleday & Co., 1981.

Cook, Blanche W. *The Declassified Eisenhower*. New York: Doubleday & Co., 1960.

Divine, Robert A. *Eisenhower and the Cold War*. New York: Oxford University Press, 1981.

——. *The Sputnik Challenge*. Oxford: Oxford University Press, 1993.

Dockrill, Saki. *Eisenhower's New Look National Security Policy, 1953–61*. New York: St. Martin's Press, 1996.

Donovan, John C. *The Cold Warriors*. Lexington, Massachusetts: D. C. Heath and Company, 1974.

Ewald, William B. *Eisenhower the President*. Englewood Cliffs, New Jersey: Prentice Hall, 1981.

Finer, Herman. *Dulles Over Suez*. Chicago: Quadrangle Books, 1964.

Giglio, James N., and Stephen G. Rabe. *Debating the Kennedy Presidency*. New York: Rowman & Littlefield Publishers, Inc., 2003.

Goold-Adams Richard. *John Foster Dulles: A Reappraisal*. Westport, Connecticut: Greenwood Press, 1962.

Grabner, Norman A. *The Age of Global Power: The United States Since 1939*. New York: John Wiley & Sons, 1979.

Griffith, Robert, ed. *Ike's Letters to a Friend*. Lawrence: University Press of Kansas, 1984.

Greenstein, Fred I. *The Hidden Hand Presidency: Eisenhower as Leader*. Baltimore: The Johns Hopkins University Press, 1982.

Guhin, Michael A. *John Foster Dulles: A Statesman and His Times*. New York: Columbia University Press, 1972.

Hoopes, Townsend. *The Devil and John Foster Dulles*. Boston: Little, Brown and Company, 1973.

Houts, Marshall, and H. Strassen. *Eisenhower: Turning the World Toward Peace*. St. Paul, Minnesota: Merrill/Magnus Publishing Corporation, 1990.

Immerman, Richard H., ed. *John Foster Dulles and the Diplomacy of the Cold War*. Princeton, New Jersey: Princeton University Press, 1990.

Kingseed, Cole C. *Eisenhower and the Suez Crisis of 1956*. Baton Rouge: Louisiana State University Press, 1995.

Krieg, Joan P. *Dwight D. Eisenhower: Soldier, President, Statesman.* New York: Greenwood Press, 1987.

Lucas, Scott. *Divided We Stand: Britain, the United States and the Suez Crisis.* London: Hodder and Stoughton, 1991.

Marks III, Frederick W. *Power and Peace. The Diplomacy of John Foster Dulles.* Westport, Connecticut: Praeger, 1993.

Mayer, David., and Richard A. Melanson. *Re-evaluating Eisenhower. American Foreign Policy in the 1950s.* Champaign: University of Illinois Press, 1987.

Pach, Chester J., and Elmo Richardson. *The Presidency of Dwight D. Eisenhower.* Lawrence: University Press of Kansas, 1991.

Parmet, Herbert S. *Eisenhower and the American Crusades.* New York: Macmillan Company, 1972.

Perret, Geoffrey. *Eisenhower.* Holbrook, Massachusettes: Adams Media Corporation, 1999.

Richardson, Elmo. *The Presidency of Dwight D. Eisenhower.* Lawrence: Regents Press of Kansas, 1979.

Warshaw, Shirley A., ed. *Re-examining the Eisenhower Presidency.* London: Greenwood Press, 1993.

Articles

Anderson, David L. "J. Lawton Collins, John Foster Dulles, and the Eisenhower Administration's 'Point of No Return' in Vietnam." *Diplomatic History* 12, 2 (Spring 1988).

Brands, H. W. "The Age of Vulnerability: Eisenhower and the National Insecurity State." *American Historical Review* 94, 4 (1989).

De Santis, Vincent P. "Eisenhower Revisionism," *Review of Politics* 38 (April 1976).

Duchin, Brian R. "The 'Agonising Reappraisal': Eisenhower, Dulles and the EDC." *Diplomatic History* 16, 2 (Spring 1992).

Gordon, Leonard H. D. "United States Opposition to Use of Force in the Taiwan Strait, 1954–1955." *Journal of American History* 72, 3 (1985).

Greenstein, Fred I. "Eisenhower as an Activist President: A Look at New Evidence." *Political Science Quarterly* 94 (Winter 1979–1980).

Herring, George C., and Richard H. Immerman. "Eisenhower, Dulles and Dienbienphu: 'The Day We Didn't Go to War' Revisited." *Journal of American History* 7, 2 (September 1984).

Huntington, Samuel P. "Civilian Control and the Constitution." *American Political Science Review* (September 1956).

Immerman, Richard H. "Confessions of an Eisenhower Revisionist." *Diplomatic History* 14, 3 (Summer 1990).

——. "Eisenhower and Dulles: Who Made the Decisions?" *Political Psychology* 1, 2 (1979).

——. "The United States and the Geneva Conference of 1954: A New Look." *Diplomatic History* 14, 1 (Winter 1990).

Keefer, Edward C. "President Dwight D. Eisenhower and the End of the Korean War." *Diplomatic History* 10, 3 (1986).

Langley, Lester D. "The United States and Latin American the Eisenhower Era." *Diplomatic History* 14, 2 (Spring 1990).

McAuliffe, Mary S. "Eisenhower, the President." *Journal of American History* 68, (December 1981).

Rabe, Stephen G. "Eisenhower Revisionism: A Decade of Scholarship." *Diplomatic History* 17, 1 (Winter 1993).
Rushkoff, Bennett C. "Eisenhower and Dulles and the Quemoy-Matsu Crisis, 1954–1955." *Political Science Quarterly* 96 (1981).

Presidency of John F. Kennedy

John Fitzgerald Kennedy Library
Columbia Point
Boston, Massachusetts, 02125
http://ww.jfklibrary.org.

Published Documents and Transcripts

Foreign Relations of the United States, 1961–1963 volumes. Washington, D.C.: U.S. Government Printing Office, 1988–2001.
Johnson, George W., series ed. *Kennedy Presidential Press Conferences.* London: Heyden, 1978.
May, Ernest R., and Zelikow, Philip D. eds. *Kennedy Tapes: Inside the White House During the Cuban Missile Crisis.* Cambridge, Massachusetts: Harvard University Press, 1997.
Nevins, A., ed. *The Burden and the Glory: The Hopes and Purposes of President Kennedy's Second and Third Years in Office as Revealed in His Public Statements and Addresses.* (Norwalk, Connecticut: Easton Press, 1988, first published, 1964).
Pentagon Papers: The Defense Department History of United States Decision-making on Vietnam. 4 vols. Boston: Beacon Press, 1971.
Presidential Recordings: John F. Kennedy: The Great Crises. 3 vols. Naftali, Timothy, ed. Vol. 1; Naftali, Timothy, and Philip D. Zelikow, eds. Vol. 2; Zelikow, Philip D., and Ernest R. May, eds. Vol. 3. New York: W. W. Norton, 2001.
Public Papers of the Presidents of the United States: John F Kennedy. Vols. 1–3. Washington, D.C.: U.S. States Government Printing Office, 1961–1963.
White, Mark J., ed. *Kennedys and Cuba: The Declassified Documentary History.* Chicago: Ivan R. Dee, 1999.

Memoirs and Diaries

Bowles, Chester. *Promises to Keep: My Years in Public Life, 1941–1969.* New York: Harper and Row, 1971.
Kennedy, Robert. *Thirteen Days: A Memoir of the Cuban Missile Crisis.* New York: W. W. Norton, 1969.
O'Donnell, Kenneth P., and Joe McCarthy. *"Johnny We Hardly Knew Ye": Memories of John Fitzgerald Kennedy.* Boston: Little, Brown and Company, 1970.
Salinger, Pierre. *A Memoir.* New York: St. Martin's Press, 1995.
——. *With Kennedy.* New York: Doubleday, 1966.
Taylor, Maxwell D. *Swords and Plowshares.* New York: W. W. Norton, 1972.

Books

Abel, Elie. *The Missile Crisis.* Philadelphia: Lippincott, 1966.
Allison, Graham T. *Essence of Decision.* Boston: Little, Brown and Company, 1971.

Beschloss, Michael R., *The Crisis Years: Kennedy and Khrushchev, 1960–1963.* New York: Harper Collins, 1991.

Blight, James G., and David A. Welch. *On the Brink: Americans and Soviets Re-examine the Cuban Missile Crisis.* New York: Hill and Wang, 1989.

Divine, Robert A., ed. *The Cuban Missile Crisis: The Continuing Debate.* Chicago: Quadrangle, 1971.

Freedman, Lawrence. *Kennedy's Wars: Berlin, Cuba, Laos and Cuba.* Oxford: Oxford University Press, 2000.

Fursenko, Aleksandr, and Timothy Naftali. *"One Hell of a Gamble": Khrushchev, Castro, and Kennedy, 1958–1964.* New York: Norton, 1997.

Giglio, James N., compiler. *John F. Kennedy: A Bibliography.* Westport, Connecticut: Greenwood Press, 1995.

Halberstram, David. *The Best and the Brightest.* New York: Ballantine Books, 1992, first published 1969.

Nash, Philip. *The Other Missiles of October: Eisenhower, Kennedy, and the Jupiters, 1957–1963.* Chapel Hill: University of North Carolina Press, 1997.

Nathan, James A., ed. *Anatomy of the Cuban Missile Crisis.* Westport, Connecticut: Greenwood Press, 2001.

Nathan, James A., ed. *The Cuban Missile Crisis Revisited.* New York: St. Martin's Press, 1992.

Parmet, Herbert S. *Jack: The Struggles of John F. Kennedy.* New York: Dial Press, 1980.

——. *JFK, the Presidency of John F. Kennedy.* Harmondsworth, England: Penguin Books, 1983.

Paterson, Thomas G., ed. *Kennedy's Quest for Victory: American Foreign Policy, 1961–1963.* New York: Oxford University Press, 1989.

Rabe, Stephen G. *The Most Dangerous Area in the World: John F. Kennedy Confronts Communist Revolution in Latin America.* Chapel Hill: University of North Carolina Press, 1999.

Salinger, Pierre. *John F. Kennedy, Commander in Chief: A Profile in Leadership.* New York: Penguin Studio, 1997.

Sorensen, Theodore C. *Kennedy.* New York: Harper and Row, 1965.

Thompson, Robert S. *The Missiles of October: The Declassified Story of John F. Kennedy and the Cuban Missile Crisis.* New York: Simon and Schuster, 1992.

Weldes, Jutta. *Constructing National Interests: The United States and the Cuban Missile Crisis.* Minneapolis: University of Minnesota Press, 1999.

Articles

Beck, Kent M. "Necessary Lies, Hidden Truths: Cuba in the 1960 Campaign." *Diplomatic History* 8, 1 (Winter 1984).

Blight, James G., Joseph S. Nye Jr., and David A. Welch. "The Cuban Missile Crisis Revisited." *Foreign Affairs* 66, 1 (Fall 1987).

Dean, Robert D. "Masculinity as Ideology: John F. Kennedy and the Domestic Politics of Foreign Policy." *Diplomatic History* 22, 1 (Winter 1998).

Dobson, Alan P. "The Kennedy Administration and Economic Warfare Against Communism." *International Affairs* 64, 4 (Autumn 1988).

Garthoff, Raymond L. "Documenting the Cuban Missile Crisis." *Diplomatic History* 24, 2 (Spring 2000).

Hershberg, James G. "Before 'The Missiles of October': Did Kennedy Plan a Military Strike Against Cuba?" *Diplomatic History* 14, 12 (Spring 1990).

Kochavi, Noam. "Kennedy, China, and the Laos Crisis." *Diplomatic History* 26, 1 (Winter 2002).

Meagher, M. E. "'In an Atmosphere of National Peril': The Development of John F. Kennedy's World View." *Presidential Studies Quarterly* 27, 3 (Summer 1997).

Monger, T. M. "Personality and Decision Making: John F. Kennedy in Four Crisis Decisions." *Canadian Journal of Political Science* 2 (June 1969).

Pelz, S. "John F. Kennedy's 1961 Vietnam War Decisions." *Journal of Strategic Studies* 4 (December 1981).

Pious, R. M. "The Cuban Missile Crisis and the Limits of Crisis Management." *Political Science Quarterly* 116 (Spring 2001).

Rabe, Stephen G. "After the Missiles of October: John F. Kennedy and Cuba, November 1962 to November 1963." *Presidential Studies Quarterly* 30, 4 (December 2000).

Scott, Len, and Steve Smith. "Lessons of October: Historians, Political Scientists, Policy-Makers and the Cuban Missile Crisis." *International Affairs* 70 (October 1994).

Zelikow, Philip. "American Policy and Cuba, 1961–1963." *Diplomatic History* 24, 2 (Spring 2000).

Presidency of Lyndon B. Johnson

Lyndon Baines Johnson Library and Museum
2313 Red River St.
Austin, Texas, 78705
http://www.lbjlib.utexas.edu/.

Published Documents and Transcripts

Beschloss, Michael R., ed. *Reaching for Glory: Lyndon Johnson's Secret White House Tapes, 1964–1965*. New York: Simon and Schuster, 2001.

Beschloss, Michael R., ed. *Taking Charge: The Johnson White House Tapes, 1963–1964*. New York: Simon and Schuster, 1997.

Foreign Relations of the United States. 1964–1968 volumes. Washington, D.C.: U.S. Government Printing Office, 1992–2003. Vol. I, Vietnam 1964 (1992); Vol. II, Vietnam January–June 1965 (1996); Vol. III, Vietnam June–December 1965 (1996); Vol. IV, Vietnam 1966 (1998); Vol. V, Vietnam 1967 (2002); Vol. VI, Vietnam January–August 1968 (2002);Vol. VII, Vietnam September–January 1969 (2003).

Herring, George C., general ed.; and Robert E. Lester, project coordinator. *Lyndon B. Johnson National Security Files: Vietnam, 1963–1969* [microform]. Frederick, Maryland: University Publications of America, 1987.

Johnson, George W., series ed. *Johnson Presidential Press Conferences*. Vols. 1 and 2. London: Heyden, 1978.

Memoirs

Johnson, Lyndon B. *The Vantage Point: Perspectives of the Presidency, 1963–1969*. New York: Holt, Rinehart and Winston, 1971.

McNamara, Robert S., with Brian VanDemark. *In Retrospect: The Tragedy and Lessons of Vietnam*. New York: Times Books, 1995.

Rusk, Dean. *As I Saw It: A Secretary of State's Memoirs.* New York: I. B. Tauris & Co. Ltd., 1990.

Books

Berman, Larry. *Lyndon Johnson's War: The Road to Stalemate in Vietnam.* New York: W. W. Norton & Company, 1989.

Bernstein, Irving. *Guns or Butter: The Presidency of Lyndon Johnson.* New York: Oxford University Press, 1996.

Brands, H. W. *Beyond Vietnam: The Foreign Policies of Lyndon Johnson.* College Station: Texas A&M University Press, 1999.

Chomsky, Noam. *The Backroom Boys.* Bungay, Suffolk: Fontana, 1973.

Cohen, Warren I., and Nancy B. Tucker, eds. *Lyndon Johnson Confronts the World: American Foreign Policy, 1963–1968.* New York: Cambridge University Press, 1994.

Dallek, Robert. *Flawed Giant: Lyndon Johnson and His Times, 1961–1973.* New York: Oxford University Press, 1998.

———. *Lyndon B. Johnson: Portrait of a President.* Oxford: Oxford University Press, 2004.

Divine, Robert. A., ed, *The Johnson Years.* Vol. III, *LBJ at Home and Abroad.* Lawrence: University Press of Kansas, 1994.

Gardner, Lloyd C. *Pay Any Price: Lyndon Johnson and the Wars for Vietnam.* Chicago: Ivan R. Dee, 1995.

Goldman, Eric F. *The Tragedy of Lyndon Johnson.* New York: Alfred A. Knopf, 1969.

Hammond, Paul. *LBJ and the Presidential Management of Foreign Relations.* Austin: University of Texas Press, 1992.

Herring, George C. *America's Longest War.* 3rd ed. New York: McGraw Hill, 1996.

———. *LBJ and Vietnam: A Different Kind of War.* Austin: University of Texas Press, 1994.

Kearns, Doris. *Lyndon Johnson and the American Dream.* New York: Harper and Row, 1976.

Logevall, Fredrik. *Choosing War: The Lost Chance for Peace and the Escalation of War in Vietnam.* Berkeley: University of California Press, 1999.

McMaster, H. R. *Dereliction of Duty: Lyndon Johnson, Robert McNamara, the Joint Chiefs of Staff and the Lies That Led to Vietnam.* New York: Harper Collins Publishers, 1997.

Miller, Merle. *Lyndon: An Oral Biography.* New York: Putnam, 1980.

Shapley, D. *Promise and Power: The Life and Times of Robert McNamara.* Boston: Little, Brown and Company, 1993.

Sidey, Hugh. *A Very Personal Presidency: Lyndon Johnson in the White House.* New York: Atheneum, 1968.

Sullivan, Michael P. *The Vietnam War: A Study in the Making of American Policy.* Lexington: University of Kentucky Press, 1985.

Woods, Randall Bennett. *J. William Fulbright, Vietnam, and the Search for a Cold War Foreign Policy.* Cambridge: Cambridge University Press, 1998.

Articles

Chace, James, and David Fromkin. "The Lessons of Vietnam?" *Foreign Affairs* 63, 4 (Spring 1985).

Dallek, Robert. "Lyndon Johnson and Vietnam: The Making of a Tragedy." *Diplomatic History* 20, 2 (Spring 1996).

Herring, George C. "America and Vietnam." *Foreign Affairs* 70, 5 (Winter 1991/1992).
Humphrey, David C. "NSC Meetings During the Johnson Presidency." *Diplomatic History* 18, 1 (Winter 1994).

Presidency of Richard M. Nixon

Nixon Presidential Material
8601 Adelphi Road
College Park, Maryland, 20740-6001
http://www.archives.gov/nixon.

Published Documents and Transcripts

Johnson, George W., series ed. *Nixon Presidential Press Conferences.* London: Heyden, 1978.
Kissinger, Henry A. *Crisis: The Anatomy of Two Major Foreign Policy Crises.* New York: Simon and Schuster, 2003.
Kutler, Stanley I., ed. *Abuse of Power: The New Nixon Tapes.* New York: Free Press, 1997.
Public Papers of the Presidents, Richard M. Nixon, 1969-1974. 5 vols. Washington, D.C.: U.S. Government Printing Office, 1971-1975.

Memoirs

Haig, Alexander M. *Inner Circles: How America Changed the World.* New York: Warner Books, 1992.
Kissinger, Henry A. *Ending the Vietnam War.* New York: Simon & Schuster, 2003.
——. *White House Years.* Boston: Little, Brown and Company, 1979.
Nixon, Richard M.. *The Memoirs of Richard Nixon.* London: Arrow Books, 1979, first published, 1978.
——. *No More Vietnams.* New York: Avon Books, 1985.
——. *Six Crises.* New York: Doubleday & Company, 1962.

Books

Aitken, Jonathan. *Nixon: A Life.* London: Wiedenfeld and Nicolson, 1993.
Ambrose, Stephen E. *Nixon: The Education of a Politician, 1913-1962.* New York: Simon and Schuster, 1987.
——. *Nixon: The Triumph of a Politician, 1962-1972.* New York: Simon and Schuster, 1989.
Andrianopoulous, Gerry A. *Kissinger and Brzezinski: The NSC and the Struggle for Control of US National Security Policy.* London: Macmillan, 1991.
Ball, George W. *Diplomacy for a Crowded World.* Boston: Little, Brown and Company, 1976.
Bundy, William. *A Tangled Web: The Making of Foreign Policy in the Nixon Presidency.* New York: Hill and Wang, 1998.
Costello, William. *The Facts About Nixon: An Unauthorized Biography.* New York: Viking Press, 1960.
Hersh, Seymour. *Price of Power: Kissinger in the Nixon White House.* New York: Summit Books, 1983,
Hoff, Joan. *Nixon Reconsidered.* New York: Basic Books, 1994.

Isaacson, Walter. *Henry Kissinger: A Biography.* New York: Simon and Schuster, 1992.

Kimball, Jeffrey. *The Vietnam War Files: Uncovering the Secret History of Nixon-era Strategy.* Lawrence: University Press of Kansas, 2004.

Kissinger, Henry A. *American Foreign Policy.* 3rd ed. New York: W. W. Norton & Company 1977.

———. *For the Record: Selected Statements, 1977–1980.* London: Wiedenfeld and Nicolson and Michael Joseph, 1981.

Mazo, Earl, and Stephen Hess. *Nixon: A Political Portrait.* New York: Harper & Row, 1967.

Nixon, Richard M. *The Challenges We Face.* London: McGraw-Hill Book Company, 1960.

Schulzinger, Robert D. *Henry Kissinger: Doctor of Diplomacy.* New York: Columbia University Press, 1989.

Shawcross, William. *Sideshow: Kissinger, Nixon and the Destruction of Cambodia.* New York: Simon and Schuster, 1979.

Sheehan, Edward R. *The Arabs, Israelis, and Kissinger.* New York: Thomas Y. Crowell Company, 1976.

Stoessinger, John G. *Henry Kissinger: The Anguish of Power.* New York: W. W. Norton & Company Inc., 1976.

Thornton, Richard. *The Nixon-Kissinger Years: The Reshaping of American Foreign Policy.* New York: Paragan House, 1989.

Articles

Hanhimäki, Jussi M. "'Dr. Kissinger or Mr. Henry'? Kissingerology, Thirty Years and Counting." *Diplomatic History* 27, 5 (November 2003).

———. "'They Can Write It in Swahili': Kissinger, the Soviets, and the Helsinki Accords, 1973–75." *Journal of Transatlantic Studies* 1, 1 (2003).

Hoff, Joan. "'Nixingerism,' NATO, and Détente." *Diplomatic History* 13, 4 (Fall 1989).

———. "A Revisionist View of Nixon's Foreign Policy." *Presidential Studies Quarterly* 26, 1 (Winter 1996).

Safford, Jeffrey J. "The Nixon-Castro Meeting of 19 April 1959." *Diplomatic History* 4, 4 (Fall 1980).

Presidency of Gerald R. Ford

Gerald R. Ford Library
1000 Beal Avenue
Ann Arbor, Michigan, 48109
http://www.fordlibrarymuseum.gov/.

Published Documents

Public Papers of the Presidents, Gerald R. Ford. 6 vols. Washington, D.C.: U.S. Government Printing Office, 1975–1979.

Memoirs

Casserly, John. J. *The Ford White House: Diary of a Speechwriter.* Boulder: Colorado Associated Press, 1977.

Ford, Gerald R. *A Time to Heal; The Autobiography of Gerald R. Ford.* New York: Harper & Row, 1979; and Norwalk, Connecticut: Easton Press, 1987.

Hartman, Robert T. *Palace Politics: An Insider's Account of the Ford Years.* New York: McGraw-Hill, 1980.

Kissinger, Henry. A. *Years of Renewal.* New York: Simon and Schuster, 1999.

Nessen, Ron. *It Sure Looks Different from the Inside.* New York: Simon and Schuster, 1978.

terHorst, Jerald F. *Gerald Ford and the Future of the Presidency.* New York: Third Press, 1974.

Wetterhahn, Ralph. *The Last Battle: The Mayaguez Incident and the End of the Vietnam War.* New York: Carroll & Graf Publishers, Inc., 2001.

Books

Cannon, James M. *Time and Chance: Gerald Ford's Appointment with History.* New York: Harper Collins, 1993.

Firestone, Bernard. J., and Alexej Ugrinsky, eds. *Gerald R. Ford and the Politics of Post-Watergate America.* Westport, Connecticut: Greenwood Press, 1993.

Greene, John R. *Gerald R. Ford: A Bibliography.* Westport, Connecticut: Greenwood Press, 1994.

———. *The Presidency of Gerald R. Ford.* Lawrence: University Press of Kansas, 1995.

Haley, P. Edward. *Congress and the Fall of South Vietnam and Cambodia.* East Brunswick, New Jersey: Associated University Presses, 1983.

Head, Richard G., Frisco W. Short, and Robert C. McFarlane. *Crisis Resolution: Presidential Decision Making in the Mayaguez and Korean Confrontations.* Boulder, Colorado: Westview Press, 1978.

Reeves, Richard. *A Ford, Not a Lincoln.* New York: Harcourt Brace Jovanovich, 1975.

Rowan, Roy. *The Four Days of Mayaguez.* New York: W. W. Norton, 1975.

Articles

Turner, Michael. *The Vice President as Policy Maker: Rockefeller in the Ford White House.* Westport, Connecticut: Greenwood Press, 1982.

Lamb, Christopher J. "Belief Systems and Decision Making in the Mayaguez Crisis." *Political Science Quarterly* 99, 4 (1984–1985).

Reischauer, Edwin O. "Back to Normalcy." *Foreign Policy* 20 (1975).

Schmitz, D. F. "Senator Frank Church, the Ford Administration, and the Challenges of Post-Vietnam Foreign Policy." *Peace and Change* 21 (October 1996).

Thesis

Raymond, William M. "Collision or Collusion? The Congress, the President, and the Ambiguity of War Powers." Ph.D. thesis, University of Michigan, 1993.

Presidency of Jimmy Carter

Jimmy Carter Library and Museum
441 Freedom Parkway
Atlanta, Georgia, 30307-1498
http://www.jimmycarterlibrary.gov/.

Published Documents

Public Papers of the Presidents, Jimmy Carter. 9 vols. Washington, D.C.: U.S. Government Printing Office, 1978–1982.

Memoirs and Transcripts

Brzezinski, Zbigniew. *Power and Principle: Memoirs of the National Security Advisor, 1977–1981.* New York: Farrar, Straus, Giroux, 1983.

Carter, Jimmy. *A Government as Good as Its People.* Fayetteville: University of Arkansas Press, 1996.

——. *Keeping Faith.* Norwalk, Connecticut: Easton Press, 1982.

——. *Why Not The Best?* Eastbourne: Kingsway Publications, 1977, first published, 1975.

Christopher, Warren. *American Hostages in Iran: The Conduct of a Crisis.* New Haven: Yale University Press, 1985.

Jordan, Hamilton. *Crisis: The Last Year of the Carter Presidency.* London: Michael Joseph, 1982.

Powell, Jody. *The Other Side of the Story.* New York: W. Morrow, 1984.

Rockefeller, David. *Memoirs.* New York: Random House 2002.

Sick, Gary. *All Fall Down: America's Tragic Encounter with Iran.* New York: Random House, 1985.

Sullivan, William. *Mission to Iran.* New York: W. W. Norton, 1981.

Turner, Stansfield. *Secrecy and Democracy: The CIA in Transition.* Boston: Houghton Mifflin, 1985.

Vance, Cyrus. *Hard Choices: Four Critical Years in Managing America's Foreign Policy.* New York: Simon and Schuster, 1983.

Books

Abernathy, M. Glenn, ed. *The Carter Years: The President and Policy Making.* New York: St. Martin's Press, 1984.

Brinkley, Douglas. *The Unfinished Presidency: Jimmy Carter's Journey Beyond the White House.* New York: Viking Press, 1998.

Caldwell, Dan. *The Dynamics of Domestic Politics and Arms Control: The SALT II Treaty Ratification Debate.* New York: St. Martin's Press, 1991.

Carter, Jimmy. *The Nobel Peace Prize Lecture.* New York: Simon & Schuster, 2002.

Dumbrell, John. *The Carter Presidency: A Re-evaluation.* Manchester: Manchester University Press, 1993.

Hargrove, Erwin C. *Jimmy Carter as President.* Baton Rouge: Louisiana State University Press, 1988.

Jones, Charles O. *The Trusteeship Presidency: Jimmy Carter and the United States Congress.* Baton Rouge: Louisiana State University Press, 1988.

Kaufman, Burton I. *The Presidency of James Earl Carter.* Lawrence: University of Kansas Press, 1993.

McClellan, David S. *Cyrus Vance.* New York: Cooper Square, 1985.

Moffett, George D. *The Limits of Victory: Ratification of the Panama Canal Treaties.* Ithaca, New York: Cornell University Press, 1983.

Muravchik, Joshua. *The Uncertain Crusade: Jimmy Carter and the Dilemmas of Human Rights.* New York: Hamilton Press, 1986.

Rosenbaum, Herbert D., and Alexej Ugrinsky, eds. *Jimmy Carter: Foreign Policy and Post-Presidential Years*. Westport, Connecticut: Greenwood Press, 1994.
Salinger, Pierre. *America Held Hostage*. New York: Doubleday & Company, Inc., 1981.
Sick, Gary. *All Fall Down: America's Tragic Encounter with Iran*. New York: Random House, 1985.
———. *October Surprise: America's Hostages in Iran and the Election of Ronald Reagan*. New York: Times Books, 1991.
Smith, Gaddis. *Morality, Reason and Power: American Diplomacy in the Carter Years*. New York: Hill and Wang, 1986.
Strong, Robert A. *Working in the World: Jimmy Carter and the Making of American Foreign Policy*. Baton Rouge: Louisiana State University Press, 2000.
Thompson, Kenneth W., ed. *The Carter Presidency: Fourteen Intimate Perspectives of Jimmy Carter*. Lanham, Maryland: University Press of America, 1990.
Thornton, Richard C. *The Carter Years: Toward a New Global Order*. New York: Paragon House, 1991.
Westad, Odd Arne, ed. *The Fall of Détente: Soviet-American Relations During the Carter Years*. Boston: Scandinavian University Press, 1995.

Articles

Brinkley, Douglas. "The Rising Stock of Jimmy Carter: The 'Hands on' Legacy of Our Thirty-ninth President." *Diplomatic History* 20, 4 (Fall 1996).
Clymer, Kenton. "Jimmy Carter, Human Rights, and Cambodia." *Diplomatic History* 27, 2 (April 2003)
Hoffmann, Stanley. "Requiem." *Foreign Policy* 42 (Spring 1981).
Katz, Andrew Z. "Public Opinion and the Contradictions of Jimmy Carter's Foreign Policy." *Presidential Studies Quarterly* 30, 4 (December 2000).
Schmitz, David. F., Vanessa Walker. "Jimmy Carter and the Foreign Policy of Human Rights: The Development of a Post-Cold War Foreign Policy." *Diplomatic History* 28, 1 (January 2004).
Skidmore, D. "Carter and the Failure of Foreign Policy Reform." *Political Science Quarterly* 108, 4 (Winter 1993–1994).

Presidency of Ronald Reagan

Ronald Reagan Presidential Library
40 Presidential Drive
Simi Valley, California, 93065-0699
http://reagan.utexas.edu.

Published Documents

Abrams, Elliott. *Undue Process: A Story of How Political Differences Are Turned into Crimes*. New York: Free Press, 1993.
Deaver, Michael K. *A Different Drummer: My Thirty Years with Ronald Reagan*. New York: Harper Collins, 2001.
Fitzwater, Marlin. *Call the Briefing! A Memoir of Ten Years in the White House with Presidents Reagan and Bush*. United States: Xlibris Corporation, 2000.
Haig, Alexander M. Jr. *Caveat: Realism, Reagan and Foreign Policy*. New York: Macmillan, 1984.

Iran-Contra Puzzle. Washington, D.C.: Congressional Quarterly Inc., 1987.
Matlock, John F. Jr. *Reagan and Gorbachev: How the Cold War Ended.* New York: Random House, 2004.
McFarlane, Robert C., with Zofia Smardz. *Special Trust.* New York: Cadell and Davies, 1994.
Menges, Constantine C. *Inside the National Security Council: The True Story of the Making and Unmaking of Reagan's Foreign Policy.* New York: Simon and Schuster, 1988.
North, Oliver, with William Novak. *Under Fire: An American Story.* New York: Harper Collins, 1991.
Public Papers of the Presidents, Ronald Reagan. 14 vols. Washington, D.C.: U.S. Government Printing Office, 1982–1991.
Regan, Donald T. *For the Record.* New York: Harcourt Brace Jovanovich, Publishers, 1988.
Reagan, Ronald. *Speaking My Mind: Selected Speeches.* New York: Simon and Schuster, 1989.

Memoirs

Reagan, Ronald, with Richard G. Hubler. *Where's the Rest of Me?* New York: Karz Publishers, 1981, first published 1965.
———. *An American Life.* New York: Simon and Schuster, 1990
Robinson, Peter. *How Ronald Reagan Changed My Life.* New York: Regan Books, 2003.
Shultz, George P. *Turmoil and Triumph: My Years as Secretary of State.* New York: Scribner's, 1993.
Speakes, Larry, with Robert Pack. *Speaking Out: Inside the Reagan White House.* New York: Charles Scribner's Sons, 1988.
Walsh, Lawrence E. *Firewall: The Iran-Contra Conspiracy and Cover-up.* New York: Norton, 1997.
Weinberger, Caspar W. *Fighting for Peace: Seven Critical Years in the Pentagon.* New York: Warner Books, 1990.

Books

Bell, Coral. *The Reagan Paradox: American Foreign Policy in the 1980s.* New Brunswick, New Jersey: Rutgers University Press, 1989.
Busby, Robert. *Reagan and the Iran-Contra Affair: The Politics of Presidential Recovery.* New York: St. Martin's Press, 1999.
Draper, Theodore. *A Very Thin Line: The Iran-Contra Affairs.* Boston: Hill and Wang, 1991.
Fischer, Beth A. *The Reagan Reversal: Foreign Policy and the End of the Cold War.* Columbia: University of Missouri Press, 1997.
Fitzgerald, Frances. *Way Out There in the Blue: Reagan, Star Wars and the End of the Cold War.* New York: Simon & Schuster, 2000.
Gerson, Allan. *The Kirkpatrick Mission: Diplomacy without Apology: America at the United Nations, 1981–1985.* New York: Free Press, 1991.
Hall, David Locke. *The Reagan Wars: A Constitutional Perspective on War Powers and the Presidency.* Boulder, Colorado: Westview Press, 1991.
Kyvig, David E. *Reagan and the World.* New York: Greenwood Press, 1990.
Mandelbaum, Michael, and Talbot Strobe. *Reagan and Gorbachev.* New York: Vintage Books, 1987.

Mervin, David. *Ronald Reagan and the American Presidency.* London: Longman, 1990.
Pemberton, William E. *Exit with Honor: The Life and Presidency of Ronald Reagan.* Armonk, New York: M. E. Sharpe, 1997.
Schmertz, Eric J., Natalie Datlof, and Alexej Ugrinsky, eds. *President Reagan and the World.* Westport, Connecticut: Greenwood Press, 1997.
Smith, Geoffrey. *Reagan and Thatcher.* New York: W. W. Norton, 1991.
Strober, Deborah Hart, and Gerald S. Stober. *The Man and His Presidency.* Boston: Houghton: Mifflin Co., 1998.
Wallison, Peter J. *Ronald Reagan: The Power of Conviction and the Success of His Presidency.* Oxford: Westview Press, 2003.
Winik, Jay. *On the Brink: The Dramatic Behind the Scenes Saga of the Reagan Era and the Men and Women Who Won the Cold War.* New York: Simon & Schuster, 1996.

Articles

Bell, Coral. "From Carter to Reagan." *Foreign Affairs: America and the World* 63, 3 (1984).
Deibel, Terry L. "Reagan's Mixed Legacy." *Foreign Policy* 75 (Summer 1989).
———. "Why Reagan Is Strong." *Foreign Policy* 62 (Spring 1986).
Hyland, William G. "Reagan-Gorbachev III." *Foreign Affairs* 66, 1 (Fall 1987).
Kegley, Charles W., and Eugene R. Wittkopf. "The Reagan Administration's World View." *Orbis* 26 (Spring 1982).
Podhoretz, Norman. "The Reagan Road to Détente." *Foreign Affairs: America and the World* 63, 3 (1984).
Schlesinger, James. "Reykjavik and Revelations: A Turn of the Tide?" *Foreign Affairs: America and the World* 65, 3 (1986).
Shultz, George P. "New Realities and New Ways of Thinking." *Foreign Affairs* 63, 4 (Spring 1985).
Tucker, Robert W. "Reagan's Foreign Policy." *Foreign Affairs* 68, 1 (1988–1989).

Presidency of George H. W. Bush

George Bush Presidential Library and Museum
1000 George Bush Drive West
College Station, Texas, 77845
http://bushlibrary.tamu.edu/.

Published Documents

Bush, George H. W., and J. McGraith. *Heartbeat: George Bush in His Own Words.* New York, Scribner, 2001.
Public Papers of the Presidents, George Bush, 1989–1993. 15 vols. Washington, D.C.: U.S. Government Printing Office, 1990–1993.

Memoirs

Baker, James A., with Thomas M. Defrank. *The Politics of Diplomacy: Revolution, War and Peace, 1989–1992.* New York: Putnam, 1995.
Bush, George H. W. *All the Best, George Bush: My Life in Letters and Other Writings.* New York: Scribner, 1999.
———, and Brent Scowcroft. *A World Transformed.* New York: Alfred A. Knopf, 1998.

Powell, Colin. *My American Journey.* New York: Random House, 1995.

Books

Greene, John R. *The Presidency of George Bush.* Lawrence: University Press of Kansas, 2000.

Nixon, Richard M. *Seize the Moment. America's Challenge in a One Superpower World.* New York: Simon & Schuster, 1992.

Parmet, Herbert S. *George Bush: The Life of a Lone Star Yankee.* New York: Scribner, 1997.

Woodward, Bob. *The Commanders.* New York: Simon & Schuster, 1991.

Articles

Charles-Phillipe, David. "Who Was the Real George Bush? Foreign Policy Decision Making Under the Bush Administration." *Diplomacy and Statecraft* 7, 1 (1996).

Cohen, David B. "From START to START II: Dynamism and Pragmatism in the Bush Administration's Nuclear Weapon Policies." *Presidential Studies Quarterly* 27, 3 (Summer 1997).

Rozell, Mark J. "In Reagan's Shadow: Bush's Antirhetorical Presidency." *Presidential Studies Quarterly* 28, 1 (Winter 1998).

Skidmore, David, and William Gates. "After Tiananmen: The Struggle Over U.S. Policy Toward China in the Bush Administration." *Presidential Studies Quarterly* 27, 3 (Summer 1997).

Index

The use of a n with a page number refers to a note on that page.

About the Author

MARTIN THORNTON is a senior lecturer in the School of History at the University of Leeds, England. He has also been Director of the Centre for Canadian Studies at the university and a visiting professor at Vanderbilt University.